Classical Civilization

GREEKS AND ROMANS
IN 10 CHAPTERS

Nigel Spivey

HEAD
of ZEUS

First published in 2015 by Head of Zeus Ltd

This paperback edition first published in 2016 by Head of Zeus Ltd

1 3 5 7 9 10 8 6 4 2

A CIP catalogue record for this book is available from
the British Library.

ISBN (PB) 9781781855027
(E) 9781781854990

Printed and bound by CPI Group (UK) Ltd, Croydon, CR0 4YY

Designed by Lindsay Nash
Typeset by Ed Pickford
Maps by Jeff Edwards

Head of Zeus Ltd
Clerkenwell House
45–47 Clerkenwell Green
London EC1R 0HT

WWW.HEADOFZEUS.COM

Contents

	List of Maps	vii
	Preface	xi
I	Troy	1
II	Athens	29
III	Sparta	71
IV	Syracuse	97
V	Utopia	131
VI	Alexandria	169
VII	Pergamon	201
VIII	Rome	219
IX	Ephesus	265
X	Constantinople	299
	Epilogue	325
	Timeline	327
	Further Reading	331
	Index	347

List of Maps

1. The World according to Herodotus   56–7
2. Greece and the Aegean   74–5
3. The Wider Greek World   100
4. Alexander's Campaigns and the   172–3
   Kingdoms of his Successors
5. Rome and Pre-Roman Italy   220
6. The Roman Empire   268–9

Many things are both wonderful & terrible,
but none more so than humankind.

Through highwalled waves of ocean storm
the species makes its way
drenched but victorious. What can't we do?

The flesh of the earth –
Gaia, weariless mother of all –
we pound, slash, and try.
Year in, year out, our ploughs scrape back & forth.

The gleeful tribe of birds
we bring down low. Roaming beasts are bound.
The nets we weave steal speechless creatures from the
    deep.
All that's wild we will outwit.
So we 'break' the urgent steed;
the massive bull, however proud, must learn to wear
    our yoke.

Words serve us too. Give voice to a thought and it
　　journeys the globe
in no time. Shelter from winter's spite
we have contrived, and more besides:
all the craft that makes a state
is part of human skill.
How not to die eludes us: true. Meanwhile,
whatever ails our mortal state we plot to thwart
with clever – and successful – cures.

Experience unbaffles us. But human cunning
leads two ways. To scheme for bad;
to work for good. Hold firm with laws
carved by centuries, and trust in solemn oaths:
so the city stands. To go the other way –
is how to bring it down.

After Sophocles, *Antigone* 332–70

Preface

Two terms in the title of this book require some definition.

'Classical' is an ambivalent word. Broadly, it can mean the period and places of antiquity in which the Greeks and Romans flourished: emphatically (but not entirely) around the Mediterranean, and chronologically from around 800 BC until AD 400. In some contexts it may denote an epoch lasting little more than the fifth century BC, a recognized summit in the landscape of Greek politics, art and literature. Associated with this sense of 'classical' is the concept of a 'classic'. This comes from a Latin adjective, *classicus*, and is used to categorize something as absolutely excellent: first class, worthy of emulation, of a standard to be aimed for. The first of these senses predominates in this book, but the second has some bearing upon how we take the word 'civilization'.

'This is very civilized', we might say, on finding a delicious meal laid out, or some other situation marked by comfort and good manners. Such a loose understanding of the term 'civilization' is not irrelevant here, but it will not serve as a starting point. 'Living in cities' is perhaps over-deterministic, but associations with a communal existence governed by expectations of property rights, mutual respect and the rule of law take us closer to what we want from the word. Of course it is proper to speak of earlier civilizations in India, Anatolia and Egypt. But one justification for this book lies in the fact that so much of our terminology for defining 'civilization' comes from the classical languages. Whether Greek ('democracy', 'hygiene', 'political', 'ethical', 'barbarous', 'sympathy') or Latin ('society', 'civility', 'justice', 'humane', 'equality', 'liberty', 'fraternity'), our ways of thinking are so conditioned by the Graeco-Roman legacy of discourse and intellectual formation ('academic', 'education', 'scholarship') that we can hardly avoid using ancient Greece and Rome as exemplary.

The story that follows tries not to idealize this exemplary status. If it fails to dwell upon the routine indignities of slavery, the subjection of women, the practice of religious superstition, and the prevalence of squalor, disease, violence and infant mortality in the ancient world, that is because it is, after all, a survey of classical *civilization*. And because there is also the adjacent sense of *classical* civilization, readers will find little by way of evoking 'everyday life' in ancient Greece and Rome. Certain archaeological sites – such as Olynthus in the Chalkidike peninsula, destroyed in 348 BC, and never reoccupied; or Pompeii and Herculaneum, caught in the volcanic eruption of Vesuvius in AD 79 – offer fascinating, if sometimes morbid, relics of domestic life. But a book that sought to encompass everything, from elite pleasures to peasant subsistence, would be a very big and potentially rather boring volume.

Our story begins in the Bronze Age, with Troy – Troy imagined, Troy as was – and it ends, under 2,000 years later, at Constantinople – not very far, geographically, from the beginning. An exceptional chapter, inadequately entitled 'Utopia', comes in the middle. This forms an interval for consideration of Greek and Roman philosophy and science. It was one of those philosopher-scientists, Aristotle, who defined our species as 'political animals'. What he meant by this definition is that humans – along with certain other gregarious creatures, such as bees, ants and cranes – tend to form societies focused upon a shared common end, or communal benefit. Some implications of this categorization are insidious (are masses of humans destined to be 'drones', serving a single royal ruler in the hive?), yet it brings us naturally to consider the household, the community and then the city, or 'city-state' (*polis*), as a defining unit of our species. Given the nexus between cities (as developed in the Graeco-Roman world) and 'civilization' as routinely characterized, it seemed obvious to organize the rest of the book according to particular cities of classical antiquity. The narrative impetus remains, however, more chronological than topographical.

A different author might have said more about medicine, mathematics, technology and the subtleties of Roman juris-prudence. But a different author might have said less about those aspects of classical antiquity that enshrine, or fore-shadow, those modern values usually described as 'liberal'. Again etymology is telling: the anticipation of tolerance, decency and humanitarian concern comes with the Greek concept of *philanthropia*, 'love of humankind', and the Latin phrase *humanitas Romana*. At the risk of wishful thinking, and doubtless in justification of a life spent largely in learning and teaching 'Classics', I have privileged those elements from Greece and Rome that underlie our concept of the 'Humanities' – time-honoured yet fragile as they are.

Nigel Spivey
Emmanuel College, Cambridge

A note on spelling and orthography

Renditions of names, places and periods generally, though not invariably, follow the example set by the *Oxford Classical Dictionary* (fourth edition, 2012). Where Greek has been transliterated, it is left in its simplest anglicized form.

I
TROY

A rather underwhelming ruin on the shores of Asia Minor; a prehistoric stronghold associated with conflict and destruction. Why begin with Troy?

It is tempting to answer that question in the melodramatic cliché, 'one man…' – with the name added in a Hollywood growl: 'Homer'. The temptation is dangerous, not least because we know so little about the existence of this individual. Yet Troy depends upon him; and this city, as he imagined it, is where classical civilization begins.

Around the middle of the eighth century BC – over 2,700 years ago – it seems that a certain professional poet, known to posterity as 'Homer', gained a reputation for reciting stories cast in epic verse. This was not rhyming poetry, but it had a strong rhythm or beat; and its subject was strong, too. 'Epic' denotes a narrative set in the age of heroes – great-hearted, muscular characters whose deeds make the lives of ordinary mortals appear puny by comparison. Homer's name is attached to a pair of epic poems that constitute the founding works of Western literature. One is the *Iliad*, which describes certain events during a protracted siege of Troy by a contingent of Greek warriors led by Agamemnon; the other is the *Odyssey*, which tells how one of those Greek warriors, Odysseus, made his adventurous way home after Troy was eventually taken.

Homer did not come from Troy. That sounds like an odd statement, since although his own epics do not directly recount the destruction, he was well aware that Troy had been burned to the ground. But Homer was probably born not far away from the site of Troy – on the island of Chios, perhaps, or at the port settlement of Smyrna (modern Izmir). He may have paid a visit to the site: in his day, it was somewhat ruined, but not entirely abandoned. 'Troy' was only one of the various names that existed for the place. Once it had been listed in the territory of the ancient Hittite empire as *Wilusa*. The Greeks knew it as *Ilios*, *Ilion* or *Troia*; sometimes Homer also calls it *Pergamos*, which can mean just 'citadel'. Dilapidated as it was, however, Troy stood proud in collective memory. The city, by the agony of its end, was symbolic of all cities; and the strip of land between the city and the sea – the 'Trojan plain', where most of the fighting took place – became a precious portion of the earth's surface where mortals were transfigured, by violence raw and refined, into demigods.

The coastline has shifted since Homer's day. But it is still possible to stand upon the excavated foundations of Troy's towers and gaze across to where the Mediterranean narrows as it prepares to join the Black Sea: the passage known as the Hellespont, or the straits of the Dardanelles. The traffic of modern shipping is continuous: one would not dare to swim the intercontinental distance without special arrangements. Little historical imagination is needed to suppose that there was once a time when Troy monitored access through these waters, and therefore that it was a contested location. Trade routes, however, did not concern our poet – rather, it was the flux of events long ago. We would describe these events as 'mythical', perhaps intending 'myth' to mean 'made up' or 'fictional', and certainly different from 'history'. Such a distinction post-dates Homer. For him, Troy once prospered as a kingdom ruled by the descendants of Dardanus, an offspring of the god Zeus. But already the city was subject to attack (by Herakles, another son of Zeus) during the reign of Laomedon; and though handsomely rebuilt by Laomedon's son, Priam, Troy would not survive.

How Troy became a rich and eminent place, and whether its wealth was enough to invite raiders, are questions of no importance for Homer. He is only aware of the poetic cause of the war that brought down Priam's Troy. In summary, this can seem whimsical, even ridiculous, but since Homer assumes we know it, the story should be outlined. It begins with an incident at a wedding celebration. The happy couple, Peleus and Thetis, have issued invitations to the Olympian deities – the gods and goddesses of the Greek pantheon, whose primary habitat was imagined upon Mount Olympus, on the confines of Thessaly and Macedonia. While these deities are gathered at the marriage feast, a strange dispute breaks out. Three goddesses – Hera, Athena and Aphrodite – are at a table where a golden apple appears. They do not know it, but this unusual fruit has been slyly placed there by another deity, one whose nature was to cause trouble – Ares, god of war. The apple carries an inscribed message: 'For the Fairest'. The three ladies reach for it – all at once.

The dispute that duly arises is not one that Zeus, as most senior of the Olympian deities, feels sufficiently impartial to judge (though liberal in his dalliance elsewhere, he is after all married to Hera). So Zeus delegates to a mortal the task of deciding which of the three goddesses is most beautiful. This mortal happens to be a young man called Paris – one of many children born to the Trojan king Priam. The divine messenger Hermes brings Hera, Athena and Aphrodite for the resultant 'Judgement of Paris'. Each goddess tries to bribe him. Hera offers the promise of kingly power (Paris, with at least one older brother, was not otherwise in line for royal succession). Athena offers him renown in war (though a good shot with bow and arrow, Paris was not the most redoubtable fighter). For her part, Aphrodite teases Paris with the prospect of love. More precisely, she promises him the favours of the world's loveliest woman.

Paris nominates Aphrodite for the golden apple. Then the grave consequences of his choice become stark. For the world's loveliest woman is not, to put it crudely, available. Her name is Helen; she is the wife of Menelaus, king of Sparta. If he wants Helen as his prize, Paris must go to Sparta and steal her.

So he does. And this is how Helen's becomes 'the face that launched a thousand ships' – for Menelaus was not the sort to endure an outrage to his honour. He called upon not only his powerful brother Agamemnon to assist with vengeance, but many other chieftains. Some, notably Odysseus, contentedly ruling his island of Ithaca, were reluctant to join the expedition to regain Helen from Troy. But their muster of a thousand ships was impressive nonetheless. Led by Agamemnon, they set sail for Troy in the faith that this force comprised 'the best of the Achaeans'.

'Achaeans' is Homer's name for them. The country of Greece did not exist in his time; actually, it did not come into existence as a nation-state until AD 1821. In any case, Homer set his story in the past. Broadly, the Achaeans equate to Greeks of a prehistoric period. Homer describes their physical presence with awe: beyond their frightening readiness for combat, the Achaean heroes are capable of tossing enormous boulders that no individual in Homer's time could even budge – and they have appetites to match, feasting nightly upon slabs of roast meat. Yet the poet enters their world without any imaginative inhibitions. All that the heroes say is heard, and cast into direct speech: so we learn, verbatim, how Agamemnon as senior commander quarrels with the most fearsome and egotistical of his subordinate warriors – Achilles, the offspring of Peleus and Thetis. Homer reports what the Olympians say, too: supernatural though they are, the deities also squabble, take sides, and have grievances to settle.

So it is that while some details of a character's background remain ill-defined – was Agamemnon king at Mycenae, or Argos? – Homer's epic narrative is both fantastic and plausible. Of course he did not himself concoct all elements of the stories; and we must remember that the *texts* of Homer were first produced, at Athens, almost two centuries later, and 'canonized' (in Alexandria) later still. But there is a widespread scholarly consensus that a single poetic voice is responsible for the *Iliad* and the *Odyssey*; and most readers will intuitively sense that these poems share a shaping spirit, at once grandiose and humane.

Two instances of Homer's engagement with his mighty protagonists are enough to epitomize the narrative style. In the sixth book of the *Iliad*, the poet shows us Priam's foremost offspring, Hector, taking leave of his wife Andromache by the walls of Troy. Holding their little son Astyanax in her arms, Andromache tearfully implores Hector not to enter the fray, foreseeing that he will leave her a widow and Astyanax fatherless. Hector reaches out to take the baby boy – who only clutches closer to his mother, for he is terrified by the sight of his father's helmet with its great crest of horsehair. Both parents dissolve into laughter; Hector removes his helmet and comforts the child, with a prayer that one day this infant will outdo his father in bloodstained glory. The vignette unites the trio briefly but significantly. It has a structural purpose, for Andromache's premonition will be realized later in the story; and the tenderness of the family group contrasts with a particularly savage pledge made earlier in the same book by Agamemnon, not only to slaughter all inhabitants of Troy but even to rip unborn Trojans from the womb. It also serves to flesh out the humanity of Hector, the great warrior. He is not exactly domesticated, but he becomes any soldier fighting on behalf of hearth and home.

Or there is the scene in the ninth book of the *Odyssey*: the adventure in which the hero Odysseus, on his way home from Troy, puts ashore to an island that turns out to be occupied by a tribe of lawless monsters known as the Cyclopes.* Seeking shelter, Odysseus attempts to ingratiate himself with one of these monsters, Polyphemus, but soon finds himself and his shipmates imprisoned inside the cave where Polyphemus dwells with his herd of sheep. Polyphemus, though gross, has humanoid form, yet soon he proves himself not civilized, or 'bread-eating': he devours two of his prisoners, and proposes to do likewise with the rest. Thereupon Odysseus forms a ruse: he offers the Cyclops wine, and then, having persuaded the giant to drink himself into a stupor, drives a fiery wooden stake into his single eye. The cave is

---

* Cyclops (plural Cyclopes) means 'round-eye'.

blocked by a boulder so huge that only Polyphemus can shift it – as he eventually does, for his flock must be let out to graze. Then the blinded Cyclops, unaware that Odysseus and his men have strapped themselves to the underbellies of the sheep, crouches by the mouth of his cave, pathetically patting the beasts as they pass, trying to recognize them by touch. Here Homer cannot resist adding the detail that Odysseus is beneath the fleece of a favourite ram, now the last of the herd to exit the cave, which causes Polyphemus to cry out:

> Dear ram, what is this – how come you are last of the flock
> to leave the cave, you who have never lagged behind the
> ewes? Usually you step out so proud – first to seek the
> pasture of succulent grass; first to browse by the waters
> of the brook, and first to heed the call of the fold when
> evening falls. Yet today you bring up the rear. Are you sad
> for your master, robbed of his eyesight by a rascal?

The soliloquy proceeds, with the audience aware that Polyphemus is being tricked all the while – and deservedly so – yet perhaps beginning to feel some pity for his plight.

Such is the poet's gift for empathy. Homer may have recycled the storylines, but the way he told them was, it seems, unprecedented. Other bards may have sung of a hero's encounter with a cannibalistic giant, even of Odysseus versus Polyphemus. But was there any rival for Homer's vivid detail, describing how the Cyclops' cave was pungent with its raised array of seasoning cheeses, or just noting how Polyphemus would whistle as he went off with his flock? A search for comparable narrative style within the literate cultures of

Egypt, Anatolia, the Middle East and Assyria yields nothing quite like this. The Mesopotamian epic *Gilgamesh*, for example, from the third millennium BC, is a fast tale of the title hero and his quest – an interestingly flawed hero at that – yet, as it comes down to us, the story barely goes beyond *what* happens to Gilgamesh and his friend Enkidu. *How* events take place – the psychology of motive, interaction of characters, and so on – is not a narrative concern; nor is there any graphic evocation of setting.*

Homer represents a long oral tradition: that much is clear from analysis of his language and from comparative studies made of oral poetry in later times. As the American scholar Milman Parry showed, bards in the Balkans, recorded in the 1930s, could recite many hundreds of lines of formulaic verse in performance – and they were illiterate. Yet was Homer in a different league of not only quantity, but quality? Accepting that audiences of epic poetry in Greece around 750 BC had never heard any performance quite so enchanting as Homer's, one proposal is that a direct effect of such poetry was to catalyze the advent of literacy in the Greek world. This hypothesis, crudely summarized, takes alternative forms. The first is that Homer himself either dictated his poems, or learned the craft of writing, in order to preserve (or memorize) his work. The second is that Homer's audience in the late eighth century reached out for some means of recording and remembering his wonderful words. Either way, letters were borrowed from the Phoenicians to form an 'alphabet' (after *alpha*, *beta* – the first letters in the sequence, followed

---

* Conversely, of course, the *Iliad* could by itself seem like a hopelessly incomplete story: much more has to happen at Troy before and after the span of Homer's poem.

by *gamma*, *delta*, and so on). These alphabetic letters were arranged to reproduce, more or less, words as they sounded when spoken.

In historical times the Greeks were well aware that the basis of their writing system, which was more efficient than any so far devised, lay with the Phoenicians. Mythically, a certain Cadmus, migrating from the Levant in search of his sister Europa, who had been seduced by Zeus in the form of a bull, came to Thebes in Boeotia, where he founded a city – and introduced literacy to the Greeks. Linguistically, Phoenician was a Semitic language with no relation to Greek; and the Phoenicians used their letters (all consonants, like Hebrew) primarily for commercial transactions.

The earliest Greek inscriptions, datable to around 750 BC, do not seem related to commerce. Dedications, gift exchange, claims to ownership – these are among the overt or likely occasions. Several of the inscriptions also appear to be scratched lines of verse in Homer's epic rhythm (the regular 'six-footed' fall of syllables known as the hexameter). The best known of these includes a direct reference to the *Iliad*'s aged hero Nestor. Is it an early sign of Homer's reputation? In his works, Homer maintained the epic poet's right to self-effacing anonymity. But his personal role in the formation of classical culture, while disputed in terms of local detail, was widely accepted in antiquity; and even if it cannot be proved that his poems were a primary motive for the Greek adoption of the alphabet, Homer as 'the educator of all Greece' is an historical phenomenon. By the early sixth century BC there was an influential guild of 'Homerists' (*Homeridai*), based on Chios, devoted to reciting Homer's lines. So flourished the cult of Homer as intermediary between myth and history, between gods and mortals – and between heroic past and ordinary present.

• • •

The people who were Homer's original patrons, inviting him to recite perhaps up to two or three thousand lines at some special event, did not themselves live in palaces. They occupied modest, low, stone-built enclosures, keeping some livestock but practising mostly arable cultivation: grains and pulses were the staples of their existence (so they liked to hear that Odysseus, during his travels, equates 'bread-eating' with 'civilized'). Some utensils and weapons of iron were in use, and the head of the house might keep a horse, possibly with a wheeled vehicle. Items of gold or silver, jewels and beads from the east, were very rare; pottery, though turned on a wheel, was mostly decorated, if at all, with geometric motifs and stick-figures.

Evidently, however, communities in the eighth century BC were aware that their ancestors had enjoyed a more magnificent lifestyle. In some parts of the Greek world – especially in the south-east Peloponnese, at sites such as Argos, Mycenae and Tiryns – the ruins of great fortified settlements were visible enough. Or there might be other monumental remains – tombs and barrows raised to the dead, conspicuously man-made. So far as we can tell, the eighth-century inhabitants of this landscape did not pillage these monuments. Rather, they affirmed a proprietorial rapport, by offering ancestral veneration at such sites. So, by some olden tumulus or earthwork, a trench would be dug, and libations of oil or wine offered to the spirits of the dead presumed buried there. The ceramic vessels used to make these libations would be left in situ; in due time, when writing was acquired, dedications 'to the hero' might be added.

Accepting the archaeological testimony of 'hero cult' in the eighth century BC, we may suppose that Homer's patrons essentially commissioned him to bring this 'heroic past' to life. Of course there were the elements of fantasy – what would be the point of poetry, or any kind of art, if it could not include wishful thinking? – but as we have seen, Homer did his best to make the evocation convincing, stitching his verses with a sustained thread of credibility. He did not compose for posterity, but sang about a generation of marvellous ancestors, to listeners for whom, perhaps, Menelaus of Sparta was claimed as a great-great-grandfather, or Ajax a mighty uncle on their mother's side.

This sense of a bloodline – a direct involvement and investment in the past – helps to explain why Homer developed such a remarkably graphic narrative style. But just how far into the past was he projecting this style? And what historical 'reality' lies behind the poetry?

• • •

It does not help that Homer was, in technical terms, rather careless in distinguishing the forging of iron and bronze – he did not measure epochs, as we do, by materials such as stone or metal. If formal athletic contests at Olympia did indeed commence, as later tradition maintained, in 776 BC, Homer ignores their existence. There was no established annalistic chronology, as there was in Egypt; only a persistent tendency, among the Greeks, to telescope the past (and to conflate, as noted, the categories of myth and history).

So Homer does not say when he thinks the Trojan War began, or when Odysseus reached home. Subsequent writers, beginning with Hecataeus in the early fifth century BC, tried to impose absolute dates, or at least a relative sequence of events, and to map a range of places. As it happens, one of their suggested absolute dates for the fall of Troy, corresponding to 1183 BC, seems not far from the date of around 1250 BC currently assigned to one of the 'destruction levels' identified by archaeologists at Troy.* But it was not until the advent of modern archaeology that an overview of Homer's part-imaginary world began to take shape. And here the professional modern archaeologist must admit, if only through clenched teeth, that the leading pioneer was an amateur enthusiast, Heinrich Schliemann (1822–1890). Schliemann did not himself define the 'Aegean Bronze Age' or 'Greek prehistory' as they are currently understood, but his excavations at Troy, Mycenae and elsewhere undoubtedly gave rise to a new science. So it is that we can say with some confidence that a war at Troy took place in the mid-thirteenth century BC; and that parts of Greece were then ruled by warrior-kings whose conspicuous wealth, physical stature and seaborne power can be shown to match, more or less, the epic image conjured by Homer.

Schliemann's own controversial career and reputation have become a study in their own right. Here we can be content to accept his own account that he heard the story

---

* Formerly known as 'Troy VIIa', but subject to reclassification.

of Troy while he was very young – and in particular that he was struck by an image of the city's destruction and of its most famous refugee, Aeneas, leaving the flames with his son by his side and carrying his father on his back. Schliemann the child determined he would find this city; Schliemann the young man made a great deal of money in order to pursue that aim; and Schliemann senior fulfilled it. It was not quite done single-handedly – the likely site of Troy had already been identified by an American diplomat in Turkey, Frank Calvert – but it was carried through with extraordinary will and bravura. Not only that, but Schliemann's persistent enthusiasm, on top of his gift for self-advertisement, was contagious. Quite literally, he made the discovery of Homer's world a topic of global front-page news. His method of excavation tended to be drastic in its quest for objects (he used dynamite to get down to 'original layers'), and his published reports confirm the acute observation of one contemporary, Adolf Furtwängler, that – for all his triumphal self-importance – Schliemann actually 'had no idea of the value of his discoveries'. Yet the scope and scale of his 'campaigns' at Troy and Mycenae – hiring squadrons of labourers, and so on – set an example of what could be done, logistically, with teamwork. Archaeology had previously tended to be a rather genteel individual hobby – and Schliemann himself had started that way, poking about for the residence of Odysseus amid olive groves on the island of Ithaca. Now it was transformed, not only in the Aegean but in Egypt and the Near East too, into a pseudo-military operation.

Beginning in 1871, Schliemann dug a great trench through Troy. Among his finds was a copper cauldron containing a hoard of gold jewellery he immediately called 'Priam's Treasure' – and later smuggled out of the country. Now in Moscow's Pushkin Museum, this hoard is more prosaically known as 'Treasure A', and dates to the second half of the third millennium BC, or 'Troy II'; insofar as he can be dated, Priam belongs to a later phase of the city – 'Troy VIIa/VIi' – about a thousand years later. Such pedantic qualification post-dates Schliemann, but he would never have had the patience for it anyway. In 1876 he moved his attention to Mycenae. The site, in contrast to Troy, was never 'lost' – its famous Lion Gate had remained visible down the centuries – but Schliemann, exploring a cemetery within the city walls, made revelations. He could not have known that graves are not usually enclosed within city walls, and therefore that the graves must pre-date the fortifications, and the Lion Gate, by some centuries. As it was, he came across five so-called 'shaft graves': rectangular pits within a closed-off area, containing the skeletons of a kinship group buried with considerable splendour.

We now see that the builders of the walls must have had special reason for making this distinctive cemetery intra-mural. For Schliemann there was never any doubt: here were the graves of ill-fated members of 'the house of Atreus' – their bodies laid out with bronze swords and inlaid daggers, golden diadems and gold and silver drinking cups, various rings, gems and necklaces, and a number of gold masks. Legend has it that Schliemann telegraphed the king of Greece to say, 'I have gazed upon the face of Agamemnon.' In fact his message was not quite so dramatic; but he did believe that the tragic story told of Agamemnon's homecoming – how he walked into a murderous domestic trap set by his wife Clytemnestra and her lover Aegisthus – reported an event in Mycenae's history.*

It was Schliemann's long-suffering colleague from the Greek Archaeological Service, Panagiotes Stamatakes, who stayed on not only to discover a sixth grave, but also to establish that these burials belonged to a date in the sixteenth century, about half a millennium before the presumed Trojan War. Already, however, Schliemann had publicized the finds as testimony to a previously unknown civilization: the 'Mycenaeans'.

Subsequent archaeological investigations have confirmed that, while Mycenae was indeed a great citadel, it was not alone. Not far away, also in the Argive plain, was Tiryns. Other centres on the Greek mainland included Iolkos (Dimini) in Thessaly; Pylos in Messenia; Thebes, Orchomenos and Gla in Boeotia; and probably Athens too. In these places there were remains of 'palatial' structures, some of them fortified with walls built of such great stones that they seemed 'Cyclopean', forming a network of associated states plausibly dominated by overlords such as Agamemnon seemed to personify. But how had such a society been co-ordinated without (as far as Schliemann could tell) a system of writing and keeping records?

In fact there was such a system – though it only came to light later – in the form of clay tablets inscribed with signs composed of squiggles and lines. These were first found at the palace of Knossos on Crete. Knossos was a site that

---

* As students of Greek tragic drama will know, Agamemnon's father Atreus had inherited a curse laid upon his father, Pelops - the hero who gave his name to the Peloponnesian landmass. The tragedy continues with Agamemnon's children Orestes and Electra, and beyond.

Schliemann had hoped to investigate, for it was associated with a king called Minos, who by legend had created a labyrinth there – an underground maze in which a terrifying creature called the Minotaur, half-man, half-bull, was kept. Schliemann was thwarted in his bid: a gentleman scholar from Oxford's Ashmolean Museum, Arthur Evans, succeeded in acquiring proprietorial rights at Knossos, where he began digging in 1900.

Before long, no fewer than three successive Bronze Age writing systems had come to light at Knossos. The first, using pictograms, was called 'Cretan Hieroglyphic', and appeared to have been invented on the island (under Egyptian influence) about 2000 BC. By around 1650 BC this had been supplanted by a more stylized script, which Evans termed 'Linear A'. This, in turn, had given way, by about 1450 BC, to a script that was apparently related but which (it later turned out) represents a different language. Evans called this 'Linear B'.

Though less inclined to showmanship than Schliemann, Evans presented his work at Knossos as revealing 'the palace of Minos' – and did not demur, eventually, from reconstructing substantial parts of its structural appearance. What had befallen the palace in the middle of the second millennium, however, only became comprehensible in the light of what Schliemann's successors uncovered on the Greek mainland. Traces of Linear B writing were found at Pylos in Messenia – the site associated with Homer's Nestor, son of Neleus – and at Tiryns, Thebes and Mycenae too. The inscriptions had evidently been made as temporary memoranda on clay tablets, which turned solid when baked in fires that eventually consumed these palaces. The signs, whatever they meant, were enough to identify the sites as 'Mycenaean'; and the Mycenaeans must be categorically different from the 'Minoans' (as Evans called them) based at Knossos and other sites on Crete and beyond. So what was Linear B doing at Knossos, the home of Linear A?

The mystery had still not been solved when, as a distinguished old man, Evans showed a group of schoolboys around a 1936 Royal Academy exhibition of British archaeological discoveries in Greece and Crete. One of the young visitors was Michael Ventris, who had already become interested in Egyptian hieroglyphics. The encounter was momentous, for Ventris went on to devote himself to the particular challenge of Linear B. The script was syllabic rather than alphabetic – that is, it was dominated by signs representing a consonant plus a vowel, such as *mi* or *ka*, along with vowels alone (*a*, *e*, *i*, *o*, *u*). In 1936, demonstrating the language expressed by these signs was still elusive.

War interrupted work at Pylos – a prime source of Linear B inscriptions – but war also brought developments in the art of cryptography. Collaborating with scholars who were attempting the decipherment of Linear B with military codebreaking strategies, Ventris found a way of consistently matching the sign groups of Linear B to an alphabetic system of consonants and vowels. By the summer of 1952 he was able to announce the result on BBC radio:

I have come to the conclusion that the Knossos and the Pylos tablets must, after all, be written in Greek – a difficult and archaic Greek, seeing that it is 500 years older than Homer, and written in rather abbreviated form, but Greek nevertheless.

How many listeners to national radio were thrilled to hear news of the proof we cannot know. But for anyone concerned with the prehistory of Greece, and Europe, this 'code-cracking' brought substantial historical implications. The Mycenaeans, then, were aboriginal Greeks: not pre-Hellenic so much as proto-Hellenic. For all that their citadels and palaces had suffered an apparently wholesale collapse around 1200 BC, the Mycenaeans did not disappear. At least, their language basically survived – to be rewritten, alphabetically, from about 700 BC onwards.

• • •

The career of Michael Ventris was cut short: four years on from his breakthrough, he died in a car crash. The information yielded by Linear B, however, continues still to flow. Much of it relates to the social, political, economic and religious structures indicated by the administrative 'book-keeping' function of the inscriptions (though society, politics, economics and religion may not be separable here). Among the bureaucratic detail we learn about numbers of livestock (some 100,000 sheep belonging to the territory of Knossos); names of particular cattle ('Dapple', 'Dusky'); stores of arms and armour, chariots and chariot wheels, and chariot wheels in need of repair – and so on. We comprehend that deities who will figure in the classical Greek pantheon – including Zeus, Poseidon, Dionysus and Athena – were recognized, with similar titles, by the Mycenaeans. We also notice certain names appearing in Linear B that seem very similar to names familiar from Homer's epic world – Hector, for example, and Achilles – and adjectives used in a way reminiscent of formulaic epithets in Homer: so a ship will be described as 'well-rounded at both ends'.

However, Linear B as it appears on the tablets so far excavated from Mycenaean palaces was not used to transcribe poetry. And we make a fundamental error of literary judgement if we try to demonstrate that Homer was a curator of Mycenaean memory. He might have wanted it to seem that way: an essential part of his poetic power consists, as noted, in persuading his audience to believe that a level of eyewitness detail prevails amid all the formulaic language of recital and performance. But, to reiterate, Homer was not an archaeologist, still less a war correspondent. Scholars sceptical of an historical Trojan War rightly point out that Homer's catalogue of the fleet assembled by Greek forces (in Book Two of the *Iliad*) omits many of the places we know, from archaeology, to have been important Mycenaean sites. But one does not have to be an expert to query the overall narrative plausibility here. The siege of Troy has been going on for the best part of a decade when the *Iliad* opens. So why have none of the great Greek or Trojan warriors become casualties so far? How come Achilles and Hector have yet even to encounter each other?

The truth is that Homer's enthusiasm for his theme carries us away. He knows just enough about the heroic past to furnish it with period pieces – helmets made of boars' tusks, for example – but he need not worry about incidental anachronisms. After all, his song comes from the Muses, daughters of Zeus: a source that is immortal, and therefore regardless of time.

• • •

With or without Homer, we may accept the Mycenaeans as prehistoric ancestors of the Greeks. Then we are bound to consider two residual questions. First, where does this leave the Minoans? And second: if the 'Mycenaean world' collapsed around 1200 BC, what happened next? – and what, we may wonder, caused the collapse?

The first issue can be simply answered. So far, no one knows what language lies behind the script of Linear A; its origins are probably Anatolian. But Minoan identity, apparent from around 2100 BC, has an archaeological definition far beyond the myth of Minos and his labyrinth. Knossos, by virtue not only of its palatial extent but also of its residential area, its support of specialist crafts, and so on, was clearly the 'capital' of Minoan Crete. Phaistos, Ayia Triadha, Malia and Kato Zakros are among the subsidiary centres located by archaeology, with their territorial boundaries conceivably marked by mountainous ritual locations ('peak sanctuaries'). Arthur Evans may have had European royalty in mind when he denominated certain spaces at Knossos (the Throne Room, the Queen's Dressing Room). However, his concept (or preconception) that a theocratic 'Priest-King' occupied the apex of power at Knossos remains broadly acceptable. The story of the Minotaur, too, finds some rationalized basis in a number of images of bulls from the site – including the well-known fresco of acrobatic 'toreadors', assembled from myriad fragments.

Seaborne expansion by the Minoans established colonial settlements around the Aegean (on the islands of Kea, Kythera and Melos, for example), and a trading range that encompassed the Anatolian coastline, Cyprus and Egypt. Wall paintings from houses at the site of Akrotiri on the island of Santorini (also known as Thera) include scenes showing a flotilla of oar-propelled boats, some decked out with awnings for VIP passengers at ease. Thucydides, the Athenian historian writing in the latter years of the fifth century BC, associated 'sea-power' (*thalassocracy*) with Minos. But was much else known about our 'Minoans' to the Greeks of historical times? In the writings of Plato, from the fourth century BC, we find a tale about an island called Atlantis, home to a great 'civilization', which was swallowed up by the sea in some natural catastrophe. Though Plato situates Atlantis beyond the Straits of Gibraltar – so in the Atlantic Ocean, likewise named after Atlas, in Greek mythology the primordial Titan who holds up the sky – there is speculation that some memory of a volcanic event on Santorini may lie at the origins of Plato's story. Geologically it seems that an eruption took place around 1700 to 1600 BC, scattering ash and pumice over a very wide area (Akrotiri was one nearby site buried under the pyroclastic flow), and very likely causing an immense tsunami or series of tidal waves in parts of the Aegean. One possibility is that Egyptian scribes took note of the catastrophe and informed Greek visitors about it many centuries later.

The classical Greeks were vaguely aware of a great deluge at some point in prehistory. Their mythology reported that Zeus, made furious by mortal misbehaviour, had flooded the earth; and in response to the inundation, a couple called Deucalion and Pyrrha had constructed a 'container' (*larnax*), and so kept afloat to survive – and then generated a son, Hellen, who in turn produced a trio of sons. These offspring gave rise to the three primary subdivisions of the Greek-speaking peoples (*Hellenes*) as subsequently recognized – the

Dorians, the Ionians and the Aeolians. Dialect was one way of making distinction among them, but – as we shall see – there were further cultural differences (not to mention further subdivisions). In any case, there is nothing to link the myth of Deucalion and Pyrrha with either the archaeology or the mythology of the Minoans – while, if only symbolically, the Hebrew narrative of Noah's Ark must be related.

It may have been a residual effect of the Santorini eruption that the Minoan presence in the Aegean became weakened. At any rate, Mycenaeans had taken control of Knossos by around 1450 BC, and the Minoans, as an archaeological 'culture' or category, disappear. So it seems to happen, as far as our knowledge goes; we create history according to the perceived rise and fall of various 'civilizations'. But what then brought about the demise of the Mycenaeans, just two-and-a-half centuries later?

Climate change, earthquakes and various other natural disasters have all been invoked. The most likely explanation is a systemic breakdown triggered by some such event. Suddenly, trading connections were cut. The internal stress latent in the centres of power, with authority vested in one kingly figure – the generic title for 'overlord', *wanax*, known to Homer, derives from Linear B – was compounded by demographic instability. Egyptian chronicles record the belligerent presence of so-called 'Sea Peoples' in the eastern Mediterranean, evidently making attacks upon coastal settlements. During the last quarter of the thirteenth century the Egyptians themselves were led by Ramesses II to a mass chariot-battle with the Hittites at Kadesh, in modern Syria. Since both sides claimed victory, the encounter is likely to have been mutually destructive. Raiding parties descended upon the Peloponnese from the north-west of Greece: a 'Dorian invasion' is sometimes invoked. The citadels of the Mycenaeans may in some cases have been robustly fortified (in contrast to the defenceless palaces of the Minoans), but, like Troy, they were not very extensive in size. At any rate, the end was swift and wide-spread. All the palaces were put to the torch. Dynastic splendour crumbled – along with all its complex economic basis and its heavy bureaucratic apparatus.

• • •

It was many years later, in the early sixth century BC, when a blacksmith of the city of Tegea, in the Peloponnese, reported that while digging a well, he had come across an enormous coffin, containing equally enormous bones. He measured the find at seven cubits – about ten feet (three metres) tall.* The blacksmith was amazed, but a visitor from another city, Sparta, presumed to know the body's identity. He excavated the skeleton and went back to Sparta proclaiming that he had with him the bones of Orestes, Agamemnon's son.

This anecdote is recorded by Herodotus, whose reputa-tion as 'the father of history' is usually qualified by the stricture that he shows little inclination to discriminate between myth, hearsay and history – the Greek *historia* implying what can be verified by enquiry. It is true that for Herodotus, who recited his *Histories* to fellow Greeks at Olympia and elsewhere in the mid-fifth century BC, there seems to have been no urgency to rationalize a story of this sort. We moderns, of course, will do so easily enough. Tegea

* A cubit was a unit based on the length from elbow to fingertips.

was a settlement situated in an Ice Age lake basin where remains of prehistoric megafauna (mammoths and such like) have been found. Similar relics, we presume, were found and put in a coffin, perhaps during the eighth century, then rediscovered by this blacksmith, before being claimed for Sparta as the bones of Orestes.

Suppose, however, that we accept the story as relayed by Herodotus. It joins many and various testimonies to the mindset of Greeks in the historical period regarding their past as something both fearful and wonderful. Credulity towards an age of heroes was clearly widespread; and while those heroes might be claimed as ancestors, yet they were categorically apart from ordinary mortals.* The active cult of heroes included veneration – or, perhaps more accurately, propitiation – of Agamemnon at Mycenae; Menelaus and Helen at the site of Therapne near Sparta; and Odysseus on the island of Ithaca. Visible remains of the Bronze Age had already become something of a heritage trail.

A number of Greek colonists established themselves at the site of Troy around 700 BC, creating 'Troy VIII'. Nearby was an ancient tumulus: of course it was denominated the tomb of Achilles. Over the subsequent centuries, Troy the city would grow again, by around 300 BC spreading far beyond its prehistoric bastion. Visitors to the site today may not be aware of this expansion – revealed so far mainly in the course of geophysical survey – but diagrams of Troy's successive phases are clear enough, showing multiple layers accumulating over the centuries, like a pile of pancakes. Such diagrams

---

* Homer was fond of likening heroes in action to certain beasts - lions, dogs, even donkeys - indicating that heroes are not only awesomely better but also (sometimes) fearfully worse than the rest of us 'two-legged animals'.

may serve to qualify the plangent verdict of Simone Weil, delivered in 1940, as her native Paris succumbed to invasion: 'The whole of the *Iliad* lies under the shadow of the greatest calamity the human race can experience – the destruction of a city.' Homer himself did not recount the story of the *Ilioupersis*, 'the Fall of Troy': that was left to his successors. But he hardly needed to elaborate. Troy, by his art, had become *the* city: the model for all that epitomizes the renewable strength, and the persistent delicacy, of 'civilization'.

II
ATHENS

Sigmund Freud, founding father of psychoanalysis, visited the Acropolis of Athens in late summer of 1904. Since his childhood he had known what was to be seen at this site, the sacred 'high city' (*akro-polis*) of ancient Athens, dominated by what remained of its most celebrated temple, the Parthenon. The reality did not disappoint. Decades on, Freud would say he had seen nothing more beautiful than these ruins. Later still, just a few years before his death in 1939, he revealed that the experience was itself a peculiar psychological event for him. As a schoolboy in Vienna, and the offspring of an uneducated wool merchant, he could only dream of standing on the Acropolis. Was he still dreaming? Was he really there? Why did it feel so unreal?

Freud diagnosed in himself a feeling of guilt. His father had worked hard to pay for the sort of education that taught the classics – that would initiate him into the significance of the Acropolis. Now, by reaching the site itself, he had 'arrived'; he had climbed a pinnacle of culture – and, in doing so, had outdone his father. So the achievement felt like an act of alienation.

As it happens, Freud considered Heinrich Schliemann to have been a supremely contented person, precisely because he had realized aspirations nursed from his early years. Freud had followed the excavations at Troy with passionate interest, and eventually came to liken his own methods of psychoanalysis to an archaeological process of 'peeling away' layers in quest of some residual 'truth' that had become 'mythical' over time.* For our purposes, however, the significance of Freud's reaction to the marble relics of classical Athens lies precisely in the sensation that caused pangs of filial piety. The Acropolis was symbolic not only of Athens at the height of her ancient glory in the mid-fifth century BC, but of 'civilized values' generally. So for Freud, and for many others, it symbolizes a bourn, a destination, for the human spirit, amid the amber glow of columns standing on a rocky mass.

• • •

The limestone platform of the Acropolis became a fortified citadel in the thirteenth century BC. With steep cliffs on three sides, and a geology that favours the sinking of artesian wells, it was obviously attractive to a Mycenaean lord. Sections of some massive late Bronze Age walls, complementing the natural defences, can be seen to this day: they were visible reminders of a past that Athenians of the historical period assumed to be heroic. Tradition told of a first king, Cecrops, born of the soil. Another early ruler, Erechtheus, was given a similar origin, sometimes with a vivid divine twist: Hephaistos, the smith god, had attempted intercourse with Athena; Athena, famously 'the Virgin' (*Parthenos*), repelled him, wiping away his semen with a rag that she threw upon the

---

* By further coincidence, Freud was on the Acropolis at around the same period as Schliemann's former assistant, Wilhelm Dörpfeld, was revealing what lay beneath the surface there.

ground; so Erechtheus arose, and was eventually honoured by the extraordinary porticoed temple of the Erechtheum (where Athenians also kept the tomb of Cecrops).

The protohistory of Athens, though vague in outline, could nonetheless be imagined in dramatic detail. So, for example, the fifth-century playwright Euripides scripted the following tragic scenario from the reign of Erechtheus: Athens is under attack by combined forces from faraway Thrace and nearby Eleusis, and the city doomed unless King Erechtheus sacrifices one of his daughters. Only fragments of this play survive, but they include some powerful passages, including a speech from the girls' mother, Praxithea:

> We have children on account of this, so that we may save the altars of the gods and the fatherland: the city has one name but many dwell in it. Is it right for me to destroy all these when it is possible for me to give one child to die on behalf of all?

Some scholars believe that the sacrifice is evoked on the marble frieze that once adorned the Parthenon temple. Certainly it would be in keeping with the fabulous ingenuity demonstrated by classical Athenians when visualizing their past. It was not until the end of the sixth century BC that Athens went through the constitutional revolution whose result was the world's first attested democracy – rule (*kratia*) by the people (*demos*). But Athenians lost no time in constructing for themselves a prelude to this revolution whereby one of the kings, Theseus, master-minded a *synoikismos*, or 'living-together', of various communities in and around Athens (the area of Attica). Some enormous bones, retrieved in the fifth century BC from the island of Skyros, were declared to be those of Theseus, and venerated accordingly.

This is the same mythical Theseus whose father, Aegeus, was taxed by King Minos of Crete with the duty of dispatching, annually, a number of young Athenians to Knossos, where their fate was to be enclosed in the Labyrinth as victims of the Minotaur. To his father's alarm, Theseus volunteered himself for this grim tribute. Myth tells how Ariadne, daughter of Minos, fell in love with the brave young Athenian, and gave him a natural torch – a ring of phosphorescent coral – and a ball of thread (the original 'clue') with which to trace his steps through the maze of the Labyrinth. Thanks to Ariadne's help, Theseus was able to kill the Minotaur and release Athens from servitude to the Cretan 'thalassocracy'. But Theseus could be careless. En route for home, he abandons Ariadne on the island of Naxos, where she will be found, and taken up in marriage, by Dionysus. He also forgets to fulfil a promise made to his father that if he returns from Crete he will change the colour of his ship's sails from black to white. Aegeus, seeing black sails of doomed youth upon the horizon, drowns himself in the sea – from which mishap those waters are called 'the Aegean'.

Theseus was said to have accompanied Herakles in a raid against the Amazons. He came back with a trophy wife, Hippolyta (or Antiope), and thereafter had to defend Athens against a raid by the Amazons. For later Athenians, this attack prefigured the invasion of Attica by Persians in 480 BC. From the east, and fighting as archers upon horseback, the Amazons symbolized Oriental danger, and perhaps also a fear (on the part of Greek males) of some society where women ruled. In any case, the theme of a 'battle of Greeks against Amazons' ('Amazonomachy') joined that of 'Gods against primordial Giants' ('Gigantomachy') as a subject repeatedly deemed suitable for the decoration of classical monuments.

Despite his misbehaviour, Theseus was enduringly regarded as a founding hero of Athens. The institution of monarchy, however, was not guaranteed its survival.

• • •

In Athens, as elsewhere in Greece, the centuries after the collapse of the Mycenaean palaces around 1200 BC are described as a 'Dark Age'. More broadly, the chronological transition is from Bronze Age to Iron Age. In the parlance of classical history, however, 'Dark Age' is used more often than 'Early Iron Age'. The term implies obscurity of historical information, drawn from an archaeological record that is patchy in its extent, and also indicates communities whose standard of living seems relatively impoverished. Literacy disappeared, along with the economic systems of central administration and storage it once served. Population levels declined by at least a half, according to estimates based upon archaeological survey. Citadels such as Mycenae and Tiryns, though not entirely abandoned, fell into disrepair. Settlements of the ensuing period, insofar as they have been excavated, seem modest by comparison. So at Nichoria, for instance, in the south-western part of the Peloponnese known as Messenia, a large hill-top town that was once part of the territory of the palace at Pylos became a self-sufficient village of perhaps 200 or so inhabitants, occupying thatched huts ringed round by fences for domesticated livestock.

Such small communities may have consisted mostly of one extended family, but signs of hierarchy can be detected all the same. To date, the site that most illuminates the Dark Age is that of Lefkandi, on the elongated island of Euboea, lying off the north-east coast of Attica. In the early 1980s a discovery was made here that still kindles the imagination. Beneath an artificial mound archaeologists came across a structure over fifty metres in length that must have been (for its time) a great hall, fronted by a porch and completed by an apsidal recess. Albeit in timber, the building was 'peripteral' – that is, with multiple columns around the walls. So why had it been buried under a mound? Because it became, upon the death of its presumed occupant, a tomb. To judge from the skeletal remains and associated artefacts, this was the burial of someone powerful. When he died, four horses were slaughtered to be buried with him. An adorned female body laid beside him may be that of his consort – perhaps also killed for the occasion.

The honorand of the tomb, given a hero's funeral, remains anonymous. In anthropological jargon he is categorized simply as a 'Big Man'; or else by the Greek term for 'king', *basileus*. However, the archaeological story does not end there. Further burials were subsequently made in the vicinity of the mound, and at cemeteries elsewhere at Lefkandi – they are not quite so grand, yet their occupants had iron swords and spearheads, and access to artefacts that may be traced to Cyprus, Tyre and the Levantine coast. The Big Man, laid to rest with his wife, may have been venerated as a hero, but he seems to have left no single heir. One possibility is that a group of 'aristocrats' succeeded him.

It is tempting to impose that narrative at Lefkandi because what we can glean of Athenian politics during the Dark Age suggests that kingship gave way to some sort of oligarchy or 'rule by the few', who would later be referred to as the *Eupatridai* – 'the well-born ones'. There are tales of a dynastic crisis, with one heroic king, Codrus, perhaps leaving no suitable successor; but already in the time of Erechtheus the office of *polemarch* ('war-lord') had been created for Ion, the king's son-in-law. Then the title of *archon* ('chief magistrate') entered Athenian political parlance. The title could attach to 'king' (*archon basileus*), and also to *polemarch* as head of military affairs; by itself, however, it carried a range of civic and legislative duties over the fixed tenure of a decade.

It seems to have been towards the end of the seventh century BC that a first written constitution for Athens was drafted. We know little about the traditional author, Draco, beyond his reputation for severity (infringement of 'Draconian' laws generally entailed the death penalty). In fact the first Athenian politician to whom we can attach much of an historical identity is Solon – and even about him there is the nimbus of legendary wisdom. Solon became chief archon around 594 BC, at a time when social tension in Athens appears to have been verging upon crisis. This, at least, is how Solon himself dramatizes the situation, in surviving fragments of apparently autobiographical verse. 'Well-born' himself, he makes a point of despising excessive wealth; accordingly, in steering a course for the city he sought to curb greed among the aristocrats and to create a constitution in which access to public offices and councils was enlarged. Property qualifications were still imposed, but Solon ordered a widespread cancellation of debts as one way of narrowing the social divide throughout Attica, and gave the population's several 'tribes' (*phylai*) greater opportunity for representation at a central 'assembly' (*ekklesia*, literally a 'summons').

As one of his elegiac fragments records, 'in matters of great importance it is hard to please everyone' – the rueful adage of any politician, perhaps. Feeling that his efforts to mould Athens into a more egalitarian *polis* had failed, Solon went abroad for ten years. By the time he returned, it was too late to prevent what he had feared: the rise of despotism.

'Despot' (*despotes*) carries the basic meaning of 'master of the house'. Already by the sixth century BC, the term had acquired a pejorative political implication of tyrannical rule. But whether the 'despotic' rule over Athens by Pisistratus and his sons during much of the sixth century BC should be regarded as good or bad remains debatable. Pisistratus was most definitely 'well-born': his family claimed descent from Homer's senior hero Nestor, son of Neleus, who once ruled over Pylos. And like Solon, Pisistratus was concerned to keep the countryside of Attica economically, socially and politically integrated with Athens the city. It was as leader of a rural faction, and after a period of factional dispute, that Pisistratus took autocratic control of Athens in 561 BC. Was this what the citizens wanted at the time? Quite possibly: we are told that they granted Pisistratus a squadron of bodyguards, presumably for fear of attack by rival aristocrats.

As it happened, Pisistratus was expelled after just five years. He almost immediately returned to power, revealing his flair as a showman by entering Athens in a chariot accompanied, so it seemed, by Athena herself (Pisistratus had found a statuesque country girl and persuaded her to dress up as the goddess). The city's most spectacular religious festival, the Panathenaia – a sort of birthday party for Athena, celebrated each summer, and on a particularly lavish scale every four years – had been formally instituted in 566 BC. The occasion was a gift to Pisistratus, who continued Solon's project of embellishing the Acropolis with new buildings. By the mid-sixth century there was a 'hundred-foot-long' *(hekatompedon)* temple for the city's divine protectress, decorated by a pediment that showed Athena striking down the Giants who had once threatened Olympian order; and a series of treasuries and shrines, all brightly painted and elaborated with sculptural scenes. In among these buildings appeared a wonderful population of figures dedicated as votive offerings: marble statues of 'youths' *(kouroi)* and 'maidens' *(korai)* set up as commemorative offerings to Athena and other deities. It is readily supposed that this formidably good-looking array represents *la crème de la crème* of 'well-born' Athenians on display. It is also worth noting, however, that among the dedications are also images of seated scribes, and plaques set up by successful potters and so on: these offer some substance to reports that Pisistratus (again, following Solon) promoted literacy and crafts at Athens. As noted in the previous chapter, the first transcription of Homer's epic appears to have been made in mid-sixth century BC Athens: Pisistratus is the likely sponsor.

Although he was forced out of power again, and eventually regained it by force, Pisistratus in person is said by later Athenian sources not to have behaved in an overtly tyrannical way. By nature mild and affable, he spent most of his time dealing with the affairs of ordinary citizens, and placed himself under the same laws as everyone else. When he died in 527 BC, he left two sons in charge, Hippias and Hipparchus. 'Pisistratid' Athens continued as such for over a decade.

There had been dynastic tyrants before in other cities, such as Corinth, and the phenomenon would recur subsequently (notably at Syracuse). But when an end came to tyranny at Athens, it brought about radical constitutional change.

That is not to say that radical constitutional change was the intention of two Athenians, Harmodius and Aristogeiton, later hailed as the 'Tyrannicides', whose bravery brought about democracy at Athens. A well-known statue group shows them heroically stripped and stepping forward with their weapons, poised to strike: whoever admires them from the front plays the part of their victim. There is little doubt that the pair were involved in some sort of anti-Pisistratid plot, and that they killed the younger son, Hipparchus, on the occasion of the Panathenaic festival in 514 BC. But accounts of their motives and actions are confused. The most plausible explanation is that Harmodius and Aristogeiton killed Hipparchus in the course of some quarrel over a love affair, or insult to family honour. Pederasty – the homoerotic relationship between an older man and a junior partner – was normal in archaic Athens: Hipparchus may have trespassed on an existing rapport. In any case the murder was done in full public view, and almost suicidally. Harmodius was immediately killed by guards, and his senior companion Aristogeiton later tortured, then killed, by Hippias.

Hippias, unnerved by the event, turned suspicious and cruel: so we are told, and the report is psychologically credible. Meanwhile, a number of Athenian families exiled by the regime were plotting to stage a return, with assistance from the Peloponnesian city of Sparta. The Spartans, as we shall see, would become arch-enemies of the Athenians in the fifth century BC. At this time they were already rivals.

One of the exiled families, the Alcmaeonids, was financing a new temple of Apollo at the oracular sanctuary of Delphi. The oracle of Delphi urged that Sparta assist in expelling tyranny from Athens. In 510 BC, with military assistance from Sparta, various exiles succeeded in expelling Hippias. They hoped, presumably, to form an aristocratic oligarchy ('rule by the few'). But they quarrelled among themselves, and in an attempt to redeem his cause, one of the Alcmaeonids, Cleisthenes, sought support from a broader constituency. To become a constituency, these supporters had to be made participants in the political process. So it was, around 508–7 BC, that power (*kratos*) was allocated to the people (*demos*).

Cleisthenes probably held office as archon at some time previous to falling out with the Pisistratids: we know little more about democracy's founder. No statues appear to have been raised in his honour by grateful citizens; it was the image of the Tyrannicides that became symbolic of Athens as a city of *isonomia*, 'equality of rights'. Perhaps Cleisthenes was so true to the ideology of egalitarianism that he shunned any kind of individual celebrity, or perhaps he was so horrified by the monster he had created that he subsequently disowned it. In any case, the constitutional changes introduced by Cleisthenes made Athens immediately different from other cities and states throughout the Greek-speaking world and beyond – and very consciously so. The Athenians could not possibly know that they were pioneers of a system that would be considered, some two-and-a-half thousand years later, the optimal form of constitution. Yet the pride Athenians took in defining themselves by democracy almost suggests the anticipation of posterity's gratitude.

Modern democracies are of course much more inclusive, socially, than Athenian democracy ever was – although extensions of franchise have only come relatively recently. However, even discounting the marked tendency in modern democracies for citizens to waive or squander their voting rights, no modern democracy has ever matched the democratic achievement of Athens. We moderns choose politicians to represent our wishes. In ancient Athens the principle of non-representation, or direct participation, was upheld as far as practically possible. The Assembly, convened on a hill called the Pnyx, west of the Acropolis, afforded a regular opportunity, at least once a fortnight, for many citizens to gather in their thousands – though it must always have been a vocal challenge, even when an auditorium was created, for an individual to address such a gathering. After Cleisthenes' reforms, diverse traditional classifications of citizen identity – by group of kinship and descent, by domicile, by socioeconomic status – became subordinate to a system of ten reformulated tribes. Each tribe was assigned a nominal founder of heroic status, legendarily associated with Athenian territory (i.e. Attica, plus the island of Salamis). The link with warrior glory provided by these 'Eponymous Heroes' was significant: for it was as a member of the tribe that the democratic citizen learned to bear arms on behalf of the *polis*. And it was from the tribe that executive officers of the democratic administration were appointed, mostly by sortition – the drawing of lots.

From each tribe fifty citizens over the age of thirty were eligible for a city council (*boule*). These took it in turn to serve as presiding officers (*prytaneis*), who in turn elected, on a daily basis, one of their number to act as chairman. From the tribes, too, came ten generals (*strategoi*), annually elected by

the Assembly. These formed a war council, soon supplanting
the old office of *polemarch*, and duly relying upon a majority
vote for any military decision. Then there was the administration of civil justice. Nine chief magistrates or archons
remained in the new dispensation, forming a sort of supreme
court that met on the Areopagus hill. From the Assembly
numerous other magistrates were chosen by lot. Meanwhile
the citizen body supplied the courts of law in the form of
dikasteries – judicial panels assigned (again, by lot) from
some 6,000 annually designated names. (To put that in
perspective, the citizen populace of fifth-century BC Athens,
i.e. men over eighteen years old entitled to vote, is usually
estimated as about 30,000.)

Even a rough summary of Athenian democracy reveals its
potential for making substantial claims upon an individual's
time. If military service is included, it would be true to say
that participating in civic business was more or less a prime
occupation for the Athenian citizen. Typically, he owned land
beyond the urban centre that comprised an agricultural
estate, but of course menial chores and seasonal tasks were
assigned to slaves, and day-to-day household management
could be delegated to a compliant wife. Light industry and
trade tended to be done by resident foreigners, who as such
were not citizens, nor could they become so: categorized as
'metics' (*metoikoi*), they paid taxes and received some legal
rights, but were excluded from politics no less firmly than
women and slaves.

No feature of this constitution says more about its ideological principles than ostracism. The term derives from
ostrakon, Greek for a piece of broken pottery or 'sherd'.
Ostrakismos was the process whereby citizens were given the

opportunity to send one of their number into exile for ten years. The procedure was as follows: once a year, the Assembly was asked if an ostracism should be held; if the vote was in favour, then magistrates arranged for the city's main public space, the Agora ('market'), to be fenced off in such a way that ten entrances were created, for use respectively by citizens according to tribe; each participant in the vote was issued with an *ostrakon*, on which he should inscribe the name of the person he wished to expel; so long as a minimum of 6,000 votes were cast, the person whose name was most often inscribed was obliged to leave Athenian territory within ten days (readers will note a certain decimal fixation at work here). His banishment did not entail loss of property; he was expected to return afterwards, with no particular loss of status or honour.

Cleisthenes is usually credited with this measure (some say he may even have been a victim of it, eventually). That 'hate campaigns' were orchestrated against this or that individual is likely, and perhaps attested by finds of *ostraka* evidently pre-inscribed with a certain name. The justification of ostracism is, however, clear enough. If any participant in democratic politics looked set to accrue too much personal power or influence, then at least citizens were offered the occasion to forestall the resurgence of a tyranny or an oligarchy. Ostracism was no obstacle to the politician capable of retaining his popularity: that is why the history of Athens in the fifth century BC features a number of prominent figures – names such as Themistokles, Kimon and Perikles. In theory, at least, the risk of exile kept these 'leaders' on their toes.

• • •

So what was it like to live in this obsessively democratic city?

Any answer to that question must begin by conceding that divisions of wealth and property persisted: there were still aristocrats in Athens, albeit they might find themselves doing jury service with a donkey-driver. These wealthy citizens were not taxed directly, but they were obliged to share some of their affluence by the discharge of certain 'liturgies' on behalf of the city – to sponsor a theatrical programme, for example, or to finance the capital cost and annual overheads of a ship within the Athenian fleet. Class divisions certainly existed. Manual labour and handicrafts were generally regarded with disdain, even if their products appeared beautiful: given a choice, no one would want to be an artisan (*banausos*). All the same, most Athenian citizens had to work for a living. Their service to the city was compensated by a daily allowance, and for some this might have comprised very necessary 'expenses'.

Conversely, some metics prospered without full political involvement. One curious example is the orator Lysias, whose father came to Athens from the Corinthian colony of Syracuse, in Sicily. So Lysias counted as a metic at Athens, and consequently was not able to take part in court proceedings. Yet he could write speeches for prosecutors and defendants, and he did so in a flexible style prescribed as a model for students of Greek to this day. So although Lysias was technically an outsider – or perhaps because he was such – his surviving speeches (the original output is reckoned at around 200) are rich in incidental detail about lives in late fifth- and early fourth-century BC Athens. An early speech,

On the Murder of Eratosthenes, for example, makes a case for the defence of someone charged with killing a man he caught having an affair with his wife: here we learn not only about the prevailing laws regarding adultery (and justifiable homicide), but all sorts of telling detail about how an Athenian household, including slaves, occupied its respective domestic spaces.

Democratic Athens was a slave economy. Certain individuals in classical Athens might possess many slaves, even up to a thousand. Lysias and his brothers had a staff of 120 slaves, deployed on the family farm and in a workshop manufacturing shields; the family of Demosthenes, another celebrated Athenian orator, kept over fifty slaves, again distributed between agricultural labour and industrial activity. Slaves were acquired through war, piracy and various vicissitudes (before Solon outlawed the practice, a free man might sell his own children, or even himself, if he fell into desperate debt). Their numbers, in any case, were considerable: by the fifth century BC, they probably made up about one third of the entire population in Attica.

A notable source of Athenian wealth in the fifth century BC was the mining of silver, by slave labour, at Laurion, near Cape Sounion.* At Laurion conditions were notoriously severe. Elsewhere, however, the rapport between slaves and free men seems to have been relatively untroubled: untroubled by any moral qualms on the part of the slave-owner; untroubled (so far as history records) by serious grievance on the part of the slave. This may have been due, in part, to state

---

* It was Themistokles who persuaded the Athenians to use revenues from the silver mines for the purpose of fortifying the city and greatly expanding its fleet of warships.

regulation. Athenian laws may be inferred indirectly, but from a celebrated public inscription recovered from the small city-state of Gortyn, in southern Crete, datable to around 450 BC, we comprehend that slaves might, at least, be accorded a specific range of legal rights – even if the principle of their subjection went unquestioned.

So was there a 'dark side' of the Acropolis? Of course. Since our vision of Athens tends to be dominated by temples and colonnades, it is easy to forget that public health was basic, infant mortality rates high, epidemics frequent and calamitous, and food shortages recurrent. Certain magistrates, we are told, were appointed to deal with the pricing of prostitutes ('flute girls'), the duties of the 'dung-collectors' (*koprologoi*), and the clearance of corpses from the streets. Athenian comedy abounds with references to the squalor of daily existence. But there was some democratic justification for the squalor. Houses, of mud-brick, were more or less the same in size, and not 'zoned' into rich or poor neighbourhoods, so a general might occupy the same sort of residence as a cobbler. In any case, citizens were supposed to spend their time in civic spaces, not at home. As for impoverished daily diet, this was offset by the numerous and regular occasions of religious festival.

It may be assumed that for well-off citizens – whose estates lay in the countryside – the concept of a 'holiday' never existed (with slaves, there was no demarcated 'work' from which to take a break). Holy days, however, made up a dense calendar: not only were there the twelve Olympian gods and goddesses to honour, but multiple minor deities, heroes, ancestors and other spirits. Thanksgiving generally took the form of sacrifice; and sacrifice most often involved the 'blood offering' of some animal at an altar. The animal should be domesticated, not a trophy of the hunt; vegetables, honey, cheese and cakes were also sometimes appropriate, or whatever lay within the budget of the worshipper.

Sacrifice was conceptually a sort of holy communion, with the deity considered as joining a meal within the *temenos* or sacred precinct. Mythology, however, sanctioned a procedure whereby the dedicated animal – a suckling pig for Demeter, a cockerel for Asklepios, a sheep for Hermes, whatever it might be – was butchered at an altar, where a fire, strewn with aromatic herbs, was lit; then the meat was roasted and shared among the sacrificants, with a parcel of offal and bones wrapped in fat and reserved for the deity.* There were certain penitential or purificatory occasions when a holocaust (complete burning) of the victim was required, but most of the monthly festivals gave Athenians, men and women alike, the chance of feasting in the cause of piety. Such rites regularly confirmed a basic tripartite system in classical thinking about the hierarchy of existence: beasts, men, gods.

We do not know if Athenian women attended the festivals for the god Dionysus that occasioned theatrical events in the city. Proof either way is elusive. If, however, the political and moral content of the plays left by the great dramatists of fifth-century BC Athens – Aeschylus, Sophocles, Euripides, Aristophanes – makes sense as if it were an extension of Athenian democracy, then a 'talking-shop' on stage was most likely intended for the all-male body of citizens. By the same analysis, going to the theatre could seem more akin to civic

---

* Legend validated this custom with the story of the primordial theft of fire from Zeus by the Titan Prometheus.

duty than a form of relaxation. The experience lasted all day, for a start: the dramatic programme as developed in the fifth century BC featured a mixture of styles and moods, conventionally labelled as tragedy, comedy and satyr play (the latter does not quite translate as our 'satire', but is related). On the occasion of the Great Dionysia festival at Athens, occurring in the spring, several consecutive days of attendance were entailed. For comfort, the theatre-goer brought his own cushion, and probably a picnic too, since on any given day there was a succession of plays to watch.

'Theatre' literally means a place to see or watch – and to be seen and watched, too, as is evident from surviving open-air structures. In Athens the principal Theatre of Dionysus, still visible set into the south slope of the Acropolis, was built around 500 BC (to be substantially 'upgraded' in the mid-fourth century BC). Local enthusiasm for the theatre as a space is usually traced to one Thespis (whence 'thespian'), a chorus-leader in the mid-sixth century BC; but where exactly the institution of choruses, and then drama, originated is still debated. The idea that proto-performances took place within the circular space reserved for threshing harvested grain remains attractive, and explains the focus upon the circular space known as the 'orchestra'. The elaboration of a stage or 'tent' (*skene*) behind the orchestra, and stone-built seating for an audience in front, soon disguised the agricultural origin of the rite; all the more so when a platform (*proskenion*), in front of the stage, and side-entrances (*parodoi*) were added.*

---

* There were plays in which actors entering from these side-entrances might mock what was being presented in the orchestra – whence 'parody'.

Priests of Dionysus and other important personages would be seated, sometimes in throne-like chairs, close to the orchestra. From there the audience was arrayed in ascending tiers. The acoustics of this structure are often praised as astoundingly clear, but it is worth noting that for music and poetic recitations a smaller roofed building (typically known as an *odeion*, or *odeum*) was preferred. Actors wore masks in the classical theatre, and to reach the upper tiers of the audience through the mouthpiece of a mask required strong delivery. Much emphasis was on words, rather than action. And since the audience generally knew the story of the play, especially if it was a tragedy, we may wonder what kept them watching. One obvious answer is that classical playwrights excelled not only at epitomizing epic storylines on the stage, but also at revealing the moral implications and complexities of those storylines for an audience of citizens. If supernatural forces – the gods, the Furies, Fate – make humans act in certain ways, perhaps extremely violent, where does that leave someone standing trial in the law-courts of the democratic *polis*?

An ancient philosophical analysis of drama's effectiveness recognized its therapeutic power (see page 159), which in turn came about because spectators at the theatre essentially forgot where they were and began to believe in the (often 'extreme', mythical and supernatural) events enacted. The *Prometheus Bound* of Aeschylus has the Titan Prometheus on stage as if undergoing the punishment (for his theft of fire) assigned to him by Zeus – to be pinioned to a cliff, with predatory birds pecking at his ever-replenished intestines. Stage directions are generally not recorded from antiquity, but from the text it seems that the actor playing Prometheus was indeed fastened to a high rock on stage, and eventually beset, if not by vultures or such like, then by the effects of extreme weather – thunder, lightning, hail. Wheeled platforms were devised for changes of scene; painters developed tricks of illusionistic perspective; and various cranes and hoists allowed for spectacular stage entrances, including the famous *deus ex machina* – the deity who appears from on high (and at Athens, of course, actors had only to gesture towards the Acropolis to suggest divine intervention).

To say that the centre of the city lay north-west of the Acropolis, in its 'marketplace' (*agora*, generically), will be substantially misleading if we do not acknowledge from the outset that the Athenian Agora was about much more than trade and exchange. Many political institutions and public offices were located there; so too law-courts, a number of temples and shrines, a library, a mint for bronze coinage, and colonnaded walkways sufficiently accommodating for schools of philosophy to gather there. Parts of this site were revealed in the nineteenth century, but its greater extent – some thirty acres, or twelve hectares – was not confirmed until full-scale excavations began in 1931. Prime funding from John D. Rockefeller Jr. enabled archaeologists to buy out existing residents of the area, and exploration continues to the present day, making the Agora a steady source of information about many aspects of classical civilization.

An inscription from the library, for example, states its opening hours and the need to pledge an oath before taking a scroll. A 'ballot box', still containing some inscribed tokens, testifies to the procedure for a jury vote. Simple clay water-clocks indicate the protocol for giving everyone a 'fair say' at a trial or council meeting. One building, tentatively identified as the state prison, has yielded a number of small medicine bottles, perhaps once containers of the hemlock administered to those condemned to death – including Socrates and Polemarchus, brother of Lysias. Direct evidence has even been found for a practice otherwise hard to imagine in such a crowded space – that of conducting cavalry drills along the thoroughfare of the processional route (the Panathenaic Way) leading to the Acropolis. In short, the Agora, along with its museum, offers abundant object lessons to any visitor who, like Sigmund Freud, comes to Athens ready primed by Athenian literature.

• • •

In relative terms, the artisans working in the Athenian district known as the Kerameikos were to be envied. They specialized in the shaping and decoration of clay vessels (their place of work, accordingly, gives us 'ceramic' as a general term for the medium). Although vases made of metal, especially silver, were doubtless more prestigious possessions, a steady demand for ceramic wares developed from the ninth century BC onwards. Shapes and styles were initially simple, but already by the second half of the eighth century BC huge pots, decorated all over with geometric motifs and stick-figures, were being produced as grave-markers. Designs and subjects of eastern provenance ('orientalizing') entered during the seventh century BC. Then, during the sixth and fifth centuries BC, Athenian craftsmen at this humble trade distinguished themselves, by sheer virtuosity, as 'artists'. A sustained study of their output, notably by the Oxford scholar J. D. Beazley, has identified numerous hands at work: Sophilos,

Exekias, Euphronios, Euthymides, Douris – their handiwork now stocks museum cabinets around the world. Not all signed their vases, so many have had to be given names: perhaps after a collection where a typical piece may be seen (the Berlin Painter), or some particularity of style or subject (the Elbows-Out Painter, the Boot Painter – the latter liked to draw women in boots). We know next to nothing of their lives, yet these industrious inhabitants of Athens offer what appears to be a candid visual commentary on culture and customs within the city. Their immediate patrons, we suppose, were citizens whose main requirement for decorated pottery was not as everyday crockery, but for special occasions: funerals, visits to the family tomb, weddings, religious festivals, and above all the gathering known as the symposium, or 'drink-ing-together'. Symposia were customarily convened in the men's quarters of the house, on couches set in a rectangular arrangement. An archaic poet, Xenophanes, describes the typical scene:

> The floor is clean, so too the cups, and everyone's hands. One attendant places woven garlands upon our heads; another comes around with a bowl of sweet-scented perfume. The *krater* stands full of good cheer, and wine prepared – wine which declares it will never betray us, soft in its jars, with a bouquet of flowers.* Among us frankincense breathes its clear scent, and there is chilled water, sweet and pure. Golden loaves are laid out for us, and a wonderful table arrayed with cheese and dense honey. The altar in the centre of the room is covered in

---

* The *krater* was a capacious vessel for mixing wine with water.

flowers, the house echoing with choruses and joy...

Symposiasts were expected to fill their cups seven or eight times during the party; given that a standard *kylix* (drinking cup) holds about half a litre, we can see why the wine was customarily diluted. Dionysus was the divine provider – in the words of another poet, 'the god who brings strength to one who is wearied, boldness to the lover, beauty to steps of a tipsy dancer' – but this gift was a *pharmakon*, both remedy and poison. 'It is no disgrace to drink as much as permits you to return home unaided', decrees Xenophanes. A small number of Athenian vases – reproduced often – show symposiasts either evidently inebriated, or else displaying an erotic abandon that suggests all inhibitions have been dissolved by wine. Wishful thinking, perhaps: the symposium was more likely to be a test of wits than sexual prowess.

There were 'drinking games'. One, called *kottabos*, involved projecting dregs from one's cup towards a particular target. Another was not so messy: one symposiast would recite a line of poetry, for his neighbour to supply the next line. Beyond declaiming from memory, or improvising, the participants also took the opportunity to sing together rousing choruses: verses, for instance, that celebrated Harmodius and Aristogeiton as heroic founders of political equality. So the symposium not only cemented a social peer group, along with its pederastic relationships and military camaraderie, but also nurtured the sort of patriotic pride that fused myth and history. A toast to the Tyrannicides was typical. But symposiasts were equally likely to raise their cups in memory of the city's most glorious victory – at the battle of Marathon, which took place just two decades after democracy's debut.

• • •

The bravery of these men will seem forever an
imperishable glory
To whomsoever the gods allot hard struggles for the
common good…

So goes the sentiment of one Athenian drinking song in celebration of the battle. However, for what happened at Marathon, a coastal site to the north-east of Athens, Herodotus is our primary source.* 'The father of history', born in Halicarnassus (modern Bodrum) on the Ionian coast (western Turkey), he probably recited his *Histories* at Athens around 450 BC. The Greek *historia* means 'enquiry', or 'knowledge gained by enquiry', and Herodotus certainly had an enquiring mind, and was well travelled. But of course he was disposed to relate events from a Greek or, more particularly, an Ionian Greek, point of view, and Ionia was the region where Greeks most suffered from the expansion of what was, by the mid-sixth century BC, the world's largest empire.

For present purposes we may call it the 'Persian empire', although its dominant ethnic groups may be either separately or jointly known as the Medes and the Persians, and it is also referred to by way of its ruling dynasty, the Achaemenids. Though originating in nomadic tribes, this empire was based in a region more or less equivalent to modern Iran. It seems that Herodotus never travelled so far as the palatial centres of

---

* In 1896, for the first modern Olympics, a long-distance race was instituted that was based on the distance from Athens to Marathon: the 'marathon' of 26.2 miles, or some 42 kilometres, was not part of the ancient games.

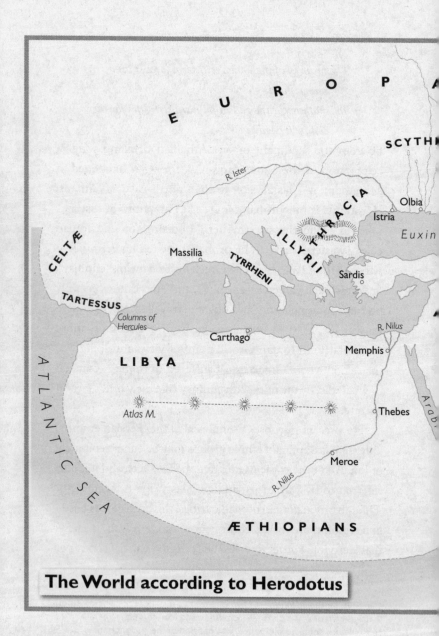

The World according to Herodotus

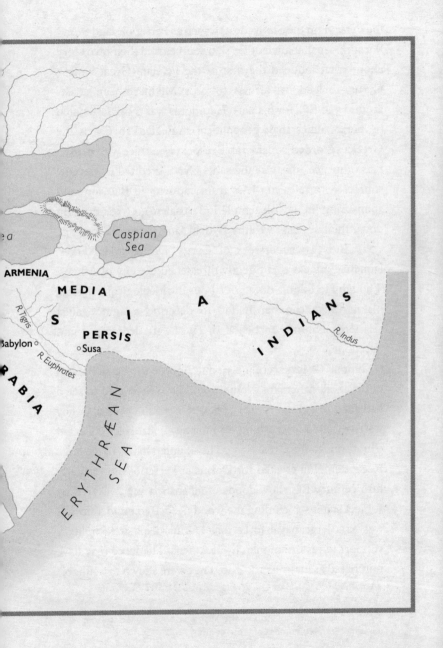

ea

ARMENIA

Caspian
Sea

MEDIA

S   I   A

R. Tigris

PERSIS

Babylon ○

○ Susa

R. Euphrates

INDIANS

R. Indus

RABIA

E R Y T H R Æ A N

S E A

the Persians in the Shiraz desert, such as Persepolis and Susa.*
We suppose that ancient Persian sources told their own story
about what induced the first of the Persian 'Great Kings',
Cyrus, to lead his armies towards Mediterranean coasts
around 540 BC; for his part, Herodotus was more fascinated
by personalities than geopolitical strategies. To Cyrus the
Greeks accorded considerable respect as a ruler with principles of justice (this was the same Cyrus credited in Hebrew
sources with releasing Jews from captivity in Babylon, and
sponsoring the Jewish temple in Jerusalem). Cyrus brought
down the famously wealthy Lydian king Croesus (see page
106). But two successors of Cyrus, Darius and Xerxes,
launched attacks that directly threatened the city of Athens.
Though Herodotus does not labour the ideological collision,
his narrative can hardly fail to describe a fight against
(Eastern) tyranny on behalf of (Western) democracy and
'freedom'.

Not all Greeks were inclined to oppose the Persians, and
not even all Athenians. Some would have been glad to see a
banished Pisistratid return to power. Persian imperial policy
was typically not crushing, so long as a local ruler collected
tribute due to the Great King. The sculpted reliefs of the huge
Reception Hall created for Darius at Persepolis in the early
fifth century BC show goods of all sorts being delivered by
subject states – including the wood needed to build a fleet. It
was as a large naval force that Darius dispatched military
support to restore monarchy at Athens. The force may have
numbered as many as 100,000. They were shown to a suitable

---

* Other Greeks did: indeed, Greek craftsmen were recruited to assist in the
monumental development of these centres.

point of disembarkation by the exiled Hippias, who by then was quite an old man (Herodotus says that when Hippias jumped down from a Persian ship, some of his teeth fell out, leaving him scrabbling for them in the sand).

The landing beach was the Bay of Marathon. While awaiting signals of internal connivance for their southwards advance upon Athens, the Persians camped here. At Athens, meantime, the alarm of invasion galvanized a rapid muster. Apart from a contingent supplied by the small Boeotian city of Plataea, Athens acted independently: the Spartans, theoretically valuable allies, were in the midst of a religious festival. Ten thousand infantry, democratically representing the ten tribes, moved at the double up to Marathon – and halted at a distance, digesting the clear mismatch between their number and that of the opposition.

Several days passed. The ten generals leading the Athenian force were divided. Five of them considered it foolish to engage the Persians, given the gross disparity of forces; the other five favoured an attack. Among the belligerents was Miltiades. A seasoned campaigner, he had been in charge of an Athenian settlement established by his uncle in the Gallipoli peninsula – then known as the Thracian Chersonese – and he knew the Persians alternately as allies and enemies. Miltiades turned to the polemarch (commander-in-chief) at the time, Kallimachos, with an appeal for his casting vote:

It is now in your hands, Kallimachos, either to enslave Athens, or to make her free and leave behind you for all future generations a memory more glorious than ever Harmodius and Aristogeiton left. Never in the course of our long history have we Athenians been in such peril as now. If we submit to the Persian invader, Hippias will be

restored to power in Athens – and there is little doubt
what misery must then ensue; but if we fight and win,
then this city of ours may well grow to pre-eminence
amongst all the cities of Greece.

Miltiades prevailed. What happened next is not entirely clear.
The Persians, aware that regiments from Sparta would eventually materialize, may have begun an operation to move
some of their forces further down the coast. It would have
been then that the Greeks launched an infantry charge – a
mass movement towards the Persian encampment, conducted
at such speed that the Persians were trapped in the bay,
unable to deploy their mounted archers, driven into an area
of marshland, and eventually forced to scramble onto their
ships for retreat. Amid the tumult of the onslaught, many
marvellous events and incidents were witnessed on the Greek
side. Some saw Theseus arise from the earth and assist in the
fighting, others a hero wielding a ploughshare as a weapon;
there was a dog who joined the charge with his master; and
Kallimachos died in accordance with the sense of his name
('he who fights well'), still belabouring Persians even though
he was pierced by multiple arrows.

We have only the Greek record of casualties at the end of
the day. It marks a massacre. The Persian losses tallied 6,400;
of the Athenians, just 192 died. It is not known how many
Plataeans, and conscripted slaves, also perished. No time was
lost in the glorification of the Athenian dead. They were
buried at Marathon, in the style of Homeric heroes (though
listed on tombstones according to the ten democratic tribes).
Centuries later, visitors to the battlefield site claimed that in
the still of night the sounds could be heard of horses

whinnying and the clash of arms. All who took part in the battle were *oligoi pros pollous*, 'the few against the many', to be celebrated in Athenian rhetoric for many decades afterwards.

Part of the story of the Persian wars must be told in the next chapter: suffice it here to say that Marathon was not the end of the conflict, nor even the beginning of the end. But the battle served as a test not just of Athens, but also of the junior democracy as a political system. The *Marathonomachoi*, or 'Marathon-fighters' as they became known, had after all conscripted themselves: the coercion to risk their lives on behalf of the city came by a collective resolve. They 'got their act together'; and they did so in the face of a foreign threat to overturn democracy and reinstate an autocrat.

• • •

A temple to commemorate victory at Marathon was about halfway built on the Acropolis when the Persians returned to the Greek mainland, in 480 BC. This time the invasion, commanded by Xerxes, was successful. The Athenians evacuated their city, decamping mostly to the island of Salamis. Persian troops occupied the Acropolis and laid to waste its shrines, altars and population of votive statues. Clearly there was then no intention of establishing a pro-Persian ruler in Athens. When the city's inhabitants returned, months later, they appear to have buried some of the wreckage, but they left the damaged temples in evident ruins, as memoranda.

A peace treaty with the Persians is said to have been brokered in 449 BC by Kallias, a veteran of Marathon. By the agreement, allegedly, the Persians agreed to limit their naval sphere of influence to Phaselis (in south-west Turkey) and the Bosphorus, while the Athenians allowed the Persians to operate in Cyprus and Egypt. Whatever the realities of the truce, it left Athens in a curious situation with regard to her allies. In 478 BC a federation had been formed to consolidate anti-Persian resistance across the Aegean. Subsequently known as the Delian League, this brought together some 200 city-states, each contributing either ships or money towards the cause of wreaking revenge upon the Persians, or at least keeping them at bay. Cash was initially kept at the sanctuary of Apollo on the little Cycladic island of Delos; but in 454 BC the treasury was transferred (for safety's sake, supposedly) to Athens. The Athenians – thanks to the initiative of Themistokles – had by far the most powerful navy: effectively, Athens was offering protection to Greek settlements in the eastern Mediterranean in return for an annual tribute.

A peace settlement with the Persians, even if it were no more than a begrudging truce, opened an opportunity for one leading politician within the Athenian democracy. Perikles, whose mother was a niece of Cleisthenes, rose to notice by his rivalry with Kimon, the son of Miltiades. He developed into a consummate performer at the Assembly. Against some strident opposition, he carried a motion to spend the cash reserves of the Delian League upon a programme of rebuilding the Acropolis. As Perikles argued, so long as Athens maintained security for the members of the League, her obligations abroad were complete. Why should the funds of the League be devoted entirely to military purposes? Was not the civilian population of Athens entitled to a share?

The social and economic effects of the great public

projects proposed by Perikles are described eloquently by his eventual biographer Plutarch:

> The raw materials were stone, bronze, ivory, gold, ebony, cypress-wood; and to fashion and work them were the crafts – carpenters, moulders, coppersmiths, stone-workers, goldsmiths, ivory-sculptors, painters, pattern-weavers, relief-makers. Then there were the men engaged in transport and carriage, merchants, sailors, helmsmen by sea, and by land cartwrights, and men who kept yokes of traction-animals, and drovers; rope-makers, flax-workers, shoemakers, roadlayers, and miners. Each craft, like a general with his own army, had its crowd of hired labourers and individual craftsmen organized like an instrument and body for the service to be performed; so, all in all, the various needs to be met distributed and spread prosperity through every age and condition.

Politically, Perikles may have been courting popularity, by opening a bounteous 'war chest' for civilian use. But that does not detract from the sense of far-reaching purpose also recorded by Plutarch. To his fellow citizens, Perikles offered the vision of creating a statement to the world, and to posterity, of what Athens the city could achieve, through the ingenious grace and creativity of its inhabitants. The cities confederated by the Delian League might now find themselves subjects within an Athenian 'empire'; nonetheless Perikles was proud to consider Athens not only as the exemplary 'school of Hellas', but as the centre of a trans-Mediterranean network that attracted goods (and skilled craftsmen) from far away. Notorious for his aloof demeanour, Perikles was not lacking in what might be called the 'common touch'. Once, it is recorded, some foul-mouthed heckler followed him around all day; yet Perikles gave no orders for this personal nuisance to be removed. And when political opponents accused him of 'prettifying' the city, as if its brightly painted buildings were like the baubles and make-up of a courtesan, he kept his dignity. His well-known Funeral Speech, delivered as a consolation to Athenians who had lost members of their families in the early phase of the Peloponnesian War, includes a sideswipe at such critics: 'We are lovers of the beautiful, but that does not make us extravagant; we cultivate the mind, but that does not make our bodies soft.'

'The beautiful', as an Athenian philosopher (Plato) later put it, 'is difficult': the result of numerous calculations, much experience and perseverance, and sheer laborious effort. A sense of such hard-bought beauty still emanates from the Acropolis, despite dilapidation. And in the mind's eye, it is possible to reconstruct some image of the experience of an ancient visitor to the sanctuary.

• • •

Though not the first phase of the project – and in fact it was never quite finished – we may as well start with the monumental entrance to the Acropolis created by an architect named Mnesikles. A monumental 'gateway' (*propylon*) for access (which had to be made from the west – the other three sides were sheer cliffs) had been created after the expulsion of the tyrants. This was demolished, and in its place an assemblage that called for 'gateway' to be made plural, and definitive – hence the Propylaia. The structure is asymmetrical and pitched on various levels, and mixes the Doric and Ionic architectural orders – and it is a triumph of functional design. Mnesikles also took care to incorporate a substantial part of the Mycenaean fortification wall. This was, after all, testament to the prehistory of the Acropolis – a prehistory in which the legendary foundations of Athens were laid.

Eventually an image of Perikles was placed in the Propylaia, as if to confirm his leading role in the commission of the glorious vista that then opened to those entering the *temenos* or 'sacred space' of the Acropolis. All was indeed brightly, even gaudily, painted – as was the custom; and the trophies of war were plentifully evident. A central bronze statue of Athena Promachos, 'Athena the frontline fighter', fashioned by Pheidias from spoils gathered at Marathon, was so tall that it could be glimpsed by mariners approaching the southern tip of Attica, at Cape Sounion. Various precious captured pieces of Persian military hardware were kept nearby. An olden statue of Athena Polias ('of the city'), made of wood and probably not very big, was housed in a temple known as the Erechtheum. This temple – perhaps also designed by Mnesikles and certainly not completed until almost the end of the fifth century BC – took its name from a shrine to Erechtheus (see page 32); King Cecrops and his daughters were also associated with the vicinity. Porches flanked the entrance to the temple: the smaller of these, facing south, was supported by columns in the form of female figures, the so-called Caryatids. Whether or not it was originally intended, a symbolic significance was later given to these Caryatids: they were reminders, it was said, of the fate of a city-state in the Peloponnese called Caryae, which during the Persian invasion sided with the invaders (subsequently its menfolk were killed and the women reduced to slavery). Moreover, the temple's layout had to accommodate an olive tree, and a fissure in the rock that gave access (allegedly) to a saltwater spring. Both features related to the mythology of early Athens – a story which was 'illustrated', so to speak, on the frontal, west-facing pediment of the most imposing structure on the Acropolis, the Parthenon. The sculptures within this elongated triangle showed two deities, Athena and Poseidon, contesting the possession of Attica. Poseidon smites the Acropolis with his trident, creating the saltwater spring; Athena plants an olive tree. Witnessing the divine dispute is Cecrops. He and his subjects will choose Athena. The olive will become the chief cash crop of Attica. Poseidon, enraged by Athena's victory, will cause a terrible deluge. But once the flood subsides he too will be accorded honour on the Acropolis.

The Parthenon was the most generously decorated of any temple in classical antiquity. But since no ancient author cared to describe in detail this wonderful monument, we can only guess at what the overall significance of the decoration might have been: a problem compounded by the fact that we are not sure what rites were served by the temple (a sacrificial altar was only added some centuries later). A painting by the Victorian artist Lawrence Alma-Tadema imagines Pheidias, as master-sculptor and 'overseer' of the Parthenon, standing on scaffolding by the relief frieze that runs along the temple's inner architrave. Perikles is shown at this 'private view', inspecting the frieze in company with his wife and his mistress; Socrates is there too, along with his young admirer Alcibiades. Pheidias has in his hands a rolled-up scroll. Much scholarly debate would be ended if such a document were found – the 'master plan' that Pheidias must have laid out for approval by the many Athenian councils and committees tasked with managing the work.* So how the temple once 'worked' in terms of its mythological imagery and its religious aura is left open to speculation.

On the eastern pediment, at the back of the building, was another supernatural scene: the birth of Athena – supernatural to the point of bizarre, since the goddess emerges fully formed from the head of Zeus. The visualization of a strange event in a naturalistic style is part of the artistic magic here. The horses whose heads occupy the angles of the pediment were, in the sculptural tableau, pulling the chariots of the rising Sun, Helios, and the setting Moon, Selene. Respectively eager and exhausted, these marble beasts continue to enchant viewers by their very 'horsiness'.

Metopes – the rectangular panels alternating with threefold mock-beams or 'triglyphs' in the Doric architectural order – were carved on each side of the temple with a different theme. On one were scenes of a battle between Gods and Giants, with Athena distinguishing herself against a Giant called Pallas; another showed episodes of a battle against Amazons, probably featuring Theseus; a third side, a struggle with Centaurs (Theseus was involved here too); and the fourth side, incidents from the fall of Troy. Ancient viewers may have discerned allegorical aspects here, if analogies were apparent with the struggle against the Persians; in any case, the temple evoked those chronological phases whereby divine order was established and Greek, particularly Athenian, identity defined.

* We label the whole venture 'Periklean', but it is worth knowing that the name of Perikles nowhere appears among the numerous magistrates and officials listed in inscriptions from the site: such was democracy at Athens.

The frieze, as already noted (see page 33), may evoke the sacrifice of his daughter, or daughters, by Erechtheus. Another suggestion is that the figures of young men, many on horseback, represent the heroes of Marathon. Numerically they can be counted as 192, which seems an astonishing coincidence with the casualty total reported by Herodotus. (Their various condition of undress makes it incredible that these figures are to be understood as taking part in the solemn procession of the Panathenaic festival.) Either way, this part of the temple would remind its beholders of sacrifice made for the sake of the city.

With such exterior embellishment, the Parthenon must have seemed 'perfect' from the outside. Its architects had also taken care to make allowances for certain optical illusions: the tendency for perfectly straight columns to appear concave was offset by letting the proportions bulge very slightly; and the base, in order to appear flat, was similarly given a raised curve. It was the inside of the temple, however, that contained the most precious element of decoration, in the form of the 'Parthenos' statue of Athena. Clad in over a thousand kilos of plated gold, this figure could be regarded as the main repository of funds from the Delian League: we learn from inscriptions that the Athenians were later able to 'borrow' from the statue, by removing parts of its drapery. The enormous figure of the goddess was done by Pheidias in the technique known as 'chryselephantine', using not only masses of gold but ivory too (for the figure's head and exposed body parts). Athena was shown crowned and erect, her spear and shield by her side. In her extended right hand she held the winged personification of Nike, 'Victory'. As a thanksgiving for success against the Persians, this was handsome. As a prayer for prospective glory, however, it might soon appear a triumph of hope over experience.

• • •

The last building of the 'grand project' of the fifth-century BC Acropolis was a small but conspicuously exquisite Ionic temple devoted to Athena Nike, 'Invincible Athena'. The marble balustrade of the temple precinct – added as a safety measure, to alert worshippers to the steep drop from the south-west edge of the Acropolis rock – was carved with relief figures of the female Victory as she had not been envisaged previously: for example, stooping to adjust her sandal, robes slipping from her shoulder. So Victory had sex appeal. By the time this parapet was added, however, around 410 BC, Victory appeared to be deserting the city. A frieze on the Nike temple showed Greeks battling against Persians. But in the end the 'Golden Age' of Athens was brought to an end not by the Persians, but by an arch-enemy much closer to home: the city of Sparta.

III
SPARTA

The direct distance between Athens and Sparta is not great – less than a hundred miles, if the sea is no barrier. Ideologically, however, the two city-states were very far apart. And this is not just an impression formed in retrospect. Beyond their historic rivalry (and occasional alliance) on the battlefield, Athens and Sparta cultivated a sort of oppositional development, with each city apparently striving to be the antithesis of the other. The written evidence suggests as much: and when we admit that the written evidence comes largely from the Athenian side, that too becomes part of the marked difference. The Athenians are eloquent, showy, studious; the Spartans, by contrast, so notoriously disinterested in verbal expression that their region, Laconia, lends its name to a general reluctance to use words beyond the minimal.

The tendency for Spartans to be *laconic* creates a particular problem for historians. We are obliged to rely very much upon non-Spartan sources – tales of Sparta told by outsiders. Immediately it might be supposed that 'non-Spartan' would then equate to 'anti-Spartan'. But the bias, if anything, goes the other way. From a distance, Sparta gains the prestige of mystery. The result is sometimes referred to as the 'Spartan mirage': a view of the city composed mostly of anecdote and projected by notions of 'good order' (*eunomia*) within the perfect state. For all its

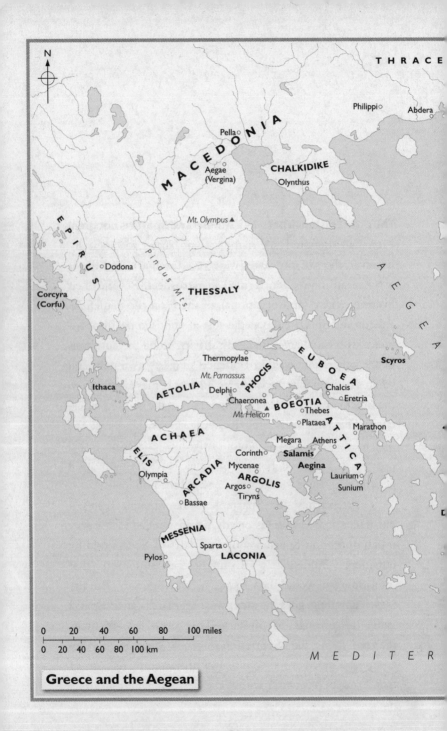

Greece and the Aegean

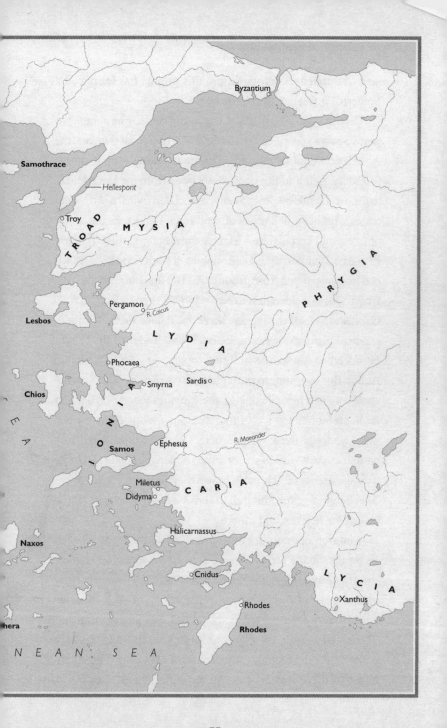

Byzantium

Samothrace

Hellespont

Troy

TROAD

MYSIA

PHRYGIA

Pergamon

R. Caicus

Lesbos

LYDIA

Phocaea

Smyrna

Sardis

Chios

IONIA

Ephesus

R. Maeander

Samos

Miletus

CARIA

Didyma

Halicarnassus

Naxos

Cnidus

LYCIA

Xanthus

Rhodes

hera

Rhodes

NEAN SEA

lack of impartial corroboration, this mirage has exercised a powerful influence down the ages.

Clarification of origins is not easily done. For about 700 years Sparta was ruled by a 'dyarchy' – two royal families, the Agiads and the Eurypontids. Tradition made the eponymous founders, Agis and Eurypon, descended from the Herakleidai, 'sons of Herakles', mythically associated with the Dorian tribes who occupied areas of the Greek mainland, the island of Crete and certain other parts of the Aegean during the early Iron Age. Uninterrupted genealogies of both royal households can be constructed from around 900 BC until around 220 BC, when Sparta yielded first to Macedonian, then to Roman rule. On either side of the lineage there are names that resonate in classical history: for example, Leonidas, leader of the 'Three Hundred' at the battle of Thermopylae in 480 BC, was an Agiad. But by tradition the legislative patriarch of the Spartan state was not himself one of the kings, rather an avuncular royal mentor called Lycurgus. We do not know exactly when this Lycurgus lived. Some ancient sources considered him contemporary with Homer; some modern scholars doubt he ever existed at all. He was, however, sufficiently 'real' in the Spartan mirage for Plutarch to script a *Life of Lycurgus*, just as he did for Perikles and others.

Plutarch does not care to hazard a date for Lycurgus, but he reports that a series of travels, to Crete and further afield – perhaps including, like Solon, a visit to Egypt – were preliminary to his comprehensive recasting of the Spartan constitution. Demographically, Sparta was already unusual. Territorial conquests made around 900 BC had given it control over the regions of Arcadia and Messenia. The inhabitants of these regions were never enfranchised, but put to work as serfs in agricultural labour. Generically known as 'helots', they remained an ill-treated underclass whose discontent occasionally surfaced as rebellion. Closer to Sparta itself were numerous so-called *perioikoi*, 'those living round about': these were not enslaved, and were liable for military service, but did not count as full citizens. (Helots, too, could be called upon to serve as lightly armed auxiliaries: this, and the deployment of *perioikoi*, undermined the widespread Greek principle that to fight on behalf of the city was to 'earn' citizenship.) So the number of 'pure' Spartans may have been relatively small – and was certainly never expanded by incomers. For Sparta, deliberately, kept a closed society.

Plutarch identifies three main aspects of the Lycurgan reforms. First is the establishment of a 'senate of elders' (*gerousia*), thirty in number (probably including the two kings). The council's members, chosen from a division of aristocratic clan groups at Sparta, were to form a guard against democracy on one hand and tyranny on the other. Several annually elected magistrates ('ephors') presided over their meetings. Secondly, Lycurgus persuaded Spartan citizens to make a complete mutual and equal reallocation of their land and property. Along with this egalitarian policy, he took measures to forestall any individual accumulation of wealth. So gold and silver were taken out of circulation – as, indeed, was any kind of currency (even lumps of iron were accorded negligible value). As a result, Plutarch notes approvingly, no travelling salesmen brought their wares to Sparta; no teachers of rhetoric came plying their trade; nor were there any pimps, lawyers, fortune-tellers or makers of knick-knacks. Necessary items of furniture were produced locally, and the city was self-sufficient in drinking vessels. Archaeology somewhat modifies this picture of proud economic independence and 'anti-banausic' prejudice; nonetheless it is true that no famous sculptor or painter is known to have come from Sparta.

The third principle of the Spartan constitution as laid down by Lycurgus was that of communal eating. All citizens should share the same food: hence the custom of the Spartan 'mess' (*agoge*). The reasoning behind this custom was consistent with a prohibition upon private wealth, and the encouragement of civic values; it harmonized, too, with an ethos of thrift and efficiency. Gathering in groups of fifteen or so, the citizens each contributed a monthly quantity of basic supplies – barley-meal, cheese, wine – with protein supplements coming from sacrificial rites or hunting expeditions. Even the kings were obliged to attend.

To these three ordinances – never, apparently, written down; and, after a briefly violent initial protest, uncontested over centuries – Lycurgus added a series of educational measures. Boys were taken from their parents at the age of seven, and put through the rigours of military apprenticeship and physical development by male citizens (who were also permitted to take an erotic interest in their charges). Girls, too, were given training in athletics, in order that their bodies might be better equipped for childbirth. Babies born weak or disabled were disposed of in a chasm by the foot of the Taygetus, the often snow-topped mountain overlooking Sparta.

The boys slept in dormitories, upon beds they made themselves from reeds; issued with meagre clothing, they rarely took baths and were generally kept 'lean and hungry' (the opportunistic theft of food was sanctioned – though a flogging awaited anyone caught doing so). Of reading and writing it was deemed proper to impart 'as much as was necessary'. Given the Spartan way with words, this perhaps did not amount to much – though Plutarch, himself a prolific author, commends the habit of making few words count epigrammatically.

Such was the institutional austerity of daily life in Sparta that war, when it came, was something of a release. Spartan warriors, allowed to grow their hair upon reaching manhood, made sure they looked at their best for fighting, and famously wore their hair long for terrifying effect. Music was played for the engagement; they marched into battle like perfectly choreographed dancers. Maternal concern, if we are to believe an oft-cited Spartan adage, went only so far as to exhort every man to come back either with his shield, or upon it: that is, having fought (and having not thrown away his shield to facilitate speedy escape), or having fallen during the fight (to be carried home with shield serving as a stretcher).

Plutarch summarizes the aim of Lycurgus:

> he trained his fellow citizens to have neither the wish nor
> the ability to live for themselves; but like bees they were
> to make themselves always integral parts of the whole
> community, clustering together about their leader, almost
> beside themselves with enthusiasm and noble ambition,
> and to belong wholly to their country.

The tone of admiration is overt: as if Lycurgus had solved an essential problem of civilized existence – how to mould individual humans, by nature greedy and selfish, into a collective body. So was Sparta a model city?

Certain features of the Spartan state were adopted in the design for a perfect community run by 'philosopher-kings' – the ideal pursued by one 'Spartophile' Athenian in the fourth century BC, Plato (see page 155 – though we do not know that Plato ever visited Sparta). Other learned onlookers were unimpressed by what passed for education at Sparta: as they saw it, the elders trained the youth to nothing more than a sort of mesmerized obedience. Plutarch, having extolled the city so far, cannot bring himself to lodge any serious criticism. He notes the allegations of a 'secret service' (*krypteia*) deployed by the Spartan authorities, and stories of mass executions carried out among the helots, 'culled' as if a subhuman species; but he does not want to believe such slander. After all, the voice of the god Apollo, delivered by his oracle at the sanctuary of Delphi – where Plutarch himself served as a priest – gave its blessing to Lycurgus. So Lycurgus became, upon his death, revered as the wisest of all political founding fathers in ancient Greece.

• • •

Viewing Sparta beyond the Spartan mirage is not easy, but worth a passing attempt. To begin with, let us notice that Sparta had an *agora*. The fact needs to be stated, since it is not immediately obvious to the modern visitor – who finds much of the ancient site occupied by olive groves. Traces have been found of a *stoa* erected after the defeat of the Persians, and of another substantial colonnade added in Roman times. A small circular structure may be the *skias*, or 'canopy', mentioned by an ancient tourist (Pausanias) as the Spartans' simple parliament. Otherwise, archaeology tends to confirm the sentiment

presciently made by Thucydides – that when future generations came to judge the actual power of Sparta by the city's
physical remains, they would never believe it once ruled much
of the Peloponnese, and exerted an influence far beyond.
Conversely, the appearance of Athens would be deceptively
awesome: at least, anyone predicting the outcome of a war
between Sparta and Athens in the fifth century BC would
have wrongly supposed Athens to be the more formidable
protagonist.

There was never, in Sparta, any building to match the
Parthenon. But surely the Spartans must have had temples?
So they did; so we find, towards the river Eurotas and still
amid olives, the ruins of what we know to have been a principal cult of the city – the sanctuary of Artemis Orthia
('Upright Artemis'). Here too, however, excavations seem to
confirm expectations. A number of sources report a practice
of worship at the altar of Artemis that became truly spectacular – to the extent that a theatre had to be built to accommodate
spectators. Its structure is visible – the place where the rites
were conducted, well into Roman times. One account says
that the altar was stacked with cheeses, and a game played
whereby priests, armed with staves and whips, defended the
cheeses from raids by the ever-hungry Spartan youths.
Another account relates how Spartan boys would test their
pain threshold by offering themselves to be whipped on the
altar. A priestess stood by, holding the old wooden cult image
of Artemis: if the image drooped below its 'upright' position,
that was a sign for the harshness of the thrashing to increase.
By all reports the ordeal was bloody, sometimes fatal.

Artemis, wherever she was venerated in the ancient world,
tended towards the severe. But her flagellation rite at Sparta

was drastic because it suited the Spartan identity as apparent in the militaristic state set up by Lycurgus. So we return, inevitably, to the stereotype. Suppose we approach it from a different perspective. Boys at the altar were demonstrating their readiness for pain, to the point of self-sacrifice. Was Sparta really so different from any other Greek state in demanding this 'aptitude' from its citizens?

• • •

One way of defining a militaristic state is to introduce the concept of a citizen army. One way of defining a citizen army is to say that whoever offers to fight on behalf of the community is given the right to participate in its government. Something like this logic operated in restricted fashion among the heroes of Homer's world, where the privileges of aristocratic authority – place of honour at a feast, with prime cuts of meat, wine cups filled unstintingly, and so on – were granted on the understanding that these came as rewards for bravery on the battlefield. Commuted to the purposes of a democratic city, such heroism necessarily became more 'ordinary', and instead of in terms of one-to-one combat, had to be expressed by the merit of service in the ranks of an infantry formation.

By way of granting such an opportunity for collective glory, a peculiar sort of warfare evolved among the city-states of archaic Greece. The technical term is 'hoplite warfare', based on the Greek word for a soldier who carried a round bronze shield (*hoplon*) large enough to cover most of himself and part of a fellow soldier. Add to the shield a helmet offering protection to the nose and cheeks, a body corselet, and greaves for the lower parts of the leg (both corselet and greaves were also of bronze), and such was the 'panoply' of the ordinary citizen-warrior – a citizen, that is, who could not afford to keep a horse. He was usually armed with a spear, or perhaps two (one for throwing, one for jabbing), and a short sword. Assembled for battle – that is, in ranks of close formation, with shields overlapped – the hoplites formed a *phalanx*. This could be deployed with or without other military modes, such as cavalry, slingers and archers. By itself, however, the hoplite phalanx has come to symbolize more than a strategy, or even 'the Western way of war'. Partly because of the premium it placed upon collective action, and partly because it operated according to rules and protocols that seem almost akin to sport or play, the settling of disputes by a hoplite encounter seems, relatively speaking, as 'civilized' as war can ever be.

To certain non-Greek observers in antiquity, this mode of dispute resolution could appear perverse – and expensive in terms of casualties. Herodotus reports (or imagines) the comments of a Persian general in the early fifth century BC, to the effect that the Greeks, whose predominantly mountainous terrain should favour protracted guerrilla-style warfare, will seek out a space of level ground where they can do battle; and, though they speak a common language, do not bother with negotiations, but rather choose to proceed with a staged mass infantry collision that leaves even the victors suffering serious losses.

This outsider's perspective on hoplite combat may miss or misunderstand an important aspect: namely, that such a custom of conducting war could not only be efficient and decisive, but also perhaps involve a reduced number of fatalities. Suppose that two city-states were in disagreement over some issue and resorted to formal hostilities. They would have to find a mutually convenient location where their respective phalanxes could be deployed. Then a date had to be set: at some time of the agricultural year when not all hands were needed for tasks on the land, and at a date within the civic calendar that did not clash with an ordained religious festival (of which there were many).

So much for time and place. Members of the two opposing phalanxes would then gather, and possibly drink quite heavily before donning their armour and falling into formation.* A stand-off could ensue, with insults traded, but considering the bronze panoply each hoplite wore, and the likely heat of the day in a plain, this cannot have lasted too long. Pipe-players were present, to sound the advance and raise morale. We must remember that a hoplite wearing the full Corinthian-style helmet, with ears enclosed and lateral vision highly restricted – and wedged into a pack whose coherence came from overlapping shields – could do little but move with the collective impetus. A big shove from the ranks at the rear would have propelled those at the front headlong towards the enemy. No wonder that epitaphs for fallen warriors sometimes emphasize that so-and-so fought *en promachois*, 'among the foremost'. But if discipline wavered within one of the advancing phalanxes and men started to scatter sideways, then the battle could be over before an actual clash of arms. In such cases the opposition might give chase for the sake of bloodshed, but more often

---

* Alcohol may have been necessary to suppress some of the ignoble effects of adrenalin-driven fear upon the human body, raucously described in Athenian comedy.

were content simply to gather up as trophies the shields and helmets that had been discarded to facilitate flight.

So hoplite warfare may be understood as a type of formal 'contest' or *agon*, sharing its category with the ordeals undertaken by athletes at sporting festivals. To accept as much is not to underestimate the psychological demands made upon combatants within a phalanx. Many discussions of virtue in classical literature invoke the quality of courage or 'manliness' (*andreia*). Nothing tested that quality like the hoplite experience, with its stress upon engaging at close quarters. Strategies for inflicting death or damage from a distance, or by stealth, were regarded as cowardly.

How should the brave man behave? 'Let him fight toe to toe and shield against shield hard-pressed; plume upon plume, helmet on helmet, chest against chest' – lines from Sparta's seventh-century BC soldier-poet Tyrtaeus evoke the compact scrummage of a hoplite collision. Holding the line, being part of the team, maintaining a collective stance in the course of fighting at close quarters: these were the tests of 'excellence' (*arete*), proven not so much by individual prowess in the manner of Homer's heroes, but rather by a steadfast resolve to serve city-state and family honour.

The most celebrated instance of such dogged Spartan bravery is the defensive action taken against the Persians at Thermopylae in 480 BC. Mustering allies and a number of helots, the Spartan commander Leonidas gathered a force much larger than his own royal bodyguard of 300, to hold a mountain pass in an area of thermal springs (Thermopylae translates as 'Hot Gates'). At stake in this action – combined with a defensive action to protect the straits at Artemision, on the northern tip of Euboea – was Persian access

northwards to Thessaly or southwards to Attica. When some
of the allies failed to prevent Persian access to a pathway
above the pass at Thermopylae, Leonidas arranged for the
retreat of the others, but stayed on with his 300 Spartans,
plus a contingent of about 1,000 Boeotians, for a final stand.
The intention was to impede the Persians for as long as
possible – the best such a relatively small force could hope
for. Legendarily, Leonidas was clear about the eventual
outcome, instructing his men to eat a good breakfast before
the battle – 'for tonight we dine in Hades'.

Leonidas was among those who fell at Thermopylae. The
action soon came to epitomize what Sparta expected from its
citizens: as Tyrtaeus hymned it, the courage to stand together
in the front line, with no thought of shameful flight. It was
another poet – Simonides, from Keos – who provided the
epigram for the Spartan dead, inscribed at the site. The
conventional translation runs: 'Go tell the Spartans, passer-by,
that here, obedient to their laws, we lie.' A more demotic
version has been offered: 'Say, stranger, go tell the Spartan
mob – we got bumped off while holding down our job.'

The Persians, as we have seen (page 61), proceeded to
invade Attica, but at least the Athenians had time to evacuate.
As Xerxes then threatened to attack the Peloponnese, Athens
and Sparta led the allied Greek defence. A naval encounter in
the straits of Salamis left the Persian fleet weakened; Xerxes
himself retired, delegating command to his general Mardonius.
The following year (479 BC), an army composed of some
40,000 hoplites from Athens, Sparta and other states gathered
to meet the Persians near Plataea, in Boeotia. Since Persian
strength lay principally in cavalry, a regular hoplite battle was
out of the question. For over a week both sides stayed wary

of an engagement – and Mardonius, we are told, attempted to exploit potential division between the Greek allies (whose overall commander was a Spartan, Pausanias, though they tended to be deployed separately). In the end, a Greek move to higher ground was misinterpreted by Mardonius as a retreat; the Persians gave chase, only for the Greeks to wheel around and use the phalanx to its full offensive effect. Mardonius died in the rout, and the Persians were expelled from the Greek mainland.

So Sparta and Athens could combine – in extreme circumstances. But the experience of coalition, for all that it brought victory, did not reconcile the two cities. Their basic binary opposition simmered, and within half a century boiled over into outright hostilities.

• • •

This was the Peloponnesian War. Perhaps we would hardly mention this protracted conflict if it had not been made subject of a 'seminal' (if incomplete) text of ancient history, generally known as the *History of the Peloponnesian War* and written towards the end of the fifth century BC by Thucydides, one of the Athenian generals who took part in some of its campaigns. Though it involved other Greek states, the dispute was primarily between Athens and Sparta; and given that Thucydides campaigned on the Athenian side and made no secret of his admiration for Perikles, we might expect little from this narrative by way of neutral analysis. But the power of the book, as far as it survives, lies precisely in its effort to set a new standard of non-partisan history writing. Thucydides used poetic diction; and while he consciously aimed not to indulge in the anecdotal whimsicality of his predecessor Herodotus, he can be shown to be no less susceptible to giving a mythical shape to the events he recounts. Nonetheless, Thucydides remains treasured for his commitment to the cause of faithful reportage. The war, as he noted, was ultimately a sordid and inglorious 'disturbance' from which no Greek could take much pride. Yet by his art it was elevated into a sort of theatrical masterpiece, whose audience should learn from what they see – or else repeat the mistakes they saw enacted.

Big books may be written on the origins and causes of the Peloponnesian War. In a few paragraphs, the following sketch will have to suffice. As the Persian threat abated and the Athenian fleet became increasingly dominant throughout Aegean waters, antagonism between Athens and Sparta escalated. Between 461 and 456 BC the Athenians built their so-called 'Long Walls' – fortifications connecting Athens to her seaports at Piraeus and Phaleron, several miles away. When we add that the same walls were torn down by the Spartans in 404 BC, to the strains of exultant piped music, there is already the historical sense that these walls were symbolic of an aggressive intent on the part of Athens to increase its power abroad, at Sparta's cost. The practical purpose of the walls – to give shelter to Attica's rural populace in case of invasion, and access to seaborne supplies in case of siege – seems almost to anticipate the mobilization of a Spartan attack.

An alliance of Peloponnesian states had existed since the sixth century BC. Dominated by Sparta, this 'Peloponnesian League' took action against Athens as requested by one of its members, Corinth, in 431 BC. Corinth, apart from being caught geographically between Athens and Sparta, maintained almost continuously difficult relations with the island of Corcyra (Corfu), which had been taken over by a renegade group of Corinthian nobles in the seventh century BC. When Athens, using her sea-power, began to take an interest in supporting Corcyra (in 433 BC), this was a signal of implicit threat not only to Corinth, but also to Sparta. Peloponnesian forces, led by the Spartan king Archidamus, duly occupied Attica and tested the efficacy of the Long Walls. So the Peloponnesian War commenced in 431 BC.

'Fortress Athens' held out. But two blows then struck from within. In 430 BC an epidemic of plague spread through the city. (Thucydides, one victim who survived, plangently describes piles of corpses in the streets.) The following year, Perikles died. The well-known portrait-type created of him posthumously, and set up inside the Propylaia as if to greet all pilgrims to the 'Periklean' Acropolis, shows him in the usual mode for an honorific image in democratic Athens, as one of the city's generals, with his hoplite helmet tipped back on his head. With Perikles, the typical image of a distinguished Athenian *strategos* has particular historical resonance. There was no one to replace him for clarity of vision and steadiness of resolve.

Military policy varied as politicians vied with each other to win support in the Assembly. To one boy growing up in Athens as the conflict dragged on, year after year, this was perhaps sufficient proof that democracy was inherently prone to pander to the short-term interest: if so, Plato never changed his mind about democracy's failure in this situation (see page 134). Meanwhile the geographical limits of the war were extended, as the erstwhile Corinthian colony of Syracuse became involved. Syracuse had advanced from being the strongest Greek settlement in Sicily to being the strongest Greek colonial settlement anywhere. But this reality appears not to have registered at Athens, where in the flux of political ambitions a certain Alcibiades gained support for a naval attack upon Syracuse. Alcibiades had been a protégé of Perikles, and a student (and would-be lover) of Socrates, and carried the glory of an Olympic victor. Much was in his favour, including his good looks. His plan for a Sicilian expedition was opposed by a political rival called Nikias; but in 415 BC the Athenian fleet set off with Alcibiades and Nikias among the joint commanders.

Whether Alcibiades felt at all responsible for the ensuing catastrophe in the waters of the harbour at Syracuse is not known. No sooner had the fleet arrived in Sicilian waters than he himself was recalled to Athens to answer charges about his personal behaviour (his temperament, as recorded in various sources, is perhaps best described as 'racy'). The more cautious Nikias carried on the mission, with some initial success in mounting a blockade against Syracuse. In 413 BC, however, and despite the arrival of reinforcements, Athenian ships found themselves trapped. Once more we rely upon Plutarch, who wrote the *Life of Nikias*, to add memorable detail. Many Athenians were captured, he says, and most perished in the great stone quarry of Syracuse, put to hard labour with meagre rations. Others were taken into slavery. Just a few were saved by their enthusiasm for the theatre. As Plutarch explains, the colonists in Sicily had a special 'yearning fondness' for the poetry of Euripides, and were thankful to any visitor who could bring them a sample. Accordingly, Athenian captives who were able to recite lines by Euripides were rewarded not only with food and drink, but with their freedom. (When they got back to Athens, they were able to thank the playwright personally.)

Nikias was put to death. Alcibiades, meanwhile, had evaded his recall to Athens, and instead defected to Sparta. From there he went to Ionia, to stir up revolt against Athens; while in Ionia he also attempted to persuade the Persians to renounce their support of Sparta. A detachment of the Athenian fleet based at Samos gave him command, and after several years of strategic success he was welcomed back to Athens. Once more, however, Alcibiades fell foul of the Assembly. He took himself to the court of Pharnabazus, who ruled the kingdom of Phrygia in Asia Minor on behalf of the Persians. This time, however, his enemies at Athens took no chances of a possible return, and had him murdered at a distance.

Readers feeling bewildered by the curriculum vitae of Alcibiades may be wondering what kind of war this had become, where one leading protagonist could move from one side to the other so fluently. Those who have tried to follow the events of a similarly extended conflict – most obviously, the Thirty Years' War of seventeenth-century Europe – will know that using the word 'war' in the singular is misleading: while one episode may seem to link as consequent to another, or can be rationalized as such, local opportunism is perhaps a more likely explanation for much of what took place over several decades. Even the Athenians were not quite sure why, in 416 BC, their forces attacked Melos with such ferocity: the island's crime was apparently no more than that of staying neutral.

'Let my spear lie idle for spiders to weave their webs around it', sings the chorus in Euripides' play *Erechtheus*. By the closing decades of the fifth century BC many Athenians may have shared that yearning for peace. A recognized end to hostilities came in 405 BC. By then the Peloponnesians had developed a naval force to match Athens. Led by the Spartan admiral Lysander – another biographical subject of Plutarch, though portrayed with little sympathy – this force was victorious at Aegospotamoi, in the Hellespont. Lysander pursued his advantage by blockading the Piraeus until formal surrender had been extracted from Athens. The Long Walls came down; Spartan troops set up a garrison on the Acropolis; and with Lysander's support, a group of Athenian oligarchs, subsequently known as the 'Thirty Tyrants', asserted themselves.

Perhaps the conduct and concatenations of the Peloponnesian War begin to make sense when we learn that the Spartans erected at Delphi an elaborate monument to their success at Aegospotamoi. Lysander was shown being crowned by Poseidon; other deities were also represented – Zeus, Apollo, Artemis and the Dioscuri; and there were statues of Lysander's pilot, his priest and no fewer than twenty-eight named captains of his fleet. So the Spartans could be showy too – and the site favoured a show. Delphi, like Olympia, was a Panhellenic or 'All-Greek' sanctuary: a site where by definition a certain 'Hellenicity' or ethnic unity was enshrined. Yet Delphi, like Olympia, was at the same time a theatre of inter-Greek hostility, as city-states took pride in their victories one over another.

A rhetoric of Panhellenism would gather momentum in the later fifth century BC, and find fuller expression in the fourth century BC, when such celebrated Athenian orators as Isocrates warmed to the theme (his *Panegyricus*, composed in 380 BC, urged all Greeks to come together under the joint leadership of Athens and Sparta). Isocrates is also credited with being the intellectual source for the concept of a Macedonian attack upon Persia – the project for which Philip II of Macedon eventually groomed one of his sons, Alexander. Before attacking the Persians, however, the Macedonians would conquer the Greek city-states – a process made all the more attractive by the fact that, despite eloquent pleas for Panhellenic solidarity, it could still be done piecemeal.

Even before the Macedonians transformed the hoplite phalanx – by increasing its numbers, training cavalry units to defend and complement the phalanx, switching from the spear to an elongated pike (the *sarissa*), and making a profession of military service – Spartan superiority on the battlefield had been undermined. The close of the fifth century BC saw Sparta apparently pre-eminent among all Greek city-states. In their king Agesilaus, though he was born lame and short of stature, the Spartans had a spirited and steady leader. Their way of life still attracted admiration: the Athenian Xenophon, distinguished both as a military man and as a writer, chose to retire to an estate in a Spartan-controlled part of the Peloponnese. However, the city, so small and self-sufficient, was constitutionally ill-suited to managing an 'imperial' foreign policy. Governors were sent to those regions formerly controlled by Athens – indeed, governors were sent to Athens, too – but it is clear enough that a Spartan education (such as it was) did not tend to produce effective administrators abroad. Accusations of Spartan hubris, greed and incompetence multiplied. Worse still, the Spartan military machine began to show signs of weakness. Agesilaus could boast that among his hoplites were no potters or blacksmiths, recruited to make up numbers in the phalanx. But the number of 'pure' Spartan citizens trained as professional soldiers, always restricted, now declined, with increasing reliance upon a draft among the *perioikoi*. Aristotle diagnosed *oliganthropia*, which is usually translated as 'lack of manpower'. But it was as much the quality as the quantity that had dropped.

The Thebans of Boeotia, who shared with Sparta a fearsome reputation for almost suicidal commitment to the phalanx, scored a significant victory over the Spartans at the battle of Leuctra, in Boeotia, in 371 BC. The Theban commander, Epaminondas, has a reputation (yet again, largely thanks to Plutarch) for strategic innovation: to say that he devised ways of attacking the phalanx side-on oversimplifies his achievement, but he nevertheless marks the development of more flexible and imaginative tactics – tactics that would be pursued with conspicuous success by the Macedonians and which left the Spartans behind. Agesilaus was not responsible for the defeat at Leuctra, where his co-regent Cleombrotas was in charge (and among the casualties); nor were his last years inglorious (Agesilaus was eighty-four when he died in 361 BC, and had just been campaigning against Persia, with Spartan mercenaries on behalf of an Egyptian pharaoh). But Sparta's heyday was over.

• • •

'Spartas Geist lebt!' – 'the spirit of Sparta lives on!' – epitomizes the appropriation of ancient Sparta in nineteenth- and twentieth-century Germany for purposes of educational ideology. First the Prussian state established cadet schools where pupils – largely of privileged background – were taught, along the lines of the Spartan 'mess', to withstand pain and hardship uncomplainingly. Then the National Socialists created institutes aimed at supplying the Third Reich with a class of warrior-leaders; these institutes, too, were overtly 'Spartanizing', as indeed was the paramilitary corps for juvenile Nazis, the Hitler Youth.

Veterans of the British public school system may feel that aspects of their experience – cold showers, enforced cross-country runs, regular floggings… at least before these schools modernized – were also indebted to the Spartan model, even if unconsciously.

Neither of these legacies is likely to endear us to ancient Sparta, in mirage or otherwise. From the vantage of liberal minds in multiracial societies, Sparta can only seem benighted in its commitment to communal living controlled by an oligarchy. Even Plato, who admired much of Sparta's practice in principle, was disgusted by what happened at Athens under the Spartan-supported Thirty Tyrants. Centuries later, the historian Arnold Toynbee would point to Sparta as one example of an 'arrested civilization'. Ultimately, then, it seems that the lesson of this proto-totalitarian city-state persists for its cautionary value: a warning against excesses of tribalism, protectionism and conservatism – and against any educational system that is essentially akin to the breaking-in of quadrupeds.

IV
SYRACUSE

According to Thucydides, the first Greeks to settle on the island of Sicily, whose existing inhabitants were called Sikels, came from Chalcis on Euboea: they founded the colony of Naxos, on Sicily's east coast, around 735 BC.

A year or two later, émigrés from Corinth arrived at the site of Syracuse, also on the east coast, displaced the Sikels there, and established a colony. Thucydides knows the name of the expedition's leader as Archias, one of the so-called Herakleidai or 'sons of Herakles'. He landed upon what was then a small island offshore (called Ortygia), expelling the Sikels who were there; subsequently the island was connected to the mainland and the colony expanded. But that is all that Thucydides knows, or cares to relate.

Stories supposed to originate from Apollo's oracle at Delphi tell a little more. The oracle was once consulted by two intending travellers, Archias from Corinth and Myskellos from a place called Rhypai. The oracle demanded to know whether they wanted wealth or health. Archias chose wealth; Myskellos health. Archias was directed to Syracuse; Myskellos to Croton, at the foot of the Italian mainland. Syracuse would prosper exceedingly; Croton would become the location of a distinguished medical school. So the oracle was justified by history. Its geographical indications for the finding of Syracuse were typically poetic:

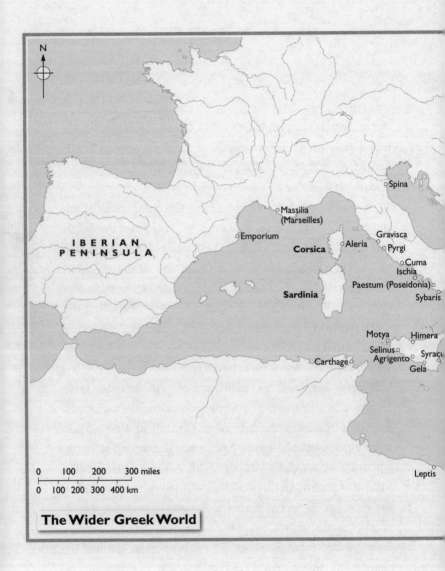

The Wider Greek World

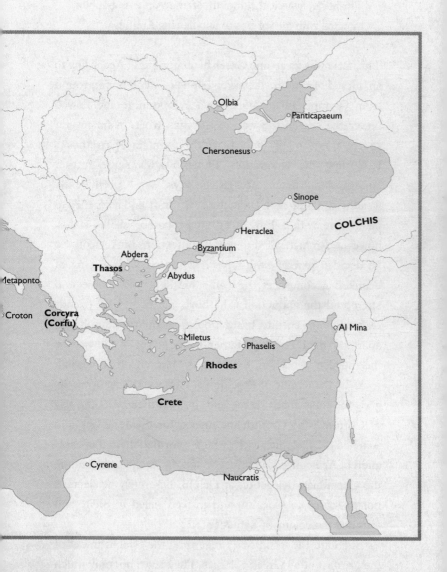

Olbia

Panticapaeum

Chersonesus

Sinope

COLCHIS

Heraclea

Byzantium

Abdera

Thasos

Abydus

Metaponto

Corcyra (Corfu)

Croton

Miletus

Phaselis

Al Mina

Rhodes

Crete

Cyrene

Naucratis

> A certain Ortygia lies in the misty deep opposite
> Thrinacia, where the mouth of the Alpheus bubbles,
> mingled with the springs of fair-flowing Arethusa.

Thrinacia was an arcane Greek name for Sicily. According to
an incredible myth, the river Alpheus went underground
from Olympia in the north-west Peloponnese and flowed
under the sea all the way to Ortygia, where a freshwater
source was (and is) known as 'the fountain of Arethusa'.
Regarding the emigration, Plutarch adds some further
circumstantial detail. Archias, he says, was a prominently
wealthy and well-born character at Corinth, and happened to
be in love with a boy called Actaeon. For all his status,
however, Archias failed to win the affections of Actaeon. So
he decided to carry the boy off by force. With a gang of
drunken accomplices, he came to the family home and
attempted the abduction. The boy's father and his friends
resisted. In the ensuing brawl, poor Actaeon was himself torn
apart and died. The boy's father, failing to get civil justice for
the murder of his son, fatally threw himself off some high
rocks by the temple of Poseidon at Isthmia, calling upon the
gods for vengeance. Plague and drought then beset the city
of Corinth. The Corinthians turned for divine advice and
solicited the Delphic oracle, which informed them that expi-
ation of Actaeon's death must be sought. Archias was among
the Corinthian delegation at Delphi. Discretely he decided
not to return to Corinth, and instead sailed to Sicily and
founded the colony of Syracuse.

Such are the testimonies regarding the establishment of
the greatest of all Greek colonies. They leave not only much
to the imagination, but also many basic questions of motive,

scope and logistics. Suppose that Archias did flee from Corinth because he was guilty of homicide and needed to bolt. How did he know where to go? The oracle's directions to Syracuse, if we reconcile one story with another, were hardly practical guidance for the navigator. Was it originally just a single boatload? Which route did the boat take? Were men, women and children aboard? And at their destination, what sort of reception awaited them from the local inhabitants? Did Archias already have connections there?

No surviving ancient source says much to illuminate these obscurities – as if they were of no ancient concern. That may be forgivable: only in retrospect, perhaps, is it clear that the Greeks developed their concept of the city-state by exporting it. So there is much that archaeology needs to contribute if we are to understand the colonization process. Fortunately, evidence is forthcoming, especially if explorations are made of the rural hinterland upon which every colony depended.

We can also attempt some useful guesswork informed by more recent historical experience. There are dangers in assuming that 'market forces' prevailed sufficiently in ancient times to constitute motives for colonization; yet it is worth pondering how far Greek colonization may be compared to the mercantile trade, from the sixteenth century onwards, and empire-building of European powers in Africa, America and India – or even to the phenomenon of penal transportation from Britain to Australia.

Whatever the results of such ponderings, there is no doubting the importance of the process of Greek colonization, at least within the parameters of this book. If Greeks had not migrated during the eighth to sixth centuries BC, there would be very little by way of 'classical civilization'. To be more precise, one part of the Mediterranean was so densely and so prosperously settled by migrants that it became known as Magna Graecia – *Megale Hellas*, or 'Great Greece' – and essentially this forms the cardinal connection implied by the hyphen in our definition of classical as 'Graeco-Roman'. And of the numerous celebrated cities of Magna Graecia – including such modern names as Agrigento, Naples, Paestum, Reggio and Taranto – none was ever so powerful, historically, nor so grandiose, topographically, as Syracuse.

No Parthenon stands on the skyline of Syracuse – though the columns and base of a fifth-century BC temple to Athena are shamelessly incorporated into the city's cathedral. For an experience of architectural splendour, travellers must go elsewhere among the Greek colonies in Italy: to Agrigento, where some half-dozen temples upon a ridge make a 'godly palisade' between the city and the sea; to Segesta, where the temple, never completed, seems for all the world to have grown among the limestone and holm-oaks; or to Paestum, where the Doric order proves it needs no adornment to be wonderful. Some sense of the grandeur of Syracuse abides at its theatre, still serviceable as such; and at a part of the ancient fortifications, which in the fourth century BC extended 20 miles (32 km) and enclosed an area of 1,830 square miles – far exceeding the dimensions of Corinth, its 'mother-city' (*metropolis*).

Yet little was known of Syracuse, archaeologically, when towards the last decade of the nineteenth century a classical scholar from Trentino, in the very north of Italy (then part of the Austro-Hungarian empire), was called to become superintendent of antiquities in that part of Sicily. His name was Paolo Orsi, and he would spend almost half a century exploring not only Syracuse and its environs, but other areas of Magna Graecia. Orsi brought rigour to excavation and elegant clarity to publishing the results: thanks to his work, and the example he set for others, a measure of the 'material culture' of Syracuse can be gauged.

The city was not only famed for its wealth. Athens may have displayed greater architectural glory, and nursed more influential poets, politicians and philosophers. But it was at Syracuse, not Athens, where Aeschylus produced his mature works; to an athlete of Syracuse, not of Athens, that Pindar dedicated one of his finest victory odes; at Syracuse where Plato attempted to realize his vision of the perfect city-state; and at Syracuse, as recounted above (pages 90–91), where the Athenian fleet suffered its most grievous defeat.

• • •

Tourist guides in Syracuse like to point out a cluster of rocky islands offshore. These, they say, are the boulders hurled at Odysseus by a monster, the Cyclops Polyphemus, furious at having been blinded, tricked and taunted by the hero. Like the legend of the fountain of Arethusa, this story, in its own way, symbolizes the cultural connectedness of Syracuse, for all its economic and military independence, to a Hellenic 'homeland'. Does the story of Archias being steered to the site by the Delphic oracle belong to similar mythology?

It is easy to suppose so. Yet the concoction of oracular blessing for colonial initiative may well have been done in good faith. Even a fleet glance at the oracle process in antiquity tells us that such procedures were matters of momentous significance. Delphi was not the only oracular sanctuary of Apollo, nor was Apollo the only oracular deity. At Dodona, for example, in Epirus – the mountainous region of north-western Greece towards the Balkans – there was an ancient oracle of Zeus. Theoretically, or theologically, supplicants came to these oracles in order to understand divine will. The supplicants might be ordinary individuals with worries about the future: Will next year's harvest be bountiful? Could this be the time for a successful pregnancy? – and such like. They might be city-states, or great rulers: famously, in the sixth century BC Croesus, king of Lydia, asked the oracle at Delphi if he should go to war against the Persians, and in 431 BC the Spartans sought Apollo's blessing to take up hostilities against Athens (a 'go-ahead', as it were, for the Peloponnesian War). Those soliciting the oracle at Delphi were admitted to an inner chamber of the temple of Apollo, where amid smoke and gloom they heard stirrings from a subterranean source and the strange cries of a priestess, the Pythia, apparently possessed by the god. At Dodona, Zeus spoke through the rustling of leaves of a great oak-tree.

What did such strange noises mean? Staff of the sanctuary were present to translate. Divine advice was usually succinct, but rarely direct: the Spartans, in 431 BC, were fortunate to be told that Apollo would stay on their side against Athens and that they would prevail so long as they fought valiantly. Responses were more often enigmatic, such as that given in reply to Croesus: that if he went to war with the Persians, he would 'destroy a great realm' – so Croesus went to war, not imagining that the great realm destroyed might be his own.

The instructions given to Archias about founding Syracuse were of the enigmatic sort. But the workings of the oracle at Delphi can be partly rationalized. Delphi, with sea access from the Corinthian Gulf, was a place more or less central to the Greeks as they scattered demographically around the Mediterranean (they called it the 'navel of the world'). If worshippers came from all parts, then conceivably the priests at Delphi could have acted as a sort of intelligence agency, compiling and collating the geopolitical information brought to them. So, although recorded in poetic language and typically cryptic terms, the message to Archias was perhaps based upon reports from the west, to the effect that a certain place on the coast of Sicily was eminently 'viable' for settlement.

In any case, the blessing of an oracle was of further use. Supplied with a sort of divine permit, colonists might demarcate the extent of their new territory by creating a 'halo' of satellite shrines and sanctuaries. Such demarcation shows up quite clearly in the archaeological survey of Poseidonia – later Paestum – on the west coast of southern Italy, a colony founded around 600 BC by emigrants from Sybaris, another colony in southern Italy. We are not told how indigenous inhabitants reacted when incoming Greeks declared that they were appropriating such and such a location on behalf of Apollo. Archaeology suggests, however, that Greek colonial sanctuaries tended to be created, like those in the homeland, within places deemed special or sacred since the Bronze Age, or earlier.

But what if Archias never went to Delphi at all? We cannot rule out the possibility that traditions of an oracular prompt for colonizing were invented, either because no one really knew why the colonists had set out in the first place – or because it was preferable not to know. Plutarch, who himself served as a priest at Delphi in the late first and early second centuries AD, does not want to press the point, but his story about Archias leaving Corinth under an impending charge of homicide can be related to a recurrent suggestion in the historical literature that early colonists were not so much seeking a future as making an escape from the past. Criminals and 'undesirables' they may have been; or else disinherited, through illegitimate birth or by simple relegation in the order of patriarchal land allotment. In this context, we may want to note estimates of demographic change across Greek-speaking areas during the archaic and classical periods: burial evidence suggests a population 'boom', relatively speaking, from about half a million around 800 BC to something like five million around 300 BC – with all the implications that has for the intensification of agriculture, and pressure upon land and resources.

Some historians of Greek colonization like to invoke the phrase 'trade before the flag'. By this they mean that the preparatory condition for establishing colonies was a pattern of seaborne exchange. Pre-modern shipwrecks in Mediterranean waters are numerous – the total of documented sites runs to well over a thousand and increases steadily – and includes some Bronze Age vessels indicative of far-ranging prehistoric trade networks. The cedar-built vessel that struck rocks off Lycia (western Turkey) at Uluburun, for example, was loaded with a variety of raw materials and 'luxury goods' when it went down around 1450 BC. Ingots of copper and tin (the constituents of bronze), jars of oil and other perishables, quantities of glass, jewellery, ivory, weapons and more – Cyprus and the Levantine coast may have been the point of departure, but these and other goods show provenance from further afield and were perhaps bound for a Mycenaean palace. With the collapse of the palaces around 1200 BC such trans-Mediterranean routes were interrupted, but not terminated. Euboean mariners are thought to have been active along the Levantine coast by around 800 BC: the site of Al-Mina (Arabic for 'the port': now in the far south of Turkey, close to Syria, at the mouth of the river Orontes), discovered in the 1930s by Sir Leonard Woolley, is usually described as a 'trading colony' or entrepôt, where east–west exchange took place, and here the signs of Euboean presence are distinctive shapes and styles of pottery from the island.

How far archaic modes of exchange of goods correspond to our modern understanding of entrepreneurial activity is debatable. Trade may have been carried out by treaty, for reciprocal benefit rather than particular gain; the market mechanisms of surplus production, supply and demand, and therefore price, are not necessarily evident. Our two most ancient Greek authors, Homer and Hesiod, register in different ways a certain disdain for maritime trade. In the heroic world of Homer's imagination, mercantile business is beneath the warrior-lord intent upon honour rather than profit: Homer associates it, disdainfully, with the Phoenicians. Hesiod is less principled, and not anti-Semitic. His didactic poem, the *Works and Days*, reveals that he had a brother, Perses, who either took up with a merchant ship or was tempted to do so. Hesiod's fraternal advice is forcefully stated. The rewards might be great, he warns, but the risks are terrible: only for six weeks or so in the year – the 'halcyon days' of high summer, from June to mid-September – are the waters relatively safe for navigation, at least across open seas (for which, of course, it was essential to be able to see the stars at night).

Hesiod's embittered summary of his own landholding in Boeotia, at Ascra by Mount Helicon – 'awful in winter, too hot in summer, and good at no time' – might, however, drive anyone to seek better conditions elsewhere. And the open grudge he holds against Perses – that the sibling had taken more than his fair share of their father's property – points us to another factor often invoked in discussions of Greek colonization, that of 'land hunger'. It is a geographical truism that Greece, in general, lacks an abundance of terrain suitable for arable farming. A less well-known aspect of Mediterranean topography is that Sicily and southern Italy, in addition to their agricultural fertility, offer a markedly 'indented' coastline, with numerous bays and inlets. This means, in effect, that coast-based colonies may more readily possess a fertile hinterland while maintaining immediate access to the sea.

A localized conflict on the elongated island of Euboea, the so-called Lelantine War between Chalcis and Eretria in the eighth century BC, probably contributed to the motives for emigration. In any case, archaeology strongly suggests that Euboeans not only established trading posts in the western Mediterranean in the second half of the eighth century BC, but settled too. A pioneer destination, around 750 BC, was the site of Pithekoussai on the island of Ischia in the Gulf of Naples. Were this merely a location for exchange of goods, it would be termed an *emporion* in Greek; were it a formal colony foundation, it would count as an *apoikia*. But Pithekoussai seems to be somewhere in between. As its cemeteries indicate, there was a 'resident' population, and from traces of iron-working we suppose that they were not only trading certain goods but making them too. Within a decade or two, a further Euboean settlement was created on the mainland, at Cumae – as if the experience at Pithekoussai had prepared the way for formal colonization.

• • •

The Euboeans were pioneers among the Greeks, but they were not alone in sailing across the Mediterranean. Phoenician ships had been plying east–west routes since the eleventh century BC, and an eloquent tirade (divinely inspired) from the Hebrew prophet Ezekiel, a Jerusalem-based priest in the early sixth century BC, catalogues the many wares that passed through Tyre, one of the principal ports of the Phoenician homeland.* Ezekiel's is an impressive list: silver and iron, tin and lead; slaves and vessels of bronze; horses, mares and mules; ivory and ebony; purple garnets, brocade and fine linen, black coral and red jasper; wheat, meal, syrup, oil and balsam; wine, wool and sugar-cane; sheep and goats; and every kind of precious stone and gold, and all manner of fabric and cloth. All will disappear when Tyre is destroyed – this is, after all, the voice of doom – yet Ezekiel recognizes the marvellous extent of the trade. 'Your frontiers are on the high seas', he cries in apostrophe to the city. And again, we can confirm by the range of archaeological testimony that Phoenician trading posts ranged far across the Mediterranean. They encompassed Memphis, in Egypt's Nile Delta; Kition on Cyprus, and Lepcis Magna and Carthage on the coast of North Africa; Motya and Eryx on or close to the west of Sicily, and several sites on Sardinia;

---

* The Greek denomination for this area, 'Phoenicia', broadly equates to modern Lebanon; 'Canaan' refers to a larger extent, deriving from a native title of Kn'n.

Ibiza and locations along the south coast of the Iberian peninsula; and, beyond the Straits of Gibraltar, Cadiz (Phoenician Gadir), and Lixus and Mogador along the Atlantic shores of Morocco. As seafarers the Phoenicians were unmatched: Herodotus reports that they were commissioned by a pharaoh in the early sixth century BC to circumnavigate continental Africa, and there is an ancient claim that they even braved the Bay of Biscay to reach Cornwall, in the far west of Britain.

Herodotus tells an interesting story about Phoenician merchants operating along the coast of Africa, beyond the Gibraltar straits (this region, for Herodotus, is 'Libya'). It amounts to a sort of 'silent trade'. The Phoenicians approach by sea and lay out their cargo on the beach. They then retire to their ships and send up a smoke signal. The indigenous people, seeing the signal, come to the shore, deposit a quantity of gold next to the unloaded cargo, then withdraw. Disembarking anew, the Phoenicians assess the amount of gold. If it is sufficient, they take it and depart; if not, they retire to their boats and wait for more gold to be added. Neither side, says Herodotus, defrauds the other. Without exchanging a single word, each deems the exchange to be fair and mutually advantageous.

But Herodotus only mentions this practice for its peculiarity. He knows that *emporia* were normally places of direct encounters between Greeks and 'barbarians' (*barbaroi*). He uses the latter term, incidentally, without prejudice. At root it implies only that the sound of a non-Greek language, to a Greek, might be transcribed as *baa-baa-baa*. Modern academic jargon prefers 'the Other'; and a point of contact between Greeks and 'Others' will be termed a site of 'acculturation'.

Those involved in trade and exchange may therefore be regarded as agents of acculturation. Herodotus knew about a merchant called Sostratus, from the island of Aegina, who prospered in westward trade: archaeologists working at Gravisca, the port of the Etruscan city of Tarquinia, have found a stone anchor dedicated to Apollo by a certain Sostratus, who may very well be the same trader. A little to the south, the site of Pyrgi says much about how 'interaction' was facilitated in the archaic period. Close to the shore, two temples were set up, by permission (or commission) of the local Etruscan ruler, who was monarch of a city inland now called Cerveteri, but known to the Greeks as Agylla. Inscribed gold plaques recovered from one of these temples record the foundation, in both Etruscan and Phoenician; dedications from the sanctuary make clear that it was a shared place of worship for Greeks, Phoenicians and Etruscans alike. The Greeks honoured Hera; the Phoenicians their mother-goddess Astarte; and the Etruscans a deity equivalent to Hera, whom they knew as Uni (and who would become, in Latin, Juno).

To assert that in general the Greeks left more of a 'cultural imprint' in Etruria and elsewhere is not to belittle the Phoenician presence. It may amount to no more than a factor of 'craft specialization', whereby itinerant Greek potters, painters, architects and sculptors found work abroad, and so exported not only their style but also the 'cultural baggage' of their subject-matter. From a tomb at Cerveteri comes one of the earliest painted vases to be signed by a Greek artist, around 650 BC. His name, written in Euboean script, is Aristonothos – literally, 'best bastard'. Perhaps he was one of those Euboeans who left because they had been denied any land at home. One pot is not of course proof that Aristonothos actually settled in Etruria. But it seems an Etruscan prized this foreign handiwork. The vase is the shape known as a *krater* – a bowl for mixing wine and water at a drinking party. Aristonothos decorated one side with an image of a sea battle; the other with a scene of a recumbent giant figure being poked in the eye by several figures wielding a long stick. We do not know what sea battle may be intended, but are fairly sure that Aristonothos sought to depict the story best known from Homer's *Odyssey* – the blinding of a one-eyed, man-eating shepherd-monster who imprisons Odysseus and his shipmates in a cave (see page 8–9). Homer vaguely locates that adventure of Odysseus in the west – not specifically in Sicily, despite the tales of the tourist guides at Syracuse. But what does it mean when presented as an image to a 'barbarian' Etruscan at Cerveteri? Did the owner of the vase already know the story, or some version of it? Could he read the inscription, effectively 'Made by Aristonothos'? Was the artist on hand to explain details – such as, behind the figure of the Cyclops, a shepherd's basket for seasoning cheeses (as Homer mentions in his description of the cave)?

These questions are intriguing enough when related to the early evidence for acculturation. The quantity of such evidence multiplies when we add a further historical element discernible in the second half of the sixth century – a knock-on effect of the Persian invasion of Ionia around 540 BC. Ionia – homeland of Homer, Herodotus, Heraclitus and many other distinguished Greek minds – was evidently also the source of a number of artists and craftsmen who emigrated westwards rather than work under Persian rule. Their presence in the west had some spectacular results – for example, an efflorescence of painted tombs around the Etruscan city of Tarquinia. It was a diaspora of creative talent that would contribute to a tradition whereby, centuries later, the Romans assumed, quite ungrudgingly, that Greeks were *the* experts in painting, sculpture and architecture.

• • •

It is one thing to admire and analyse the visible results of culture contact and culture change. What about ethnic inter-action at, let us say, a more basic biological level? Greek sources record a piquant anecdote about the foundation of the colony of Massilia (modern Marseilles) in the south of France by Ionians from Phocaea, around 600 BC.* A certain Phocaean – perhaps a merchant who supplied the Celts with wine – became a friend of the local king. Happening to be in the area on business, he found himself invited to the wedding of the king's daughter. The Phocaean perhaps was not aware that a number of suitors were present at this occasion, nor that protocol expected the princess to mix a cup of wine and offer it to the man she wished to become her bridegroom. Our sources do not describe the general reaction when the girl presented her nuptial cup to the Greek guest – though the possibility is aired that it was an error. In any case, the king took the event as divinely ordained and gave his blessing, and our Phocaean rose to the occasion, renaming his surprise bride Aristoxene ('best foreign girl'). The couple went on to produce a long line of descendants.

* Phocaea is now Foça, a somewhat desolate former fishing village on Turkey's western coast.

To this legend we can add the results of an extensive field project around the colony of Metaponto, located on the instep of the boot-heel formed by Italy's geographical shape. By surveying superficial remains turned up by modern agriculture, archaeologists have been able to chart patterns of occupation in territory beyond the ancient city of Metaponto. Every city needed its *chora*, or 'hinterland' (often, in the colonizing process, this might be assigned by measured allotments, or *kleroi*). In the countryside around Metaponto it is clear that the density of small farms increased steadily from the late sixth century BC onwards. Investigation of rural cemeteries, and study of dental and skeletal remains found there, suggest that male incomers intermarried with local women, and by the fourth century BC it seems to have been a truly 'mixed' population.

The pattern of interaction varied. At Syracuse, we are told, the first colonists formed an elite of 'land-holders' (*gamoroi*) who made serfs of the indigenous Sikels. And, as if prime farmland soon came at a premium, or the colonists fell out among themselves, certain colonies 'cloned' themselves. So, on Sicily, the first colony Naxos gave rise to Leontini and Catana, and from Gela (founded in 688 BC by Dorian emigrants from Crete and Rhodes) came Agrigento (Akragas) a century or so later. Rivalry between colonies was persistent, and not much mitigated by the rise of what might be considered a common enemy. The Phoenicians kept outposts on Sicily, but it was their North African city Carthage, originally a colony from Tyre, that sought to assert itself militarily in the western Mediterranean. The vulnerability of the Greek settlements on Sicily to Carthaginian attack is sometimes invoked by way of explaining why, when Athens was exemplifying the political virtues of democracy, the Sicilian colonies tended towards tyranny, or 'military monarchs'.

A number of these autocrats are known as historical 'characters', beginning with Phalaris, tyrant of Agrigento in the early sixth century BC. His name became a byword for gratuitous cruelty: when his blacksmith devised a huge hollow bronze bull in which Phalaris could confine an enemy, then revolve it over a fire and so roast his victim alive, the blacksmith found himself used as a test of the contraption. Other rulers would gain celebrity by more conventional means. But there was an experimental spirit in politics at large. A Syracusan tyrant offered the philosopher Plato the opportunity to realize an ideal state (see page 154); it was among the colonial cities of southern Italy that Pythagoras and his followers not only set up schools but also constitutions.

Epitomizing the prosperity of the Greeks abroad were the Sybarites – the colonists of Sybaris, a foundation of around 720 BC in the Gulf of Taranto, towards Italy's 'toe'. An ancient discussion of luxury reports that the Sybarites led the way in banning industry and roosters from their city (as disturbances to sleep); while among the pursuits that gained them fame were all-night drinking bouts, steam baths, and training their horses to dance to piped music. One Sybarite described how watching someone digging a ditch had given him a pain in his back; a fellow Sybarite groaned, saying that just hearing about this had made him feel faint. Ancient historians note, with particular satisfaction, that Sybaris was destroyed towards the end of the sixth century BC in a conflict with her neighbour, the colony of Croton. The site, however, remained attractive to settlers. So it was chosen, around 444 BC, as a suitable location for a most unusual venture – a joint Greek colony.

Thurii was its name. Athens, under Perikles, took the lead, but the invitation to colonists was impartial, and the ideology ostentatiously democratic. The layout of the city was assigned to Hippodamus of Miletus: so deeply is his name associated with orthogonal town-planning that 'Hippodamian' is enough to conjure visions of streets and buildings within a regular grid. Hippodamus had refashioned his home city this way after its destruction by the Persians, and he organized the Piraeus area of Athens similarly. At Thurii this urban architectural ideal was accompanied by constitutional principles drafted by Protagoras, a philosopher from Abdera (an Ionian colony in Thrace) who had already made his name as a purveyor of wisdom at Athens (see page 149). His code of civil laws does not survive, but its tenor may be epitomized by the motto ascribed to him, 'man is the measure of all things'. As a colony, Thurii may not resound loudly in the pages of history, but it was where the historian Herodotus chose to spend the last portion of his life.

• • •

The dispersal of hundreds of relatively small Greek communities around the Mediterranean and Black Sea did not strain the notion of 'Greekness'. On the contrary, distance only heightened an awareness of *to Hellenikon* – the Greek identity defined by Herodotus as 'the blood we share, the language we share, our common cult places and sacrifices, and our similar customs'. For all its perils, seafaring was nevertheless much cheaper and quicker than journeying overland (and many journeys were made with the shore kept safely in sight). So far-flung communities 'networked' through the maritime movements of traders, priests, poets, philosophers, artisans and mercenaries; certain sanctuaries developed as places where Greeks abroad could occasionally unite.

Delphi, of course, was one such sanctuary, and the motives for making the journey there were not confined to functions of Apollo's oracle. Unlikely as it may seem, given Delphi's steep-terraced situation, there was a stadium, high up in the site, where athletic contests could take place; a horse- and chariot-racing arena must also have existed in the vicinity. From the early sixth century BC onwards, so-called 'Pythian Games' were held at Delphi every four years, and these were open to contestants from around the Greek world.

Music, dancing and poetry featured among the competitive activities at the Pythian Games, befitting the god honoured by the festival. Other sporting festivals were established elsewhere, notably the Isthmian Games at Corinth (in honour of Poseidon) and the Nemean Games (for Zeus) at Nemea in the territory of Argos. Both Isthmian and Nemean Games were, like the Pythian, Panhellenic, but these three never matched the prestige of the fourth Panhellenic venue – Olympia.

Olympia lies in the north-west Peloponnese, on the fringes of a region known as Arcadia. The romantic reputation of Arcadia stems from its natural landscape of mountains and glens, its cult of the goat-god Pan, and its relative isolation: to this day, Olympia shares an aspect of that remoteness, despite the numbers of visitors it attracts. Once it lay close to a minor town called Pisa (unconnected with the Italian city of that name). A Bronze Age tumulus was raised at the site, legend-arily the burial place of the hero Pelops, who had come from Ionia to win the hand of Hippodameia, daughter of a local king called Oinomaus. According to the myth, Oinomaus had a history of challenging his daughter's suitors to a chari-ot-race, which they would lose on pain of death. Pelops contrived a way of winning the race. His victory involved some trickery, and a curse that would eventually bring grim tragedy upon his descendants, from his son Atreus onwards ('the house of Atreus' includes Agamemnon, Clytemnestra, Iphigeneia, Orestes and Electra, and other unhappy lives). Still, Pelops got a wife, and by doing so in a chariot-race set the scene for Olympia the testing ground par excellence.

The ancient Olympic Games continued almost without interruption from the date assigned to their official inception, 776 BC, until an official shutdown was ordered towards the end of the fourth century AD. Coming under Roman control in the second century BC, the sanctuary was considerably 'upgraded' in terms of its facilities: many of the ruins now visible belong to the Roman era, and some may be credited to particular benefactors, such as the emperor Nero. Prior to these improvements, however, Olympia was indeed a testing destination. For centuries athletes and spectators simply camped at the site and endured its inhospitable surrounds. True, it was well watered by two rivers; but Olympia is also a place that gets oppressively hot and humid in high summer (when the quadrennial festival was held), and the area became malarial as the rivers silted up. A microclimate favouring spec-tacular thunderstorms encouraged the cult of Zeus at the site, from the Bronze Age onwards. Originally there may have been some kind of festival involving horses and other domesticated animals, but the sporting contests that became part of this cult were not intended to be 'fun'. In Greek these contests were *agones*, and it is no accident that we derive our 'agony' from this word. Herakles was by one tradition credited with pacing out the stadium at Olympia and with instituting contests of strength and combat: it is worth remembering that Herakles was obliged to perform twelve 'Labours' as penitence to a king, and that these trials of body and spirit were called *athla*. In this sense every 'athlete' was, like Herakles, trying to redeem his mortal state by going through the 'agonies' of hard training and harsh competition.

Mythologically, Herakles was born after a liaison between Zeus and a mortal princess. Tormented from an early age by the jealous anger of Zeus' wife Hera, the brawny hero was goaded into a fit of violent madness in which he killed his own wife and children. This was the appalling misdeed for which he had to serve atonement to Eurystheus, a king of Argos. A number of his Labours were mythically located in the Peloponnese and called for skill in wrestling, but in any case Herakles was a proper model for any athlete. The glory of Herakles, at the end of his tests, is apotheosis – to be made one of the Olympian gods. His followers could not hope for that, yet a sort of immortality beckoned – so long as they won. A crown of olive leaves was the notional prize, but much more followed.

The great temple of Zeus at Olympia, erected around 460 BC, displayed a series of metopes representing the Labours of Herakles. Within the temple, an enormous statue of Zeus enthroned – a 'chryselephantine' image of gold and ivory fashioned by Pheidias later in the fifth century BC – took the epithet of Nikephoros, 'Victory-bearer'. A winged Victory figure issued from the extended right hand of Zeus. An athlete should agonize to his utmost for the sake of winning; theologically, nevertheless, victory came by the grace of Zeus. All athletes, plus their trainers and supporters, prayed to Zeus as the festival commenced; after it was over, the successful ones (with their entourage) thanked the deity with sacrifices and feasting on a grand scale.

Olympia became pre-eminent as a sporting occasion in large part because the organizers of the festival devised, during the sixth century BC, a programme of challenges that was varied and exciting. They kept the standard of contest high by summoning the athletes a month prior to the festival, to allow for some kind of 'seeding' among the competitors (any Greek-speaking individual could enter, but hopeless contenders were sent straight home). After a tussle with Pisa, the small city-state of Elis gained control of the sanctuary and supplied referees. No absolute records of performance were kept, so we do not know how far ancient athletes could jump, or throw the javelin, and so on. But the names of victors were preserved, and whoever won the sprint-dash of the stadium – from one end to the other, a little short of 200 metres – became eponymous to the entire occasion. In turn, eventually, the Olympic Games provided Greeks everywhere with a common chronology. So 776 BC (by our reckoning) would be the 'First Olympiad; stadium race won by Koroibos of Elis'. Thereafter any historical event could be pitched according to the sequence of Olympiads – although other ways of measuring time were available.

The Olympic victory lists, though incomplete in their survival, are themselves historically significant. In the early years, athletes with a Peloponnesian provenance feature; there are plenty of Spartan names. By the mid-sixth century BC, however, the pattern is changing. We notice that the colonies, especially those in the west, are becoming increasingly more successful. The city of Croton not only reared the most redoubtable wrestler of antiquity, Milo, who won a succession of Olympic titles (his first as a youth in 540 BC); it also provided the first seven runners in the stadium race of one of the Olympiads in the late sixth century BC. Around that time, about a dozen Greek cities, predominantly colonies, established their own so-called 'Treasuries' at Olympia – small but conspicuous buildings overlooking the main precinct of the sanctuary and the route to the stadium. Official delegates from the colonies represented on this terrace – including Gela, Metaponto, Sybaris and Syracuse – could arrange meetings at their respective treasuries. But above all these were shrines to victory, and not only athletic victory. Military trophies were also put on show: the shields and helmets, for example, gathered from the field when the hoplites from one city-state defeated a rival phalanx.

Success at the Olympic Games clearly carried transferable symbolic value. It is epitomized by the story that when Croton went into action against Sybaris, its army was headed by Milo the champion wrestler, wearing his several olive wreaths of Olympic victory and clad also in a lion skin – as if a second Herakles. Conversely, it is tempting to see the sporting festival functioning as a sort of 'drive-discharge' within Greek society. Some of the athletic disciplines were dangerously rough, in particular the *pankration*, or 'all-in fighting'; though boys competed apart from grown men, there were no weight categories in wrestling and boxing, nor much protection by way of padded gloves and gentlemanly rules. Yet athletics proved a relatively harmless mode of expressing aggression. An ancient literary evocation of archaic Athens imagines how Solon once gave a guided tour of the city to a visitor from 'barbarian' Scythia (the Russian Steppes). The visitor is horrified by the sight of young Athenians at exercise – grappling in sandpits, clouting and kicking each other, a mess of sweat, blood and bruises. Solon gives the broad civic justification – that these are apprentice citizens being hardened for the rigours of military service, or defenders of the city keeping fit for their role, and so on – then adds a point of civil law: elsewhere – in Scythia, no doubt – it may be normal for a man to walk about town with a knife on his person; in Athens it is illegal.

The educational and civic values of organized sport were redeveloped in modern industrial society largely in tandem with the archaeological discovery of ancient Olympia. Converting aspects of pagan and Panhellenic cult into a chivalric-Christian and international movement, the French aristocrat Pierre de Coubertin retained the term 'Olympic' for whatever might ensue after launching a new series of contests at Athens in 1896.* The divergence of modern from ancient ethos was made stark by de Coubertin's insistence that participation, not victory, was of paramount importance. All the same, the justification of sport as a civic virtue was revived, and abides still. *Mens sana in corpore sano*, 'a sound mind in a healthy body': the slogan is in Latin, not Greek, and was penned by a Roman satirist (Juvenal), but we hear it quoted often enough. Perhaps there is no more pervasive legacy of the classical world at present than the obligation to 'go to the gym'

---

* By then archaeologists had already been working at Olympia for some two decades – and excavation continues still.

and 'keep fit'. We have not embraced the Greek habit of athletic nudity – a *gymnasion* literally implies a place where nudity is to be expected – but neither did the Romans.

If any of us ever wonders about the purpose of such essentially unnecessary effort, it is worth knowing that even in antiquity there were critics. Here is a fragment from the archaic philosopher-poet Xenophanes:*

What if a man win victory in swiftness of foot, or in the pentathlon, at Olympia where lies the precinct of Zeus by Pisa's springs, or in wrestling? What if by cruel boxing or that fearful sport men call pankration he should become more glorious in the citizens' eyes, and win a place of honour in the sight of all at the games, his food at the public cost from the State, and a gift to be an heirloom for him? What if he triumph in the chariot-race? He will not deserve all this for his portion so much as I do. Far better is our art than the strength of men and of horses! These are but thoughtless acclamations. It is not fitting to set strength before goodly art. Even if there arise a mighty boxer among a people, or one great in the pentathlon or at wrestling, or one excelling in swiftness of foot – and so stands in honour before all tasks of men at the games – the city would be none the better governed for that. It is but little joy a city gets of it if a man conquer at the games by Pisa's banks; it is not this that makes fat the store-houses of a city.

From this resentful outburst we see just how profoundly, by the late sixth century BC, athletics had permeated civic life. State

---

* His description of the Greek symposium is given above, page 53.

recognition of the winning athlete took various forms: free meals for himself and his family, front seats at the theatre – and, at Sparta, the honour of fighting in the king's bodyguard. A winner at the festivals of the Panhellenic 'circuit' of Delphi, Olympia, Isthmia and Nemea received a simple crown of foliage. But as the passage of Xenophanes indicates, there were plentiful further rewards and privileges from the community to which the athlete belonged. The games staged at Athens, as part of the Panathenaic festival, offered jars of oil to its victors – in quantities that had considerable economic value. A successful athlete could expect to make a good living. Beyond that was the sort of status we may be tempted to describe as 'celebrity', perhaps resorting also to the Greek word *kudos*.

One way of comprehending such celebrity or *kudos* for athletes is to remember that the military mode of the hoplite phalanx, with its emphasis upon collective action and esprit de corps, reduced the potential for an individual to distinguish himself on the battlefield. Locked into the ranks, a man's courage was certainly tested: the Spartan poet Tyrtaeus lauded the gritty type who kept steady under pressure, no matter if he were a prize-winning athlete or not. But if one wanted to emulate an Achilles, an Ajax or any hero from the past, where was the opportunity to prove oneself 'best of the Achaeans' – if not at the games?

• • •

A sprinter called Exainetos won the stadium race for the second successive time at the ninety-second Olympiad, in 412 BC. The homecoming welcome arranged for him by his city, Agrigento, was extravagant. A team of 300 chariots, drawn by white horses, was mustered to escort him into the city. In order for the procession to take place, a section of the city walls was knocked down.

The demolition may have had symbolic meaning: the city's defence lay in the quality of its manpower, with Olympic victory marking a sprinter with the same warrior attribute as swift-footed Achilles. But the gesture also came at a high point in the political fortunes of several Greek cities in Sicily; and the festivals at Delphi and Olympia had already revealed the potential for political leaders to confirm their authority by coming back as winners. The well-known bronze statue of the 'Delphi Charioteer' is the partial relic of a group dedicated in honour of victory at the Pythian Games by Polyzalos, a tyrant of Gela, around 480 BC. Polyzalos is not the long-robed figure whom we see, calmly holding the reins: his credit as victor may mean nothing more than that he owned the horses, the chariot and the chariot-driver. But his was the honour nonetheless. To be honoured by a so-called 'epinikian' or 'victory-related' statue made a firm claim upon posterity. By the fifth century BC certain sculptors were specializing in such commissions, notably Myron, who created the original 'Discobolus', or 'Discus-thrower' – an action piece; Polykleitos, whose approach towards 'harmonizing' the athletic body in vertical repose was so carefully calibrated that he wrote a treatise on ratios and geometrics by way of explanation.

The immediate and the long-term influence of these 'winning bodies', known mainly through a good number of Roman copies or respectful adaptations of the originals, can hardly be overstated. Placed prominently as commemorative monuments in cities of the classical world, images of successful athletes came to represent 'pillars of society'. Some, indeed, became properly heroized, with shrines and altars set up for their worship as demi-gods. On top of this virtual presence came epinikian poetry, a genre of 'victory song' whose best-known exponent was Pindar, active throughout the first half of the fifth century BC.

So far as we know, Pindar himself was no athlete, and his poems show little interest in the physical or technical accomplishments of sportsmen. His genius lay rather in creating a magnificent vision of victory – sonorous odes evoking not only the ecstasy of being saluted as the best, but also a sense of 'deep time' culminating in this moment of transfiguration. So legend and genealogy figure large in Pindar's poetic salutations to this or that victor on the Panhellenic circuit: some story from the heroic or primal past will teach a lesson that leads to righteous blessedness, or sow some seed whose ultimate fruit is the garland of victory.

Born in Boeotian Thebes, Pindar worked for patrons in various parts of Greece. He was proud that his verses could travel across the seas 'like Phoenician merchandise'. His faith in aristocratic values was proud, too. However much it strained his powers of invention, Pindar's emphasis upon inherited worth always seems earnest: *noblesse oblige* was a valid motive for entering an athletic contest, and the winner should act accordingly. So it happened that Pindar himself travelled to Sicily, in 476 BC, and produced some of his finest work in marking equestrian victories associated with two tyrants on the island, Hieron of Syracuse and Theron of Agrigento.*

* These two, not otherwise the best of friends, combined forces to defeat a large Carthaginian army by Himera, on Sicily's north coast, in 480 BC; later Hieron married Theron's daughter or niece.

Unconditional flattery is not Pindar's style. The leaders have shown their 'excellence' (*arete*) – and must continue to do so beyond the racetrack. As Pindar addresses Hieron, towards the close of his First Pythian Ode (celebrating Hieron's victory in the chariot-race at Delphi, in 470 BC):

> Since envy is better than pity, do not abandon great deeds. Steer your subjects with the rudder of justice; temper your tongue on the anvil of truth... The first prize in life is good fortune; next is a good reputation; whoever gains and maintains both of these has won the greatest crown.

The subsequent history of Syracuse, before the city eventually yielded to Roman conquest in the late third century BC, includes episodes of oligarchy, democracy, further tyranny, and monarchy. Pindar's advice would need to be quoted again and again. But could it be taken further? Could Syracuse be recreated as the perfect state? As already mentioned, Plato thought so. And that leads us to a point in our survey of classical civilization where we must pause, geographically, to consider a place that appears on no atlas.

V
UTOPIA

Utopia is not a known location.* **Merely as a word it is** ambivalent. Rendered into Greek, it could be either *outopia*, 'no-place', or *eutopia*, 'good-place'. So it lodges between nowhere and paradise. Yet Utopia belongs by right in any topography of classical civilization – if we allow it, albeit indulgently, to symbolize the general project of philosophical enquiry in Greece and Rome. That is not to say that all Greek and Roman philosophers were idealistic 'dreamers'. *Philosophia*, a 'love of knowledge' (or of knowing, or just *trying* to know), may encompass various forms of intellectual activity – including those anticipating the modern 'empirical' method of science – that propose a theory on the basis of observed or experimental phenomena, as well as abstract speculations about 'life, the universe and everything'.

Arguably the central work of classical philosophy is Plato's *Republic*, which, although it is nothing like a handbook of political 'republicanism', does attempt to describe the best sort of city-state – a sort of *eutopia*. Yet even here a good deal of rational energy is consumed by the effort of wondering how any of us might behave if we found a ring that made us

---

* 'Utopia', in St Thomas More's imaginative vision of a perfect society (1516), denotes a fantasy island somewhere in the Atlantic. Though More wrote in Latin and was influenced by Plato's myth of Atlantis, and though the word sounds Greek, 'Utopia' is not a classical concept.

invisible. Would we use the ring to steal, settle scores and generally cause mischief? Do we only behave well for the sake of *seeming* good (as Protagoras and the Sophists maintained)? This virtual scenario seems bound up with individual morality, but it has essentially civic implications. Given that humans live in societies, and are therefore obliged to balance personal interest with the 'group dynamic', the rapport between self-government and group-government is more than a metaphorical conceit. Might the state produce citizens who – if they *could* become invisible, thanks to a magic ring – would choose to do good rather than evil? Or: if such individuals became the leaders of the state, would that state not prove to be the best imaginable?

The historical context of those questions may broadly be defined as Athens at the end of the fifth century BC – a time when democracy was in crisis (see page 89). Plato's uncle Critias was prominent among the Thirty Tyrants who, with the connivance of the Spartans, seized power, and the young Plato may originally have been a supporter; it is clear that he never approved of democracy, or at least deplored the opportunities it offered to demagogues and politicians appealing to the collective desire for immediate gratification. Even Perikles he judged to be a crowd-pleaser. He was soon nauseated by the excesses of the Thirty Tyrants; nevertheless Plato maintained the hope that his theory of good government could be implemented. He journeyed across to Sicily several times with a mission to exert philosophical influence upon the rulers of Syracuse – first Dionysius I, and then his son and successor Dionysius II. None of these missions, it seems, was effective; yet in his old age Plato produced a detailed and prescriptive manifesto for the perfect constitution, the *Laws*.

In this respect Plato seems quite apart from his own mentor Socrates, whom he deploys as principal spokesman not only in the *Republic*, but throughout a series of relatively well-preserved and absolutely elegant 'dialogues' that purport to be the record of thematic interchanges between Socrates and various young Athenians. Cult figure as he may have been, the historical Socrates was no philosopher-king, nor does he seem to have nursed any desire to be a politician. On the contrary, he took pride in being a maverick – an 'idiot' (*idiotes*), in Greek, simply signifies one who goes his own way – and Socrates used this basic status to challenge the intellectual complacency of anyone and everyone, himself included (irony was one of his favourite tactics, and never more effective than when edged with self-deprecation).

Found guilty, in 399 BC, on various counts of impiety and 'corrupting the youth', Socrates – then in his seventieth year – was condemned to take his own life. He did so by way of a draught of poison (hemlock), and with an apparently tranquil acceptance that the court's verdict must be fulfilled. Several of his friends and followers stood around, lamenting: Socrates bade them be calm also. What was there about death, he reasoned, to fear or deplore? It was either like going to sleep – a sort of passive oblivion; or else it was as the poets imagined, a fantastic voyage to some netherworld where all the spirits of the past were stored. Who would not feel glad, Socrates suggested, to meet up with some of these foregone spirits, such as Ajax and Agamemnon, and be able to commune with them?

His enforced suicide was not a deliberate melodrama. But if the politicians of the day thought that they were getting rid of him, they were wrong. By the act of his death, Socrates was magnified. Plato proved the most reverent custodian and transmitter of the master's influence – though it should be stressed that when Plato uses Socrates as a mouthpiece, this is not verbatim reportage. Amid Plato's gracefully abstracted prose, it is easy to forget that there was a local, historical context for Socrates.

There is some 'solid' archaeological evidence: the house of a cobbler called Simon, said to have been regularly visited by Socrates, has been located in the western limits of the Agora. We also know from Athenian comic drama that Socrates figured as a conspicuous eccentric to his contemporaries: in a play of the 420s BC by Aristophanes, the *Clouds*, he is directly lampooned, with some intimation that his teaching will lead to trouble with the civic authorities. More generally, we have only to look at some of the surviving repertoire of the theatre during the fifth century BC to realize that moral quandary – especially the state of impasse or blockage where Socrates liked to lead his disciples, the sense of not knowing where to go next, termed *aporia* in Greek – was already a staple of tragic drama.

In the *Antigone* of Sophocles, for example, Athenians were obliged to witness the tragic result of a collision between the claims of personal, family-based values and the prevalent laws of the state. Antigone must bury her brother Polynices, so that his soul can pass on; but by royal decree Polynices, deemed (let us say) a 'terrorist', should not be given these rites. What, if anything, *justifies* the course taken by Antigone – to defy authority and cast the necessary 'handful of dust' over the exposed body of her brother?

In the theatre of Athens, such mythical dilemmas were rehearsed and enacted as if they were occurring there and then. The force of the drama lay precisely in the fact that the audience knew *what* should happen in the story, but not quite *how* it unfolded; they were therefore not only psychologically engaged, but also virtually serving as a jury in a court case. While the dialogues in which Socrates features are not always dramatically compelling – too often, it seems, an adversary in argument is reduced to basic assent: 'Quite so, Socrates'; 'Assuredly'; 'Yes, indeed!' – they are nevertheless rooted in an Athenian tradition of debate and discussion.

Socrates accepted death, but clearly enjoyed his active personification of the 'contemplative existence' (*bios theoretikos*, as later defined by Aristotle). 'The unexamined life is not worth living' – a maxim for his immediate apostles – makes a basis for individual virtue, but also appeals to anyone who would resort to dialectic and deductive reasoning as a means of understanding the world. In what follows, we shall survey the philosophy of the classical world more or less on its own terms: withholding the observation, for example, that it is much easier to lead an examined life when one has slaves to do the daily chores; and refraining from supercilious wonder that, for all the ethical finesse of certain Greek and Roman philosophers, not one of them ever questioned the institution of slavery, nor so much as mentioned – as a topic – the subjection of women. (It is noticeable, however, that much philosophical discourse concerns individual freedom and 'self-rule', or *autarkeia*.)

A good deal of ancient speculation about the physical world, and the human body, we can briskly summarize: they had no telescopes or microscopes, so it is futile to expect insights beyond guesswork. Nonetheless, the groundwork for modern empirical science and deductive thinking was achieved; if there were any doubt regarding our debt to the classical world, the mere terminology of learning bears witness: 'academia' is a direct inheritance from Greece, so too 'school', while 'education' has Latin roots.

Socrates plays a cardinal role in this story. It is a measure of his absolute historical importance that all Greek philosophers before his time are referred to as the 'Presocratics'.

• • •

The importance of Socrates has not been exaggerated for the sake of creating an historical character. His status as intellectual hero – 'the thinking man's thinking man' – persisted throughout classical antiquity, with his unmistakable features carved or painted as a virtual presence in numerous Roman houses. But the designation of the 'Presocratics' only arises in the nineteenth century, thanks to the patient and enduring labours of two German scholars, Hermann Diels and Walther Kranz, who successively collected diverse attestations of archaic Greek philosophy to be found in later sources.* The vocation of philosopher was hardly articulated before Socrates, even if some of the Presocratics apparently made a living from their claims to expertise in various fields – including medicine, astronomy, engineering, politics and 'physics' (deriving from the Greek word *physis*, 'nature', this could encompass all sorts of enquiry).

The earliest of the Presocratics are located at the colony of Miletus, on the western coast of Asia Minor. Rising amid

---

* Diels defined the discipline of 'doxography', literally 'opinion-writing' – the literature of philosophical doctrines reported indirectly.

cotton-fields in the accumulated silt of the river Maeander, it is not a site that bears substantial witness to the 'Milesian school' of philosophers once nurtured there. The ruins visible today are mainly those of a Roman city: scarcely anything can be seen of the Greek port and settlement rebuilt after vengeful destruction by the Persians in 494 BC, let alone of the colony that flourished in the seventh and sixth centuries BC. So imagination is needed to give any sort of context and character to the name of Thales, effectively the 'founding father' of classical philosophy. In company with other Presocratics, Thales left no direct evidence of his life and teaching: what we know of his career in sixth-century BC Miletus comes from citations of his ideas by later writers and anthologists, plus a number of anecdotes. One story tells of how Thales used his expertise in star-gazing and meteorology to make a forecast relating to the olive harvest in a particular year; he then made himself rich by cornering the market in oil-presses. Further testimonies relate to his invention of navigational devices, again derived from astronomy, and to a sojourn in Egypt, where his knowledge of geometry enabled him to measure the height of the pyramids by using his own shadow. However, along with two other names associated with Miletus in the following generation, Anaximander and Anaximenes, Thales evidently did not limit himself to what we would call 'applied science'. 'Big questions' – what lay beyond the heavens, how the cosmos originated – were boldly addressed.

Thales, as reported by later sources, proposed that the earth floated upon water, and that water was the base element of all matter. We can only guess the empirical observations that lay behind this hypothesis – the sea evaporating to salt? gold retrieved from rivers? humans perspiring when hot? Yet we suppose, nevertheless, that the hypothesis was grounded in observation and offered, like any hypothesis, for refutation or development. It fell to Anaximander to propose the origin of life in the marine element. As for Anaximenes, it is enough simply to list examples of problems he tackled. Why do winds blow? What makes a rainbow? Why do earthquakes happen? Why do we not feel heat from the stars?

Shadowy as they may be, the Milesians left their mark. Anyone subsequently claiming to be a 'wise man' was obliged to hypothesize upon such topics arising from observed phenomena. Ionia was the principal area of the Greek-speaking world that gave rise to the Presocratics, but it is a feature of their biographical profiles – such as survive – that these thinkers tended to be itinerant. How much of their 'knowledge', and indeed their spirit of enquiry, was indebted to the senior cultures of Egypt and the Near East (especially, for astronomy, Babylon) is hard to say. Miletus, in common with other cities along the Ionian coast, had trading connections with the Nile Delta. Thales was said to have come from Phoenician stock. Pythagoras of Samos, who is perhaps, by reputation, best known of the Presocratics (if 'best known' is the right phrase for such a mysterious figure), allegedly travelled as far as India. There appears to be something of the Asian shaman tradition in the Presocratics; and no doubt, if they did plagiarize ideas, they preferred not to reveal their sources.* Or is it mere coincidence that non-mythological explanations of the world appear around the same time from three apparently separate sources: the Presocratics, the Buddha and Confucius?

* Greek intellectual activity was typically competitive, but the competition was Greek against Greek, and never involved claims of superiority over other cultures.

What we know about Presocratic thinking and teaching derives entirely from second-hand reports – essentially the scattered material gathered by Diels and Kranz, though new fragments occasionally come to notice. With such citations sometimes consisting of no more than one or two words, the task of reconstructing Presocratic ideas can be formidable. The 'utterances' attributed to Heraclitus of Ephesus are a notorious case in point. Some, relating to the pervasive principle of change and strife in the world, remain nicely quotable: 'All is flux'; 'You cannot step twice into the same river'. Other remarks, on the face of it simple enough, presumably create meaningful analogies ('Dogs bark at everyone they do not know'). With Heraclitus the image of an embittered prophet is hard to resist, as his scornful eye is cast upon the sacrificial rites of conventional piety ('They vainly purify themselves with blood, just as if one who had stepped into the mud were to wash his feet in mud'). No less scorn is reserved for the performers of epic poetry and their fanciful cosmologies ('Homer should be turned out of the lists and whipped').

Already, then, we sense that these archaic 'philosophers' positioned themselves apart from priests and poets, rival claimants to extraordinary insight. The hostility towards Homer we shall re-encounter with Plato, who gives more reason for his distrust. Yet the Presocratics were not above couching their ideas in verse form. The 'literary' relics of Empedocles, of Agrigento, convey with memorable elegance observations about the four 'elements' (fire, water, earth and air), the succession of night and day, and such like.* Such relics give credence

* Empedocles, in company with several of the Presocratics, believed that the earth was round.

to the tradition that Empedocles invented the art of rhetoric – and reprimand our modern expectation that scientists cannot write, while 'writers' do not understand science.

So these archaic philosophers might, like poets, be called upon to perform at aristocratic gatherings and symposia. Xenophanes not only gave symposiasts advice on how they should comport themselves (see page 53), but also provided 'food for thought', delivered in elegiac metre. Xenophanes was no atheist, but his critique of anthropomorphic religion was trenchant: the supernatural must lie beyond human imagination, so why then did Homer and Hesiod insist upon giving the gods such mortal failings as deceit, theft and adultery? Being provocative seems to have been part of his performance: his denunciations of celebrity athletes for their civic and economic redundancy sound like a deliberate antidote to epic and lyric poetry.

Pythagoras, by contrast, appears to have valued athletes as potential pupils and is said to have trained Olympic victors. His name is beguilingly familiar, on account of a 'theorem' about triangles traditionally associated with him. From the tangled mass of later anecdotes and references it does indeed seem that arithmetic and geometry were part of the 'Pythagorean' curriculum – for Pythagoras, as Aristotle noted, everything could be expressed by numbers, including music. But perhaps what is more important for our present purpose is that Pythagoreanism was a 'way of life'. From Samos Pythagoras migrated to the colony of Croton in the far south of Italy, where his instruction attracted a society of disciples in the second half of the sixth century BC. How far this instruction was strictly dogmatic is impossible to assess: reports tell us, for instance, that Pythagoras himself was a pioneer of vegetarianism, while one of his pupils was the famous Olympic wrestling champion Milo, by legend also a redoubtable carnivore. To what extent the society formed a political faction is likewise hard to judge: in other cities of southern Italy, if not at Croton, 'Pythagoreans' apparently entered government as such. In any case, the founder's charisma seems to have rested largely in offering not only holistic wisdom about diet, physiology, mathematics, music and so on, but something like a religious doctrine. This did not involve the rejection of conventional rites, but rather galvanized them with particular commitments in preparing for an afterlife (for example, keeping silent for meditation).

Greek religion, as already noted, had its mystical elements. Various cults, including those connected with the names of Dionysus and Orpheus, promised some sort of rebirth to their initiates. With Pythagoras comes the articulation – albeit indistinct as it is related second-hand – of a 'soul' (*psyche*) that is the essence of personality and that can move, conditional upon a series of 'purifications', from one body to another. Pythagoras himself claimed that in a previous life he had been a (minor) character in Homer's *Iliad*. But the body inhabited by this or that soul was not necessarily human. One well-known story about Pythagoras tells how he stopped a man from beating a dog because he heard, in the dog's yelps, the cry of an ancestor. This belief in *metempsychosis* – the transmigration of the soul – may have been, for Pythagoras, an ideological reason for not eating animals. At any rate, for better or worse, he introduced a concept of body-and-soul 'dualism' into the repertoire of classical thought.

• • •

Another distinguished inhabitant of Croton in the late sixth century BC was the physician Democedes, one of the earliest known exponents of Greek medicine. Again it is not clear how much of early medical practice was indebted to expertise gleaned from Egypt and Babylon: Herodotus was certainly aware of intellectual traffic, and his mention of Democedes implies that it went two ways, for such was the reputation of Democedes that he was hired as physician to the Persian court of Darius the Great. Croton became renowned as a centre of medical knowledge, and joins a number of sites where 'families' of doctors were established. The island of Kos is the best known of these: here it was that Hippocrates made a name for himself in the second half of the fifth century BC. The text of the 'Hippocratic Oath' – a version of which is still used in many medical schools today – describes senior physicians as 'fathers', their apprentices as 'sons', and fellow pupils as 'brothers'. So medicine becomes almost a hereditary skill, and its practitioners a sort of priesthood. Indeed, the premises where these ancient doctors worked were typically sanctuaries to the healing god Asklepios. The oath begins with an appeal to Apollo – the god whose power was to punish mortals with a disease that came to 'lodge among the people' (the literal meaning of 'epidemic'), and equally to relieve such afflictions. Asklepios was a son of Apollo; sometimes named or represented in company with divine personifications of Hygeia ('Health') and Panacea ('Cure-all'), he was sire to the medical profession.

The divine connection may seem perplexing. For Hippocrates is usually styled as the originator of clinical medicine, meaning that he is considered to have pioneered the development of a medical method rooted in diagnosis of symptoms, the experimental investigation of the causes of disease, and a willingness to seek practical ways of curing disease. Some would contrast this with 'faith healing', or the acceptance of ill health as divinely ordained. So why were Hippocrates and others of his 'trade' established at temples, and why does the Hippocratic Oath invoke Apollo?

The answer to that question – and the reason we have raised it at this point in our story, between Presocratics and Socrates – must lie in the peculiar status of collective cult observance in the classical world. There were crimes of impiety – Socrates himself would be condemned on such a charge – but no theocracy prevailed: priests were not so powerful that they made civic laws. It was not impious to allow Zeus only a symbolic role in the phenomenon of thunder; and, of course, 'polytheistic' religion – a diversity of deities – tended to deter sacred authoritarianism (did a priestess of Demeter rank above a priest of Dionysus?) If certain Presocratics were openly scornful of aspects of traditional cult, such scorn did not necessarily equate to atheism, agnosticism or blasphemy. And for practitioners of medicine, the search for causes and cures was not tantamount to a rejection of faith. As becomes clear from the various texts gathered in the so-called Hippocratic Corpus – a collection of medical writings from the fifth to fourth centuries BC, none of them directly ascribed to Hippocrates – the causes and remedies of sickness were considered within the scope of a patient's 'lifestyle'. Hippocratic diagnosis looked at habits, heredity, personal temperament and physical environment (including climate). The wisdom gained by gathering numerous case notes was pooled with a broader theory about balancing elements inside and outside the body. But the psychosomatic

part of finding a cure was not underrated. Healing sanctuaries created under the auspices of Asklepios and his doctor
descendants offered dormitory accommodation, not only so
that a patient could be kept under observation, but also to
allow a residential regime of therapy that encompassed
prayers, analysis of dreams, hypnosis, bathing, exercise,
special diets and purges – and even, for the therapeutic benefits of tears and laughter, going to the theatre.*

Physicians taking the oath pledged themselves to a code
of conduct, including a promise not to abuse their knowledge
or trusted position, and a refusal to assist death or conduct
abortions. Evidently there was an open market in offering
cures, and plenty of 'alternative medicine' available. Who was
to be trusted in this marketplace? The Greek word *pharmakon*
is ambivalent, meaning either a healing remedy or a poison.
Botanical potions or philtres, harmful and beneficial, are
referred to from Homer onwards. By the first century AD a
five-volume guide to herbal effects, produced by one
Dioscorides, would be available. Whether this counts as phar-
macology, as we would understand it, is questionable: to
sample the text of Dioscorides is to become aware that almost
every plant in some way offers a beneficial effect for a discon-
certingly broad range of afflictions.

But drug-based cures are hardly mentioned in the
Hippocratic writings: the emphasis there is upon restoring
balance of bodily forces and substances. From this developed
the theory of constitutional 'humours', according to which an
individual's physical health and personality are determined

* The theatre in the sanctuary of Asklepios near Epidaurus, in the eastern
Peloponnese, is one of the best preserved from antiquity.

by the relative proportions of certain liquids in the body. Depending on the dominant presence in their bodies of blood, phlegm, gall or bile (*chole*) or black bile (*melaina chole*), people are, respectively, sanguine, phlegmatic, choleric or melancholic. A surplus or imbalance of one of these fluids could exert a negative influence on health and character. With a Pythagorean love of numerical symmetry, this fourfold system was related to the four seasons, the four elements and four prime qualities (hot, cold, wet, dry).

The Asklepieion on Kos continued as sanctuary and sanatorium for over a millennium. Indeed, the genealogy of Asklepios runs continuously through the classical world.* Ultimately, it was a physician from Pergamon, Galen (born AD 129), who proved most influential in the history of Western medicine. After junior experience gained in patching up wounded gladiators, he was appointed to serve the Roman emperor Marcus Aurelius. The emperor cannot have been a hypochondriac, for Galen found time not only to conduct much anatomical and physiological research, but also to write an extraordinary number of books, many of which survive (though not a fond account of his own library, which is lost). Galen was proud of his knowledge and determined to show where it differed from rival claims to knowledge. His writings therefore tell us a great deal about his predecessors.

Considering what the practitioners of medicine in the classical world lacked – such as microscopes, chemistry, and permission to carry out post-mortem examinations – it is astonishing, and commendable, that so much was achieved

* Doctors at Rome were regularly of Greek origin, even if they were given Latin nicknames: the first surgical specialist recorded at Rome, Archagathus, was referred to as *Carnifex*, 'the Butcher'.

in pursuit of cures for injuries and illness that were 'safe, swift, and pleasant'. That aim is attributed to another Greek doctor working at Rome, named (predictably) Asklepiades. It reminds us that the defining trait of Asklepios, and the principal commitment of the Hippocratic Oath, was *philanthropia*, 'humane kindliness'.

• • •

Hippocrates was more or less contemporary with Socrates. So far as we know, they were never acquainted. But both men lived and worked in an ambience of intellectual autonomy and intellectual rivalry; within this ambience there was already a preoccupation with 'epistemology' – our knowledge about knowledge, our thinking-through of how we think. Here, historically, it is possible to identify Presocratics who were 'Protosocratics'. One such was Parmenides, from Elea (Velia), the colony set up on the Italian coast by Ionians displaced by the Persian advance towards the Aegean around 540 BC. To Parmenides are ascribed the first principles of methodical argument, and he presents an enduring challenge to cosmologists by his denial of the possibility of 'what-is-not', but for our story his importance lies in the report (from Plato) that he came across to Athens while in his mid-sixties and conversed with the young Socrates.

With him on this visit Parmenides brought his own youthful 'Eleatic' follower, Zeno. This Zeno – not to be confused with Zeno the Stoic, whom we shall encounter later – remains known mostly for his 'paradoxes': mental exercises, in effect, designed to thwart or perplex the opponents of Parmenides. Whether playfully or not, Zeno showed how a course of reasoning depended on 'premises' – what was assumed or 'given' at the outset of discussion. So if 'movement' is reckoned to be a distance covered in a certain amount of time, and that distance is divisible, then the following paradox arises: imagine that Achilles (famously swift-footed), when challenged to run a race against a tortoise, graciously gives the tortoise a head start. Then Achilles can never catch the tortoise, because while the tortoise crawls along, Achilles has to traverse a series of infinitely divisible distances: he can never complete the series, so never catches up with the tortoise. Similarly, if an arrow shot from a bow is always in one place at any given time, how does it fly anywhere? In quoting these paradoxes (and they have forever only been quoted) it is easy to ridicule them as examples of what happens when philosophers pose questions about the world. But Zeno was not addressing the physics of motion, nor the mathematics of infinity: both he and Parmenides were fundamentally concerned to establish ground rules for the development of argument, scientific or otherwise.

Three further Presocratic thinkers who demand mention are Anaxagoras, whose doctrine that Mind (*nous*) was the original and ordering principle of all matter reportedly impacted upon at least two prominent Athenians apart from Socrates (Perikles and Euripides); Democritus of Abdera, in Thrace, who with Leucippus theoretically reduced matter to atoms – 'indivisible things' – thereby not only anticipating modern particle physics, but also offering a possible account of the cosmos in which deities played no part; and Protagoras (also from Abdera), who in his 'great speech' as transmitted by Plato (in the dialogue called *Protagoras*) saw humanity created as physically inferior to many other living creatures, yet rendered superior by its intelligent capacity for cooperation and communal existence.

The influence of Gorgias, who came to Athens from Sicily during the second half of the fifth century BC, should also be registered. Gorgias and Protagoras are counted as Sophists: technically, *sophistes* means no more than 'learned', but it came to denote (as defined in the *Oxford English Dictionary*) 'one who undertook to give instruction in intellectual and ethical matters in return for payment'. As such it could become a term of disparagement, in particular when connected to the emergent art of rhetoric – the public 'presentation' of knowledge. Was this, indeed, a skill (*techne*), or merely a 'knack' (*tribe*)? Plato, in a dialogue featuring Gorgias, was evidently suspicious of the sophistic emphasis upon persuasive effort. It was as if no truth existed, only points of view. Modern commentators are more sympathetic, and salute Gorgias for recognizing that prose could operate no less artfully than poetry. (Plato would not have accepted that the denial of rhetoric might also be deemed a rhetorical strategy.)

Socrates, then, has an intellectual context, if not a pedigree or apprenticeship with any one of his predecessors. He may once have pursued an interest in physics, before turning to the sort of moral reasoning for which he became famous. Essentially, however, there was no Socratic 'doctrine', except the obligation to ask questions – to submit any doctrine to critical scrutiny. He was not an atheist, but religious practice did not lie beyond the scrutiny of reason (it is easy to see how this approach could be deliberately misrepresented as 'impiety'). It was above all the spirit of independent judgement, shared in an open and amicable manner, that Socrates personified.

And Socrates made a caricature of himself: that was (and is) part of his appeal. For one who emphasized the moral implications of beauty, he was in person quite different from the classical stereotype of a good-looking man: balding, thickset, dishevelled and paunchy. His courage and resilience when on military service were attested by fellow soldiers, and his snub-nosed features did not deter youths of Athens from forming what we would call a 'crush' on their teacher: most notoriously Alcibiades, who attempted (without success) to engage Socrates erotically by way of supplementary wrestling lessons. Yet Socrates evidently enjoyed the role of anti-hero. He remarked that one good reason for keeping fit was to be able to run away fast from a battle. As for his own appearance, he made use of it as a philosophical point. Asked by one of his friends, Critobulus, to take part in a beauty contest, he agreed – immediately posing a question: 'So tell me: what do you mean by beauty? Is beauty confined to a man, or found in other things?' Critobulus replies that a horse or an ox can be beautiful, and indeed inanimate objects too, such as a shield or a sword. Socrates presses him to say what makes such diverse things beautiful. Critobulus says that something is beautiful when it is well made or well formed according to need or use. This gives Socrates the opportunity to pounce, with dialogue along the following lines:

Socrates:	Very well. Do you know what use we have of our eyes?
Critobulus:	To see.
Socrates:	In that case my eyes are more beautiful than yours.
Critobulus:	How so?

Socrates:	Yours just look straight in front. Whereas mine, bulging as they are, give me lateral vision too.
Critobulus:	So the most beautiful eyes of all are those of a crab?
Socrates:	Evidently so!
Critobulus:	And what about noses – which is more beautiful, yours or mine?
Socrates:	The gods gave us noses for the purpose of smelling. Your nostrils are set downwards. Mine however point upwards, so can receive smells from all over the place.

There is no doubt, in Xenophon's account of this repartee, that young Critobulus would have been judged by any onlooker as more handsome than Socrates. But here we see at work the sort of argumentative technique brought to the point of parody by Zeno. Of course Achilles can outrun a tortoise; of course Socrates could not be described as beautiful (Alcibiades likened him to a satyr). Admitting as much, how then is relative motion, or beauty, to be defined?

• • •

Pity all human attempts to comprehend the world as it really is. We barely know what is going on around us. It is as if we were all prisoners in some great cave, shackled in such a way that we can only look at the back wall of this cave. Behind us there are figures moving around, some carrying dimly recognizable objects, and beyond them a flickering light that casts their shadows upon the wall. We see no more than a shadow-play. Such are the limits of the senses we are born with. The majority of us will suppose that this is 'reality'. But is there a way out – towards the light?

The cave is Plato's analogy for mortal existence, and Plato supplies the answer. We escape the imprisonment imposed by our senses by following the way shown by Socrates and becoming philosophers, striving ceaselessly to find the truths of concepts we glimpse as shadows on the wall. Love, courage, justice, beauty, goodness: the soul has an inkling of what constitutes such qualities – it perceives their 'forms' – but must be trained to pursue them. It will be an upward, outward struggle for enlightenment.

Tradition relates that Plato, whose name implies broad shoulders, was in his day a champion wrestler. His school, founded in 387 BC, was located within the precincts of a gymnasium in a suburb of Athens that took its name from an obscure hero, Akademos, who was supposedly buried there. So the 'Academy' was already a place for physical exertion when Plato developed intellectual rigours for the mind. It follows from the analogy of the cave that our bodies, prone to desire and disease and annual depreciation, impede the path towards truth. So knowledge vies with pleasure as an attainment; and so, in the search for the ideal truth of love, 'Platonic love' must entail an affection that transcends sensual impulse.

A twentieth-century philosopher, A. N. Whitehead, famously summarized all Western philosophy as 'a series of footnotes to Plato'. Inaccurate as most witticisms tend to be, this will serve to lead us beyond the summary of Plato as idealistic and dualistic, towards his more particular signifi-cance for 'classical civilization' – that is, his serious fantasy of the perfect city-state. In the *Republic* it is acknowledged as fantasy – as Socrates is made to say, who would criticize a painter for creating a picture of something not matched in nature? In the *Laws*, however, the older Plato adds a programme of practical measures to realize something at least compromising with the ideal. Both visions are, in any case, extensive in scope, encompassing ethics, aesthetics, metaphysics, political theory, and more besides: in this sense it is fair to say that Plato set an agenda for many subsequent philosophers. Whether he also carries responsibility for the stereotype of philosophers as aloof, eccentric and unworldly is debatable. That was certainly not his intention: for in the philosopher's fantasy state, philosophers rule.

Of aristocratic lineage himself, Plato scorned the notion that ordinary citizens could combine to steer the ship of state. Captains were called for, skilled in astronomy, navigation and seamanship. The city-state must be governed by those who know best. *Hoi polloi*, 'the many', caring little for wisdom, were like herds of cattle or swine, shambling from one feeding place to another: how could they know what was best for everyone, in the long term? So leadership devolved to a type idealized by Plato as the 'perfect guardian' (*phylax panteles*), or 'philosopher-king'. Incorruptible, just, wise, watchful, reasonable and caring – the attributes of a philosopher-king make up a wish list that we might hope would apply to any political figure. By Plato's analysis, however, the consequences for the state or *politeia* are profound – and, to many modern readers of the work, unpalatable.

Both the *Republic* (the title derives from its Latin translation, *Res Publica*) and the *Laws* are complete manifestos, each making sense as a whole. It is unfair to make excerpts of Plato's proposals – but unavoidable. Two examples will suffice here. Regarding aesthetics: Plato deplores the 'mimetic' quality of much art and poetry – that is, the quality of (say) a painted bunch of grapes that looks just like a real bunch of grapes, so convincing that birds might come to peck at the painting; or of epic verse that reports speeches from Zeus and Apollo as if the poet had actually heard and transcribed them. How were people to learn the difference between truth and falsehood if artists and writers kept creating virtual reality? If the perniciously engaging texts of Homer could not be destroyed, then at least they must be rewritten and the city also purged of any kind of illusionistic art.

Or, regarding the family as a social unit: the interests of close kinship are always likely to collide with those of the wider community. Private property fosters greed. Therefore abolish the family and the home. Instead there might be a community of wives and, instead of parents, state-run nurseries for the children. Sexual reproduction will be assigned to strong, good-looking people; any infants born deformed will be discreetly destroyed.

From this second example we see immediately how Plato's treatise unsettles. On the one hand he seems to be a proto-feminist, wanting women to be freed from their traditional domestic and child-rearing roles so that they may play proper parts in the public sphere; on the other, he advocates a system of eugenics, as a further means of ensuring that the state is as excellent as possible. No wonder Plato is liable to be presented as a totalitarian maniac, a pro-Spartan, an arch-enemy of the 'open society'. And no wonder, perhaps, that at neither Athens nor Syracuse did Plato achieve anything that could be counted as a political success. In the leafy surrounds of his Academy, an aristocrat in the company of well-born and affluent young men inclined to *symphilosophein*, 'theorize together', it may have been too easy for Plato to forget that humanity is – in the phrase of a later European philosopher (Immanuel Kant) – naturally, and irredeemably, a sort of crooked timber.

• • •

When Plato died in 347 BC, leadership of the Academy passed to his nephew Speusippus. The intellectual star of the next generation, however, was Aristotle, a doctor's son from Stagira in northern Greece. Aristotle had entered the Academy at seventeen years of age and spent two decades studying with Plato. To judge from his surviving works – of which there are many, though still more are lost – Aristotle was probably ready to graduate; his own philosophical and scientific interests were leading him away from the Platonic curriculum. As it happened, a former Academician called Hermias became tyrant of a minor territory on the coast of Asia Minor, and he invited Aristotle to join him at its capital, Assos, an idyllic site overlooking the Aegean. It was here, and subsequently while resident at Mytilene on the island of Lesbos, that Aristotle was able to pursue the studies of marine biology that are among his most enduring contributions to the sum of human knowledge. His career as philosopher took another turn when he was invited to the Macedonian court, to serve as personal tutor to the young prince Alexander. Later on, after his pupil had taken up the challenge of conquering the world, Aristotle returned to Athens, where he set up a school that became known as the Lyceum. One of its buildings was a covered courtyard or *peripatos*, so students were sometimes called 'Peripatetics'. He died in 322 BC, a year after Alexander's death, and after anti-Macedonian sentiment at Athens had forced him to leave (he was always a metic, excluded from citizen rights). The Lyceum was thereafter guided by Theophrastus, a popular lecturer, able biologist, and astute observer of social types (*The Characters of Theophrastus* is an early classic of people-watching). But no one could replace Aristotle.

Il maestro di color che sanno: 'the master of those that know'. That salutation, made by Dante in the thirteenth century, epitomizes Aristotle's extraordinary status beyond his own age, a reputation that has also done some injury to his original ideas. Even in the twentieth century it was possible for a comedian (Woody Allen) to mock the Aristotelian system of formal logic, with a mischievous twist of a classic 'syllogism' – the process of argument whereby two propositions lead to a certain conclusion ('All men are mortal. Socrates was mortal. Therefore all men are Socrates.*'). In late antique and medieval times, interest in Aristotle's ideas came from both Islamic and Christian scholars, among them such distinguished names as Avicenna (Ibn-Sina), Averroes (Ibn-Rushd), al-Ghazali and Thomas Aquinas: reconciling their theological priorities with the ideas of 'the master' was bound to cause some distortions.

A strange legend about Aristotle, probably concocted in fourteenth-century Europe, told how he fell victim to a practical joke set up by his pupil Alexander. A courtesan called Phyllis was hired to seduce the great philosopher. He became

---

* A line from *Love and Death* (1975). Correctly: All men are mortal. Socrates was a man. Therefore Socrates is mortal.

besotted: so much so that he allowed Phyllis to bridle him and ride him around like a horse, a whip in her hand. This kinky image served to illustrate a Christian homily on the frailty of pagan wisdom. Yet while it remains historically undocumented, the episode is not completely out of character with Aristotle's teaching. Where Plato idealized human nature, to the point of myopia, Aristotle was more pragmatic. Humans were subject to passions, making some of their actions 'involuntary'. Doubting Plato's faith in the immortality of the soul, Aristotle sought to establish a practical system of moral behaviour that would produce happiness or 'well-being' (*eudaimonia*) in this life, not for eternity.

One way of calibrating the difference between Aristotle and Plato is to remark what Aristotle has to say about drama. Plato, as noted, was austere with regard to poetry of an imitative nature, and saw nothing clever or funny about (say) a man who could mimic a chicken. Aristotle, by contrast, seems to have understood that humans naturally enjoy the very act of representation – however it is done – and find the experience of drama therapeutic. We will voluntarily go to see a play in which terrible events are represented on stage. The representation may be so convincing that we forget where we are and forget that it is only acting (usually of mythical events), and we are moved to tears. Soon enough we will recover, but meanwhile this sharing of pretended yet credible emotions has given us a *catharsis* or 'purging', a let-out of anxieties accumulated during day-to-day life.

Aristotle did not specify the importance of installing theatres at great healing centres such as Epidaurus; nor do we have his lecture notes on comedy, analysing (perhaps) its value as a tonic. However, his observations upon the universal validity of myth as a basis for drama, and his implicit recognition of how we identify with the characters enacting these stories, show Aristotle as sympathetic to the psychology of the stage. Aristotle's identification of 'dramatic unities' (of place, time and persons upon the stage) was for many centuries a concern for playwrights in the Western tradition; some of his precepts regarding dramatic structure are still taught in courses promising to divulge the secret of a successful Hollywood script.

A glance at the range of Aristotle's works is enough to attest his encyclopedic concerns. Some titles cannot be certainly assigned to Aristotle as author, and some are really no more than compilations of empirical data, quite possibly collected by his students – for example, notes on the habits of wasps, or the way in which human semen liquefies as it cools. All the same, the intellectual expertise of Aristotle embraced philosophical logic, physics, astronomy and meteorology, sense perception, memory, metaphysics, sleep, dreams, biology (human, animal and marine), botany, engineering, ethics, politics and constitutional history, rhetoric, 'poetics' (literary theory), and education. Plato's Academy was devoted to teaching; Aristotle's Lyceum added the enterprise of research – and in that sense may be described as the prototype of the modern university.

Indeed, Latin translations of Aristotle's works made up much of the curriculum for the first universities of medieval Europe, such as Paris and Bologna. The pre-eminence of a pagan philosopher amid institutions more or less under Christian authority was not without its problems, but as affirmed centuries later by Cardinal Newman, the 'idea of a university' is the pursuit of 'universal' knowledge beyond any dogmatic agenda; Aristotle's empirical method of gathering data, presenting it according to the logical-deductive process of definitions, hypotheses, conclusions and so on, remains standard practice across most academic disciplines.

• • •

The meeting of Aristotle's erstwhile pupil Alexander the Great with Diogenes the Cynic (probably at Corinth around 336 BC, though the story varies) is perhaps the most piquant encounter between a monarch and an intellectual. Diogenes, by philosophical vocation 'of no fixed abode', was then using a large storage jar for shelter, and happened to be airing himself when young Alexander passed by. The newly crowned king halted and asked if there was anything he could do for Diogenes. Retorted Diogenes: 'You can stop blocking my sunlight.' Invented as it may be, this anecdote introduces us nicely to the development of philosophy after Aristotle, or within the 'Hellenistic world' that emerged after Alexander's death in 323 BC. Princely or destitute, who was truly happy and free? It is traditional to identify four styles or schools of philosophy with different answers to that question: the Cynics, the Stoics, the Epicureans and the Sceptics.

The establishment of monarchies around the eastern Mediterranean and the ethnographic enlargement of the Greek-speaking ambit would join to undermine the ideal of a city-state that was small and self-sufficient. As if in acceptance that the opportunities to act as a 'political animal' were severely reduced – unless one became a courtier – philosophers resumed the Socratic posture of civic eccentricity. Or rather, they focused their teaching upon practical strategies for achieving the sort of fearless serenity displayed by Socrates when tested to extremes.

True, Alexander was not yet an all-conquering master of many dominions when Diogenes told him to get lost. All the same, it took some nerve, and made a point. Celebrity and beggar are not two categories we commonly associate: but from his stance as celebrity beggar, Diogenes demonstrated his refusal to make another association – that of virtue with power and wealth.

Cynicism, in modern usage, tends not to be virtuous. But when its ancient founder, Antisthenes, began collecting followers at Athens, in the early fourth century BC, the definition and attainment of *arete* – 'excellence' or 'moral virtue' – were paramount. Antisthenes had been devoutly present with Socrates on his deathbed, and emulated Socrates in favouring the precincts of a gymnasium as a place for discussion. In this case it was the Cynosarges ('White Dog') training ground, which may have given the Cynics ('canines') their nickname. Antisthenes did not, it seems, set out to recruit followers to his cause of virtue as the sole aim in life, and was rather irritated by the persistence of a would-be disciple in the form of Diogenes. But it was Diogenes who won the Cynics their eventual notoriety as philosopher-dogs or strays. If virtue alone mattered, what use were riches or home comforts? So the Cynic went mendicant, and Diogenes practised begging from statues – in order, he said, that he could accustom himself to a stony response.

The Cynics admired Socrates for his resilience to hardship and his disregard for social niceties. But they went a good deal further than Socrates in proving their independence. Not content with mere heckling at the Assembly, or even while Plato was lecturing, groups of Cynics might feed themselves on plants known to cause flatulence, so that when some speaker reached a particularly sonorous or sensitive moment in his oration, they could give vent to coarse and noisy rejoinders. Diogenes is said to have masturbated openly in the Agora: when rebuked for lack of self-control, he claimed that he was, on the contrary, showing great self-control – if only Paris had done likewise, the Trojan War need never have happened.

Such tests of civic convention were harbingers of a trend towards self-sufficiency developed by the movement known as Stoicism. But with the Stoics we must immediately register a theological motive to their attitude. The Presocratic Heraclitus had, in his telegraphic manner, stated the case for an omnipresent divinity: God pervasive in day and night, and the seasons; God in war and peace, in plenty and in famine – in other words, there was a pattern to the universe that was dappled light and shade over mortal existence, and beyond the prayers of mortals to change. Stoicism grew out of a similar sentiment. As a philosophical school it was founded around 300 BC by Zeno, who came to Athens from Kition on Cyprus. To say 'school' is, as with Plato's Academy and Aristotle's Lyceum, to raise unrealistic expectations of classrooms, timetables, lessons and so on: convened in a busy public space of Athens, it must always have been a relatively informal meeting of minds. The site was the Stoa Poikile ('Painted Portico') on the north side of the Agora, so called because its wall was decorated with large-scale frescoes of major events in Athenian history or myth-history, including the battle of Marathon. But Zeno and his followers were not concerned with patriotic imagery. They regarded the cosmos as shaped by fire, yet guided by divine reason (*logos*). Fire would consume all things eventually, and generate new worlds: in any case the process was faultless and unchangeable.

So much (in bald summary) for Stoic physics and theology: what were the implications for individual conduct? One word, in Greek, provides a possible epitome – but will need explanation, because its modern equivalent involves a shift in sense. We might render the Greek *apatheia* as 'apathy', and consider it a trait of the feeble or careless person. To the Stoics, however, apathy was a leading virtue. The wise man acts in accordance with, and acceptance of, divine reason. Divine reason is manifest in whatever happens in the world. Therefore it is not only futile but wicked to complain about illness, hardship or misfortune. These things happen within the harmonies of necessity. Good sense and happiness consist in staying unmoved by vicissitudes. The ups and downs of life do not affect the properly apathetic adherent of Stoicism.

Zeno's successors at the Stoa included some distinguished names, notably those of Cleanthes and Chrysippus. But it was among the Romans that Stoicism really flourished. One influential person in transmitting Stoic doctrines to Rome was Epictetus, who came from Hierapolis in Asia Minor – as a slave, during the time of Nero in the first century AD. It is recorded that his master once tortured him. 'If you continue like this,' said Epictetus, calmly, 'you will break my leg.' The master persisted. There were no screams, but after a while Epictetus announced, no less calmly, that his leg was indeed broken, and he was now temporarily useless to his master. Fortunately, freedom was eventually granted, and Epictetus taught first at Rome, then at Nikopolis in northern Greece.

His *Enchiridion* ('Handbook') collects a series of guidelines for personal tranquillity, based upon knowing one's station as decreed by divine destiny – a primer of fatalistic contentment which closes with the image of Socrates going placidly towards his death.

Stoic morality made an obvious appeal to Romans already inclined to vaunt the austerity of their humble republican origins as 'character-building'. 'If a man is to know himself, he must be tried', wrote Seneca (the Younger), who served as tutor to Nero and was ultimately one of the emperor's victims (implicated in a conspiracy, Seneca committed suicide by slitting his wrists in a bath). Two centuries on, the satisfaction of suffering happily found a voice in an emperor, no less – Marcus Aurelius, whose *Meditations*, though composed privately as exhortations to himself, were known in late antiquity and first printed in 1559. Taken as a whole, these memoranda are rather monotonous and repetitive. Individually, however, they paraphrase into some good one-liners ('Why should the smell of your brother's armpit offend you?'); from the consistency of sentiment it is difficult not to accept that the author was, as his portraits suggest, a resolutely placid figure at the centre of power, doing what he could to further the Stoic belief in brotherly love. When required to attend the amphitheatre games in Rome, he ordered that the combats be fought with blunt weapons, or swords with buttons on their tips.*

Another Hellenistic philosophy that found favour among the Romans was Epicureanism. Its founder Epicurus was

* The well-known gilded bronze equestrian statue of Marcus Aurelius in Rome's Capitoline Museums in the Piazza del Campidoglio probably also once featured the figure of a fallen barbarian, begging for mercy.

about twenty years old when Aristotle died, and seemingly had little time for the mastermind, deeming him 'dissolute'. But then Epicurus was scathing about many philosophers, past and present; his teaching, conducted more or less contemporaneously with (and not very far away from) Zeno the Stoic, was notoriously singular. Though born on Samos, Epicurus had, via his father, citizen rights at Athens. He bought a house with a garden and set up his school there. Women and slaves were not excluded from this community of the 'Garden of Epicurus', and the resultant gossip must have made it difficult for Epicurus to adhere to his own motto of *lathe biosas,* 'live in obscurity'. Contrary to the Stoics, he advised staying away from politics and public duties, and denied the providential activity of a supreme deity. Death was not to be feared – it was simply an end, with no supernatural terrors – and life was to be enjoyed. This has been caricatured as vulgar hedonism ('living for the day'), or even gluttony; the Epicurean ideal of trying to live without pain becomes, in Latin, *indolentia*, and thereby synonymous with laziness. But Epicurus offered the philosophical life as one way of being contented with relatively little, in material terms (and the stomach, after all, is not an insatiable organ). Immoderate desires are the route to distress and disappointment; the secret of autonomy and happiness is to curb rather than indulge oneself.

So Stoic side-swipes against the Epicureans – 'I do not desire to be pacified by a cake, but by right principles', said Epictetus – seem unfair. Christian sympathy was hardly to be expected, given the Epicurean denial of divine intervention (Epicurus was not an atheist, but conceived of the deities as supremely unconcerned by human affairs). That staunch adherents were at large in the Roman empire is proved by an extraordinarily verbose inscription (estimated at 25,000 words, on a stoa wall some sixty metres long) set up in the city of Oenoanda, in the western part of Turkey once known as Lycia, during the early second century AD. Its sponsor, another Diogenes, begins with the declaration that before dying he wants to share the secret of his happiness with all and sundry. What follows, as far as it can be reconstructed, is a full gospel of Epicurean beliefs. Meanwhile it fell to a Latin writer, Lucretius, to elaborate those doctrines in an extended poem, *De rerum natura* ('On the Nature of Things'), around 50 BC. 'Man's greatest wealth is to live on a little, with a contented spirit': once more, Greek philosophy was shown to be congenial to the Roman republican virtue of frugality. But Lucretius was also able to weave in a powerful account of atomic physics, with a description of the infinite universe that in places seems to anticipate aspects of modern quantum theory.

• • •

There would come a time when Greek philosophers were invited to the imperial court at Rome. Hadrian, who was the first Roman emperor to grow a beard – to create a philosophical look, allegedly, though it may also have served to cover a scar on his chin – liked to engage in erudite dialectic, and routinely triumphed over his guests.* Such nice disputes were fashionable – and, when couched in consciously 'declamatory' mode, they characterize a period and intellectual tradition

---

* As one of them, called Favorinus, later confided, it was wise to lose an argument to someone in command of thirty legions.

known as the 'Second Sophistic', which began in the late first century AD and continued till the early third. A typical author of this period was Lucian, cosmopolitan in formation, eclectic in his ideas, polished in style and amusing in effect. Thereafter, Plato's ideas were to enjoy a distinct revival (in the form of Neoplatonism: see page 314).

Our account of classical philosophy ends, however, not with sophistry but with Scepticism. Maybe it is only right that we should conclude with the doctrine that there are no doctrines; that the one thing worth knowing is that no one really knows anything. The origins of this intellectual stance lie with a teacher from Elis (the city near Olympia) called Pyrrho. Pyrrho is said to have travelled to India with the army of Alexander the Great. It may have been from exposure to multiple beliefs and philosophies that he developed his faith in 'non-assertion', or principled doubt. Things might *appear* this way or that, but contradictory opinions were always possible. So the Sceptic should act impartially. This was not for the sake simply of being negative. The final purpose of 'querying' or 'doubt' (as the word *skepsis* translates) was a sort of 'imperturbability' (*ataraxia*).

Pyrrho did not expound this in writing: to have done so, perhaps, might have seemed too assertive. Followers adopted the non-dogmatic dogma in various ways thereafter. But a full account of Scepticism only came around AD 200, from a medical practitioner called Sextus Empiricus. Aware that Pyrrho had once been an artist, Sextus used an anecdote about antiquity's most famous painter, Apelles, to illustrate the benefits of Scepticism. Apelles was painting a horse in action, and trying to represent flecks of foam about the horse's mouth. But for all his skill, he could not get the right effect. In a fit of temper, he gave up and hurled a studio sponge at the picture. By sheer chance, the sponge landed where the horse's mouth was depicted – and created exactly the image that Apelles had desired. The lesson was that the Sceptic, by abandoning all efforts to make an objective or reasoned judgement, finds unexpected gratification.

Whether Apelles took it this way is not recorded. One suspects that any reliance upon chance would have been an insult to his professional pride. In any case, the mere mention of his name is enough to haul us away from spheres of contemplation and back into the world of action. For Apelles was officially painter to a historical figure famous for his instinctive ability to seize an opportunity, unhampered by doubt or hesitation: Alexander the Great.

VI
ALEXANDRIA

Few portraits survive of King Philip II of Macedon. His image perhaps was not important to his rule. Or at least, he did not trade upon personal charisma. Archaeologists excavating a monumental tomb at Vergina, in north-east Greece – the site probably corresponding to the Macedonian royal centre of Aigai – claim to have found the remains of Philip's skull. According to one forensic analysis, this skeletal relic suggested a face scarred by some violent trauma of the right eye socket. The damage is consonant with the historical report that Philip, while inspecting ballistic equipment deployed for attack upon a city in northern Greece in 354 BC, was hit in the eye by an arrow.

Scholars continue to dispute the identity of the occupants of this tomb – and much else about ancient Macedonia. But that report tells us something about Philip's style as a military commander. He exposed himself to danger: he did not ask others to take risks he would not take himself. It also hints at one reason why the hitherto compact kingdom of Macedon became an empire. Philip was a pioneer of siegecraft – the strategy of encircling an enemy city or stronghold to cut off its supplies and communication. The ordnance developed for this mode of warfare – including large catapults, assault platforms, battering-rams and tunnelling sheds – is mostly known by description in the histories of Polybius and others.

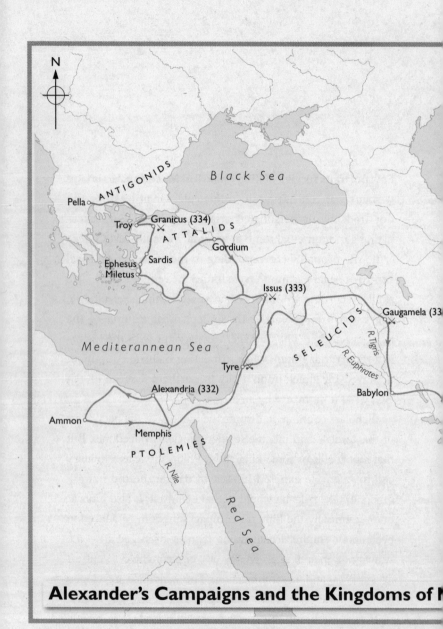

Alexander's Campaigns and the Kingdoms of N

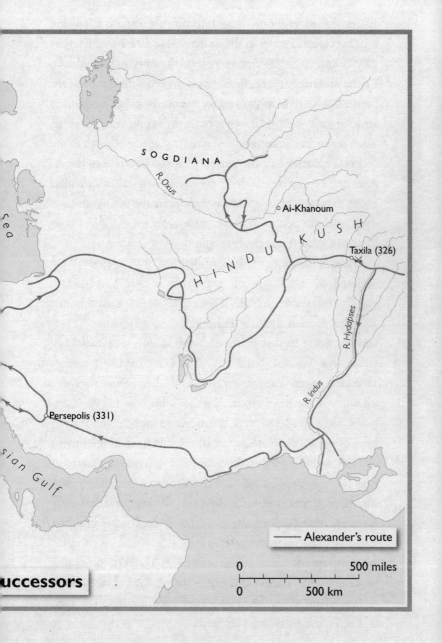

Its consequences for urban architecture are obvious to anyone touring classical ruins in the eastern Mediterranean. Even as picturesque ruins, the circuits of solid masonry walls at Alinda, Priene and many places besides, assembled with obvious care for neatly squared ('ashlar') edges and overlapping ('isodomic') structure, still testify to the civic necessity of preparing for siege. Such defences can usually be dated from the late fourth to the second centuries BC, the period of Macedonian dominance. And one of our best sources for archaeological information about the classical Greek city is the elegiac site of Olynthus, in the Chalkidike peninsula – so completely bombarded by Philip in 348 BC that it was never rebuilt.

Philip's sobriquet 'Monophthalmos' ('One-eyed') was adopted, as if a badge of honour, by a later Macedonian ruler, Antigonus; in turn Demetrius, son of Antigonus, awarded himself the title 'Poliorketes' ('the Besieger'), such was his pride in this method of war. It was not invariably successful: famously, the city of Rhodes held out against Demetrius for a year (305–4 BC), and when Demetrius gave up, the thousands of bronze missiles lobbed by his siege-engines were collected and transformed into an enormous bronze statue, the Colossus of Rhodes. But the development of such military hardware was typical of Macedonian dedication to equipping a full-time, professional army. Gone was the hoplite phalanx of called-up citizens and off-duty farmers. Massed formations of the Macedonian infantry, wielding pikes up to five metres long, were drilled in complex manoeuvres. Cavalry units worked in concert, providing protection for flanks and rear. Eventually, as this army advanced into Asia, formidable breeds of horses were joined by even more fearsome elephants.

Philip subjected various Greek city-states to the power of this army. None could resist. At the battle of Chaeronea in 338 BC a combined force of Greek city-states led by Athens and Thebes attempted to block the Macedonian advance from the north (Chaeronea marks a valley route southwards through Boeotia). This was the occasion when Philip delegated a subordinate cavalry command to one of his sons – Alexander, aged eighteen; it was also the occasion when the 'Sacred Band of Thebes' was massacred. The Sacred Band – 'a regiment of lovers' – was a Theban phalanx formed of pederastic couples, famously cohesive as a fighting unit. Plutarch, a native of Chaeronea, says that after the carnage even the battle-hardened Philip was shaken to see that the men of the Sacred Band had died as they fought – shoulder to shoulder, arms entwined.

Victory at Chaeronea led Philip to extend Macedonian control over almost all the regions of Greece. At Athens, the most articulate voice of resistance belonged to the lawyer and orator Demosthenes, whose anti-Macedonian speeches were so pointed against Philip that they became a byword for any highly personal attack ('Philippic'). How far the Macedonians represented a distinctly 'foreign' threat to the Greeks remains debatable – and a topic that lives on in modern political and ethnic sensibilities. Beyond linguistic affinities with non-Greek peoples – mainly Illyrians and Thracians – Macedonians exhibited certain cultural habits that the Greeks regarded as barbaric (drinking wine undiluted, for one). Yet their monarchs followed a policy of Hellenization. The last plays of Euripides were written for the court of Archelaus at Pella; and when Philip came to choose a tutor for the young Alexander, he called for Aristotle, pre-eminent by far among the Greek philosophers of the day (Aristotle's father Nicomachus had been royal physician).

Nonetheless, in the eyes of Demosthenes the Macedonian dynasty – sometimes named 'Temenid' after its founder, though descent was ultimately traced to Herakles – was fundamentally antithetical to Greek democracy. In due time, it is true, the military success of Macedon created a Greek-speaking or 'Hellenistic' world based upon the autocratic institution of the court. We should, however, take note that the court precinct as developed by Philip at Vergina measures some 12,500 square metres. This could of course be regarded as an index of regal megalomania. Alternatively it appears tantamount to putting an agora, or public space, within the ruler's palace, so bringing 'the people' into the court (Vergina could accommodate an audience of some 3,500, seated). Such architecture of royal accessibility is backed up by anecdotes of humble peasants being able, during formal receptions, to petition the Macedonian king directly. The model of a paternalistic king who was a 'saviour' (*soter*) to his subjects would become an important aspect of the success of kingship in the Hellenistic age – and also had significant religious implications.

Philip's assassination, aged forty-six, in 336 BC was a drama that took place not at court, but in the theatre at Vergina, during a royal wedding celebration. The deed was done by one of the Royal Guard – but why, or at whose prompting, remains a matter of speculation. Some historians accuse Olympias, mother of Alexander the Great, and even implicate young Alexander in the plot. Philip had several wives, and a number of offspring by them and other women: in other words, various individuals or factions at court were competing for succession. At the time of his death he was poised to launch his boldest campaign of all – an invasion of Persia. In the event, Philip seems to have been buried swiftly but handsomely, and the inheritance of the mission passed directly to the twenty-year-old Alexander.

Alexander's ready assumption of command, and his inspired extension of Philip's foreign policy, can be briefly outlined. The adventure may be woven into legend, and its details liable to revision, but the following summary is widely accepted. In 334 BC Alexander crossed over to Asia with an army of about 50,000 men – not only Macedonians, but Greeks and other recruits. Reclaiming the Aegean seaboard of Anatolia as 'Greek' was an initial aim, and made feasible by a successful first encounter with the Persians, by the Granicus river not far from the Hellespont. Affirmation of the young commander's cultural roots – and his heroic alter ego – was made when Alexander stopped at Troy and paid sacrificial honours at the tomb of Achilles. Advancing southwards, his strategy was to take from the Persians their access to the Mediterranean. This took him down through the Levant and into Egypt; en route, another major encounter with the Persians at Issus, in Cilicia, in 333 BC allowed Alexander to display an Achilles-like fury in leading a cavalry charge. The battle is said to have left 100,000 Persians dead, and the reputation of the Persian king Darius III undermined: whether the king fought bravely or made an abrupt retreat is not clear, but at any event he abandoned his wife and other royal women-folk behind for capture (respectfully done by Alexander). Depriving the Persian fleet of its Mediterranean bases was not easy: the effort of besieging the Phoenician island-city of Tyre took ten months and involved building a causeway to the mainland. But Egypt capitulated readily, acclaiming Alexander as a liberator, with full pharaonic titles.

By 331 BC it was time to move inland towards Mesopotamia, where Darius had assembled an army from all parts of the Persian empire (a sizeable contingent of Greek mercenaries was also included). Alexander crossed the Euphrates and met the Persians near the village of Gaugamela, to the north-east of Mosul in modern Iraq. The battleground was the choice of Darius, who hoped it would favour his war chariots, their wheels bristling with blades. But again Alexander's versatile deployment of heavy and light cavalry units around a compact phalanx proved superior. Darius fled the field, to be murdered the following year by members of his own staff; Alexander meanwhile occupied the principal centres of Persian administration and ceremony. Although his troops sacked Persepolis, Alexander took measures to integrate his rule with that of the Persian 'Great King', whose title he appropriated after the death of Darius. He began wearing the royal diadem, which was a highly potent symbol: it signified a living god. It also entailed that eastern possessions once subject to Darius must be claimed for Alexander. These territories included Bactria in the north of modern Afghanistan, where Bessus, one of the conspirators against Darius, had installed himself as 'King of Asia'. So Alexander set out to campaign in areas hitherto beyond the scope of any Greek geography, and with names still evocative of the exotic – the rivers Helmand and Oxus, the territory of Sogdia around Samarkand, the mountains of the Hindu Kush.

By 328 BC Alexander had taken Bessus and the Bactrian capital Balkh. He recruited thousands of fresh troops locally. Why should he stop at the limits of the old Persian empire?

An oracle in Egypt had told him he could conquer the world: by now Alexander believed it. But this faith, it seems, did not extend throughout his forces. They had reached the Punjab, with the entire Indian subcontinent in prospect, when at last, in 326 BC, Alexander's closest subordinates – the so-called 'Companions' (Hetairoi), who had grown up with him and fought with him in the heavy cavalry unit – announced, on behalf of the whole army, a refusal to continue. Alexander, it is reported, went into a long solitary sulk (like Achilles). Eventually he conceded defeat. But he made it a condition of withdrawal that the troops build a mock encampment on a gigantic scale: tents, beds and equipment made to look as if they had belonged to a force of superhumans. It would be supposed, then, that these giants had refrained from crossing the river for reasons of their own. Had they so wished, it would have been easily done – and woe betide anyone who tried to stop them.

• • •

'Alexander the Great' is posterity's recognition of his military achievement. The title reflects his grand vision, and suggests his megalomania (*ho megas* is Greek for 'the Great'); it allows, too, for his assumption of regal supremacy in Persian style. But any account of Alexander's military achievement is incomplete if it tells only of battles. We know well enough from recent world history that winning a war is not only a matter of forcing surrender from an enemy. A more formidable challenge lies beyond: the winning of 'hearts and minds' in enemy territory. Without Alexander's success on that front there would have been no Macedonian empire. And so, if momentarily, we return to the philosophers. Whether Aristotle had any influence in shaping his pupil's authoritative 'look' is open to speculation. But it is hard to deny that a fourth-century BC fascination with physiognomics impacted upon the image of Alexander as we find it in statues (of various sizes), on coins and in paintings and mosaics.

Before analysing the components of Alexander's image, we should take stock of the fact that there is, so far, no way of knowing what he *really* looked like – insofar as no posthumous reconstruction of his features can be effected from his skeletal remains, because these have not yet been located. Alexander died in 323 BC, at Babylon. Ancient sources relate that a funeral cortège from Mesopotamia was organized by one of Alexander's generals, Ptolemy, two years later. Whether the plan was to follow Alexander's alleged wish to be buried in an Egyptian oasis, or to return his (presumably embalmed) body for deposition in the royal cemetery at Vergina, we do not know. At any event, Ptolemy diverted the destination to Alexandria. So it is conceivable that one day the tomb of Alexander will be found there, and found to contain the mummified remains of the man. If so, we may have some chance of measuring the distance between art and reality.

That is a matter of pure curiosity – heightened because so many literary sources record the 'charismatic' effect of Alexander in person. A number of anecdotes relate to the potency of Alexander's image. For example, there is the report about his fellow Macedonian, Cassander. Cassander, eldest son of Alexander's appointed regent in Macedonia, went on his father's behalf to Babylon to meet Alexander – and was not well received; a victim of Alexander's sudden and violent temper, he was beaten up in public. Years later, when he had become king of Macedon (and exacted some revenge on Alexander's family), Cassander happened to be walking through Delphi and caught sight of a statue of Alexander. In Plutarch's words (from his *Life of Alexander*), the sight 'smote him suddenly, with a shuddering and trembling of the body from which he could scarcely recover'. Psychologically this is a highly credible episode; incidentally it says something about the power of a portrait to create a virtual presence. It involves a fascinating interaction between politics, physiognomics and aesthetics. How far did artists make Alexander the Great great?

A repeated assertion in ancient literature is that three artists in particular gained Alexander's trust. One was the painter Apelles of Kos, whom we encountered in the last chapter. He may have been commissioned to depict the sort of battle scenes that would be the model for the well-known Alexander Mosaic, which seems to evoke a crucial moment in the battle of Issus.* There was also a gem-cutter, Pyrgoteles, who would have shaped the miniature but visually arresting images of Alexander that appeared on coins. Then there was Lysippus. Only Lysippus, it was said, could capture Alexander's essential *ethos*. Other sculptors, fixing too selectively upon Alexander's habitually tilted neck and 'melting, liquid eyes', were liable to lose the leonine 'manly' aspect. As it happens, there is no single surviving image of Alexander that we can attribute to Lysippus; and indeed, though a large number of Alexander 'portraits' do exist, these are nearly all demonstrably posthumous. Nevertheless, we can collect

---

* The mosaic once adorned a house in Pompeii; it is now in the National Archaeological Museum in Naples.

several recurring features from these portraits, which together may give us the essential aspect as determined by Lysippus.

In the first place, the image of Alexander was always youthful. He died before he grew old. That is a well-known fact, but calls for some comment. He was in his early thirties when at Babylon he succumbed to a fever (possibly compounded by alcoholism); like his heroic model Achilles, he was spared the degenerative transformations of senior years. As one later writer observed, all images of Alexander conveyed 'the same look of youthful freshness'. It is, however, possible to distinguish an Alexander whose status is 'Crown Prince' – that is, still a teenager, before taking his father's place. A mesmerizing head from the Athenian Acropolis has good claim to be one such image. Among the finds at Vergina are a number of small 'dynastic' images in ivory, including one that looks as if it could plausibly represent the young Alexander.

Alexander did not to grow a beard. Long before the invention of the safety razor, this was not an easy option; ideologically, an association (among Greeks) of effeminacy with smooth-faced men might have acted as a deterrent. But Alexander's choice was no doubt followed by his immediate Macedonian Companions, and thence diffused through the numerous ranks of his army, so a 'fashion' prevailed. It invested the leader with a certain legacy of athletic success – the statues of Olympic victors from the fifth century BC tended to be beardless. It also contributed to a divine resemblance that suited Alexander – to be 'shining', like Apollo (even if his drinking habits were firmly Dionysiac).

Images also traded, of course, upon his prowess as a warrior. Alexander may have convinced himself that he was, like Achilles, invulnerable. Alternatively, if he wore no helmet into battle, then it was part of his military genius: making himself conspicuous, a point of morale-raising focus for his own officers and troops, and a source of panic to the enemy. In the Alexander Mosaic we see him charging into a mêlée, eyes wide with excitement, hair flashing gold, intent upon the figure of Darius; the Persian king, for his part, shows only alarm, wheeling his chariot around in search of escape. We may wonder if anything like this scene could actually have happened. But credible sources do attest that Alexander, astride his favourite horse Bucephalus ('Ox-head'), would indeed lead a cavalry charge, and did so on occasion without warning his Companions.

The sources also tell us that Alexander, though well proportioned, was not a physically large man. When he tried to sit upon the throne of the Persian kings, his legs swung well short of the ground, and minions hurriedly fetched a stool. His friend Hephaestion was of more impressive stature; after Issus, the ladies of the defeated Persian king's harem instinctively threw themselves for mercy at the feet of Hephaestion, not Alexander. Yet Alexander, by consensus, possessed a commanding presence, radiating from his eyes. These generated much comment, regarding their size, colour and glistening quality, but above all their contribution to a 'heavenwards gaze'. Accordingly, many images of Alexander show him as if transfixed by some distant prospect. Admirers took this as a symptom of his 'divine inspiration' (*enthousiasmos*). He appeared superhuman.

There was something of a culture shock when, in 327 BC, Alexander sent instructions to the Greek cities that he expected divine honours from them. Logically this was a consequence proceeding from his assumption of the status of the Persian Great King. At Persepolis it had been normal for visiting dignitaries to prostrate themselves in the royal presence: this might involve falling to one's hands and knees, and looking up only when bidden to do so. But Herodotus tells us that when Spartan ambassadors came to Xerxes in the fifth century BC, they had refused to do so, as a matter of religious principle. Such grovelling adoration, known to the Greeks as *proskynesis*, was reserved for the gods. So Alexander's request was greeted with protests, and some recorded non-compliance, even among his Macedonians. The controversy did not, however, deter him from parading various divine associations: with his claimed ancestor Herakles, with Helios the sun-god and with an Egyptian configuration of Zeus, Zeus Ammon (or Amun). The latter guise involved wearing headgear with ram's horns, and Alexander would appear at banquets thus attired. He was pleased when Apelles did a painting of him wielding a thunderbolt, like Zeus. Numismatic manifestations of his presence would exploit such associations, especially in regions where a tradition of rulers with divine status had long existed. In Egypt, for example, veneration was due to the pharaoh as son of Amun-Ra, the Egyptian deity uniting supreme divine power with cosmic solar control. Alexander personally consulted the oracle of Amun/Ammon at the oasis of Siwah, deep in the Libyan desert. For Alexander, clearly, it was better that he adapt to local custom than attempt to impose upon it whatever was demanded by Macedonian protocol. If certain aspects of his supernatural posture upset Greek sensibilities, so be it: the Greek cities were, after all, a relatively minor part of his domain.

In taking over the Persian empire, Alexander had almost

thirty different ethnic identities among his subjects. This is why his image counted for so much: for while Greek might be introduced as a common language (the ecumenical dialect of *koine*), visual messages were broadly and immediately accessible. And so Alexander and his image-makers played upon cross-cultural appeal. The physiognomists had defined the brave man as sharing certain features with a lion. Naturally the leonine man must have a thick and tousled head of hair framing his wide, and typically bulging, corrugated brows. In Alexander's case the mane-like effect may have been heightened by his (alleged) practice of sprinkling his hair with gold dust. A vigorous forelock marks many of his portraits. But what is most important is the mass of the hair: its power is primal. The strength of the Old Testament strongman Samson derived from his hair; Spartan warriors used to grow theirs long; and eventually the Latin word for 'mane' or 'luxuriant hair', *caesaries*, would enter (via Julius Caesar) the title of Roman imperial power.* Long hair, again, recalled the Homeric hero as traditionally represented. Alexander's proven bravado in front-line fighting simply reasserted an archaic association of shoulder-length coiffure with abundant virility.

• • •

Alexander's closest friend, Hephaestion, died in 324 BC. Alexander may have instituted a cult for Hephaestion as a way of expressing his own profound grief; he also indicated how his own death was to be marked – as an apotheosis. As it

---

* This is one reason why a Roman *imperator* (beginning, ironically, with Caesar himself) might be sensitive on the topic of his baldness.

happened, such was his reputation that he would live on for centuries, in various ways and in various parts of the world – in India, in Islamic writings (either directly as 'Iskender', perhaps also obliquely as the 'Two-Horned One'), even in Jewish scriptures. In medieval Europe he was adopted as one of the chivalric 'Nine Worthies'. But in the short term, of course, Alexander's image was as precious to his 'Successors' (the Diadochoi) as it had been in providing a figurehead for his empire. For although Alexander had taken, beyond the concubines that were a warrior's claim, a wife – the famously exquisite 'little star', Roxane, daughter of a Sogdian warlord – he left no designated heir (nor any kind of will). So far as we know, there was never any presumption, among Alexander's chiefs of staff, that one of them would eventually take sole charge of all the Macedonian conquests. Some may have harboured claims of fraternity, and as Companions some may have been closer than others, but none could match Alexander for charisma. When they came to divide Alexander's territory, therefore, they organized his cult reverently, and kept his image conspicuous. He was, after all, a talisman of their own right to power.

The division was acrimonious. According to one version of events, Roxane was pregnant when Alexander died, and produced a son, who could have become Alexander IV. But the prospect of a regency seems only to have intensified the struggle for power among the Macedonians. To simplify a complex and bloody sequence of events, the territory that Alexander had made subject to himself as King of Kings was apportioned as follows: Macedon, already somewhat separated, fell to Cassander; the Black Sea region and Thrace went to Lysimachus; Asia Minor was claimed by Antigonus;

and Asia beyond the Euphrates by Seleucus. Predictably, they fought with each other; within Asia Minor, a shrewd official entrusted by Alexander to keep guard over accumulated war booty at a site called Pergamon, in the Troad area, would eventually manage to create yet another domain: compact, but culturally so important that it awaits our attention in the next chapter.

Here we shall focus upon Egypt, annexed by Ptolemy. As one of Alexander's Companions since boyhood – he would later claim to be a half-brother – Ptolemy participated fully in the conquests. And while Alexander included among his entourage an official chronicler, Callisthenes, and there was apparently a daily 'Royal Diary', Ptolemy kept his own narrative record. The text has not survived, but it was the primary source of information for a later historian called Arrian, whose account of Alexander's campaigns, though partisan, remains the most credible known to us.

That Egypt was regarded as a prize is suggested by the fact that Ptolemy's former colleague Perdiccas promptly launched an invasion attempt, which Ptolemy repelled: one advantage of Egypt was precisely that it could be effectively defended. The Persian satrap had surrendered without a fight, and an administrative centre at Memphis came already supplied with a royal treasury. Ptolemy was content to follow Alexander's lead in adopting the ancient modes of rule by a pharaoh, but he moved the capital from Memphis. And although the new capital bore Alexander's name, and Alexander's grandeur of design, it was very much a Ptolemaic creation – and it became one of the great centres of classical civilization.

• • •

Like his father Philip, Alexander had practised the royal custom of holding court. Theoretically, any of his subjects could gain an audience, but the throng could be intense, and elbowing one's way to the front of it a challenge. An architect from Rhodes, called Dinocrates, who had an ambitious proposal for Alexander's attention, came up with an eccentric solution to this challenge. He dressed himself in the garb of Herakles – so essentially wearing nothing more than a lion skin and carrying a knotty club – and, in this strange costume, paraded ostentatiously at the back of the crowd. Sure enough, his presence caught the royal eye, and Alexander beckoned him forward. Dinocrates then explained his proposal. An entire land mass, the peninsula of Mount Athos extending south from Chalcis, was to be fashioned into a likeness of Alexander. The king would be shown as a vast, semi-natural effigy, recumbent. In his right hand, a city would be built.

The concept was designed to appeal to a monarch's vanity. Alexander, however, spotted a practical problem. How was the city's water to be secured? For all we know, Dinocrates had already thought of that, and had some bold hydraulic scheme to unfold. But monarchs like to think that they know best about all sorts of things, and perhaps discretion demanded that Alexander be allowed to have made a wise appraisal. In any case, Dinocrates did not leave disappointed. The king liked his audacious approach. Dinocrates should indeed be commissioned to build a city, yet in a sensible place: by the great commercial thoroughfare that was the Nile Delta, opening Egypt to the Mediterranean.

An ancient list of cities founded by Alexander during his campaigns includes eighteen Alexandrias, plus two foundations named after his horse Bucephalus (which died in battle by the river Jhelum, on the north-west frontier). In some cases, only echoes of the name survive (e.g. Kandahar); others remain to be securely located. It seems that the easternmost foundation is that of Ai-Khanoum, by the river Oxus, towards the foothills of the Hindu Kush. Here a French mission managed to record the presence of a proper classical city – that is, with temples, theatre, gymnasium and so on – before the site was spoiled by war in the 1980s. This may well be the city of Alexandria Oxiana. Among the finds is a Greek inscription raised by one Klearchos, conceivably the follower of Aristotle with that name. He exhorts citizens to heed the wise precepts of Apollo at Delphi. Paraphrased, these are: 'As children, learn good manners. As young people, control your passions. In middle age, be just. In old age, give wise advice. Then you can die – with no regrets.' Delphi, regarded by Greeks as the 'navel of the world', was very far away, but resonant nonetheless here in northern Afghanistan.

Beyond making a beacon of Hellenic values, what was the purpose of such a foundation? It is noticeable that most of the 'new' cities were in fact located at sites previously important in the networks of Persian rule, so they made a statement about continuity. They also afforded places for Alexander to settle the soldiers who had fought for him.* Above all, however, there was a commercial motive. War and occupation of a territory by a large army were destructive: the city foundations went some way to making amends and promoting the development of trade between east and west – though the

---

* To this day there are claims by certain tribal groups in Pakistan – the Kalash, the Pathans – that they are descended from Alexander's troops.

age-old Silk Route continued to provide a primary mercantile channel.

And if Europe was to benefit from Asia's wealth, then there had to be suitable ports on the coast. After Alexander's death, a city eventually called Alexandria Troas was developed as such on the Aegean shore. But for centuries the city laid out by Dinocrates to the west of the Nile Delta was pre-eminent. Back in the sixth century BC, Ionian Greeks had established – by special concession from Pharaoh Ahmose, known to the Greeks as Amasis – a residential trading post in the Delta at Naukratis. Naukratis, lying 45 miles (70 km) inland, had declined by the fourth century BC, partly as a result of the silting process of the Nile as it flooded annually. While the location of Alexandria now seems ideal as a port, it was not so clear when Alexander surveyed the scene in 331 BC. All that existed along this shoreline was a small fishing village called Rhakotis. Pharaonic Egypt had been a notoriously 'closed' society; apart from the Naukratis concession, it had shown little interest in doing business with the rest of the Mediterranean. Furthermore, supplies of fresh water were not locally available. But Alexander and his architect thought that they could remedy that lack and proceeded to mark out the extent of a 'big city' or *megalopolis*.

Macedonia had its royal capitals, at Vergina and at Pella; a fine city was also created at the cult centre of Dion, at the foot of Mount Olympus; but there was nothing on this scale. Athens and Syracuse might both claim greater extent, in terms of city limits, but neither could match the dense conurbation that developed at Alexandria. Dinocrates signalled the scale by creating a broad longitudinal axis: ancient reports estimate this central thoroughfare at 30 metres (100 feet) wide. It was more likely 15 metres but still a magnificent boulevard at that. Gridded streets intersected, and overall the city incorporated five residential districts, demarcated by letters of the Greek alphabet. One of these became home to a large Jewish community; and it is to Philo Judaeus, one of the prominent members of this community in the first century AD, that we owe much incidental information about Alexandria as it flourished under the Ptolemies and beyond. Such written sources as survive are particularly valuable because lamentably few traces of ancient Alexandria remain.

'Abandon all hope, archaeologists who enter here': the sentiment gained currency in the nineteenth century, when the practical and bureaucratic obstacles to excavating in Alexandria were enough to discourage even such an optimist as Schliemann (he had come in search of Alexander's tomb, which had been a site of homage by Roman emperors but was 'lost' by the fourth century AD – and remains elusive to this day). Over the centuries, subterranean exploration disclosed the secret of the water supply – a complex of cisterns and conduits, fed by a canal from the Canopic branch of the Nile and by seasonal rains. More recently, underwater explorations in the harbours of the city have yielded some colossal eroded relics from the Ptolemaic period. But the situation now is not much changed from 1922, when English novelist E. M. Forster wrote a guidebook to Alexandria. We see the ancient city primarily through the lens of its literary reputation – as transmitted in modern times by Forster and others, including the Greek poet C. P. Cavafy.

Ancient Alexandria was much more than a city of letters, but there are particular reasons why its literary reputation became so strong. Ptolemy, as noted, was himself something of an historian. Declaring himself king in 304 BC and extending his territorial possessions to Cyprus, Palestine and parts of the Aegean, he yet found time to compose his memoirs of Alexander's wars. He was also a bibliophile and passed on a respect for literature to his chosen successor, a son by his third wife Berenike, who took the title Ptolemy II Philadelphus. For a few years father and son shared power, before Ptolemy I died, peacefully and at an old age, in 282 BC. It is hard to say how much was owed to paternal initiative, but it seems that administrative and financial systems for Ptolemaic Egypt (and beyond) were institutionally established under Philadelphus, as he extended the Brucheion, or royal quarter, of Alexandria. Important as these were for Egypt's governance and economy, however, two other institutions within court precincts are more celebrated: one is the library, the other the museum.

Neither was an invention. Collections of scrolls existed at Athens, and a pro-Macedonian statesman from Athens, Demetrius of Phaleron, may have been involved in transporting the concept of a *mouseion*, a 'shrine of the Muses', to Alexandria. Demetrius was a pupil of Theophrastus at the Lyceum, where a *mouseion* consisted of books and teaching materials. But the Alexandrian project was on a different scale. As developed with the generous patronage of the Ptolemies, library and museum here interacted as if at once arts centre and research institute.

The Muses, usually nine in number, were described by Hesiod as daughters of Zeus. Mount Helicon, not far from Hesiod's home in Boeotia, was one of the places particularly associated with them. They were divine forms of inspiration in poetry, music, dance and various intellectual activities;

eventually their names were assigned special 'fields', such as Clio (history), Terpsichore (dance) and Urania (astronomy). A 'museum' at Mount Helicon kept texts of Hesiod's poems, and statues of poets and others considered mortal conduits of divine inspiration. The museum at Alexandria was a much more active establishment. It offered paid (and tax-free) residencies to scholars from around the Greek-speaking world. Estimates of their number at any given time vary from 100 to 1,000. There was a grand communal dining hall, a series of lecture rooms and promenades – and, of course, access to the library.*

Schole is Greek for 'leisure': schools and scholarship should therefore rightly be considered not as work, but what we can do when freed from the labours of everyday survival. That sense of leisurely pursuit lingers in Plato's dialogues, but it was already evaporating when Aristotle set up his Lyceum. The Ptolemies effectively professionalized the scholar's vocation. In the fifth century BC, Sophists and others had lectured to audiences who paid a fee for attendance. Now research could be pursued for its own sake. Some of it might well have given rise to practical and even lucrative applications: one of antiquity's most ingenious engineers, Archimedes, legendarily used his time in Alexandria to develop the water-screw device that served farmers in Egypt and elsewhere for irrigation projects.† Otherwise, in Aristotelian fashion, the library indulged disinterested curiosity. And as the library flourished, the disciplines of philology, palaeography and literary criticism originated. If a text of Homer's *Iliad* materialized, it was

* The main library was nearby; another was created further along the coast.
† When he returned to his native Syracuse, Archimedes deployed his expertise in levers and moments for catapults against Roman besiegers.

put to scrutiny. What constituted a 'sound' or 'corrupt' manuscript? How could the poet's original diction be distinguished
from interpolations by others, or from a copyist's
misunderstandings?

It is well known that the library at Alexandria was
destroyed by fire, but it is still unclear at what point in history
this happened and whether the destruction was intended. In
a sense, however, the library's actual fate does not matter.
What matters is that it created a model for other cities to
emulate (Pergamon, Rhodes, Antioch and more), and that its
associated scholars effectively defined and refined the 'classics' of Greek literature and learning. 'Of making of many
books there is no end', laments the Hebrew prophet known
as Ecclesiastes. His melancholic eloquence may be dated to
around 200 BC – he was well aware, then, of the ceaseless
industry of learning at Alexandria.

The reputation of Alexandrian scholarship is not alto-
gether glowing. It is of course possible to be a high-ranking
academic without being particularly intelligent, and clever-
ness has never been exclusive of vanity and petty disputes:
stories from the Ptolemaic court attest those persistent truths.
But one particular dilemma deserves our notice. If works of
the past were recognized as setting an absolute standard, how
were writers of the present supposed to respond? Systematic
cataloguing of the library, whose holdings are estimated to lie
between 100,000 and over half a million scrolls, is attributed
to Callimachus, who was himself a highly productive poet. He
fell out with one of his pupils and fellow librarians, Apollonius,
over the question of whether a poet should attempt epic:
'Don't look to me for thunder ,' declared Callimachus, 'that
comes from Zeus.' The quarrel was so vexatious that

Apollonius eventually removed himself to Rhodes, where he composed, as if to prove his point, his *Argonautica* – the saga about Jason's voyage in quest of the Golden Fleece.

Readers must judge for themselves which of the antagonists in this literary feud comes out better to posterity. If Callimachus is assessed by one portion of his surviving output, a number of epigrams, then we ought to cite one memorable translation, for it honours the ideal of elegant but satisfying brevity:

> *They told me, Heraclitus, they told me you were dead,*
> *They brought me bitter news to hear, and bitter tears to*
> *   shed.*
> *I wept, as I remembered how often you and I*
> *Had tired the sun with talking, and sent him down the*
> *   sky.*
>
> *And now that thou art lying, my dear old Carian guest*
> *A handful of grey ashes, long, long ago at rest*
> *Still are thy pleasant voices, thy nightingales, awake;*
> *For Death, he taketh all away, but them he cannot take.*

The bibliographer's disposition is nicely reflected in the eventual formation of poetic 'garlands' – the gathering of 'literary flowers' implied by the Greek term *anthologia*, and represented by the *Greek Anthology*, a collection that has charmed readers down the centuries. Yet a roll-call of poets at the Ptolemaic court contains enough by way of distinguished names to prove that veneration of 'classic' forebears did not deter fresh creative effort. Theocritus, a migrant to Alexandria from Syracuse, contrived the genre of pastoral: lyrical 'little visions' ('idylls') of an idealized countryside where shepherds while away time by singing of love, transience and death. Posidippus, who came from Pella, pioneered the word-picture known as *ekphrasis* ('speaking out'): he may be regarded as the prototype, poetically, of the informative head-set that many viewers of paintings and sculptures in modern museums like to use. And Herodas, perhaps from Kos, amused the court with 'mimes' that parodied the low life on the streets outside. There was a price to pay, in terms of flattery: Ptolemy I styled himself as *Soter*, 'saviour', and the poets did not balk at hailing him as omnipotent Zeus. A particularly unctuous poem by Callimachus told how a curl of hair from the head of Berenike (III) became a constellation. But such is patronage. The poets could dutifully trill a monarch's praise; it cost an astronomer nothing to name a new star after the queen; and mathematicians of genius, such as Eratosthenes, who calculated the earth's circumference to an unprecedented degree of accuracy, could simply dedicate their equations to Ptolemy.

• • •

While the Ptolemies were diligent custodians of high culture, they also exploited the potency of 'pomp and circumstance' – what is sometimes called the 'theatre state', a monarchical style built upon lavish shows and spectacles. Processions featuring giant automata of deities, along with liberal rations of wine distributed to every household, ensured Alexandria's fame for its carnivals and religious parades. Ptolemy I shrewdly assessed that his kingdom, founded in a spirit of inter-ethnic unity or 'single-mindedness' (*homonoia*) perhaps taken from Alexander, needed a cult figure (apart from himself) without sectarian associations. So he introduced the god Sarapis. The origins of this deity remain obscure, and possibly they always were. Functionally Sarapis was versatile, connecting with fertility, universal order and the Underworld; for a consort he took Isis, long revered by the Egyptians as 'Lady of All'. How priests of the new cult squared Sarapis with the old tales of Isis searching for the dismembered Osiris, her brother and husband, is a theological topic beyond the scope of this book. Suffice it to say that Sarapis flourished throughout the classical world for half a millennium. As envisaged by artists he is bearded and benign, with a mass of curly hair: his headgear, looking unfortunately like a plant pot to modern eyes, was a measure of grain that symbolized his Underworld connection – and suggested his part in providing the corn harvest on which Egypt's prosperity depended.

That Alexandria was set up by the Ptolemies as a cultural beacon to the 'inhabited world' or *oikoumene* is clear enough. But of course, as a major port, it also needed a beacon for shipping. Alexander and Dinocrates presumably had this in mind when choosing the site, for like Tyre it offered a small offshore island that might be connected to the mainland by a mole. Two harbours were thus created, and the island, called Pharos, became the site of a lighthouse wonderful to behold (as well as practically effective).

The structure of the lighthouse had to be solid enough to withstand the heat of fires kept burning at its base, and tiered so that light could be reflected – by a system of mirrors, probably of burnished bronze – from a tower about 100 metres high. Its luminous range at sea was variously attested at between 30 and 300 miles. The edifice eventually collapsed in the fourteenth century, damaged by a series of earthquakes, and a Turkish fort took its place. But we can reconstruct its design from images on coins and from small terracotta models evidently sold as souvenirs, for the Pharos of Alexandria joined a list of Seven Wonders that ought to be seen in the ancient world. One of the many books by Callimachus was a compendium of 'sights' (*theamata*) that were also 'wonders' (*thaumata*) – a list which seems to have been trimmed to a must-see distillation of the following: (i) the Great Pyramid at Giza; (ii) the Hanging Gardens of Babylon; (iii) the statue of Zeus at Olympia; (iv) the temple of Artemis at Ephesus; (v) the Mausoleum at Halicarnassus; (vi) the Colossus of Rhodes; and (vii) the Pharos of Alexandria.

It is commonly claimed that of this list, only one survives: the Great Pyramid of the pharaoh Khufu, of the third millennium BC, whom the Greeks knew as Cheops. (Herodotus set the tone of wonder for the monument, albeit with some disapproval, and exaggeration, of the labour involved.) Depending on one's definition of survival, the picture is not quite so bleak. At Ephesus, a solitary column of the temple of Artemis may be seen (crowned, as it usually is, with a stork's nest). At Olympia, moulds, chippings and other debris from the making of Pheidias' massive statue of Zeus have been excavated from the sculptor's workshop. And at Halicarnassus, a number of impressive sculptures and architectural fragments have been recovered from the site of the Mausoleum – the towering tomb of Mausolus, the fourth-century BC local dynast who ruled that town and its region of Caria in Asia Minor on behalf of the Persians. Nonetheless, the wondrous effect of these monuments is mostly gone, and irretrievable.

As is the Ptolemaic city of Alexandria. So we will take our leave by way of a verbal evocation of its characteristic magnificence. This is Shakespeare's rendition of Plutarch's account of how Cleopatra VII, ruling in the late first century BC, 'pursed up' the heart of the Roman general Mark Antony when she arrived to meet him, by river, in the province of Cilicia:

> *The barge she sat in, like a burnished throne*
> *Burned on the water. The poop was beaten gold;*
> *Purple the sails, and so perfumed that*
> *The winds were love-sick with them. The oars were silver,*
> *Which to the tune of flutes kept stroke…*
> *… For her own person,*
> *It beggared all description. She did lie*
> *In her pavilion – cloth of gold, of tissue –*
> *O'er-picturing that Venus where we see*
> *The fancy outwork nature…*

> *Antony and Cleopatra*, 2.2.196 ff.

Within a few years the dynasty was finished by submission to Rome. But up until the end, the Ptolemies did things with wonderful style.

VII
PERGAMON

The sense of the term 'classical', as observed in the Preface to this book, is mutable. It may encompass all of Graeco-Roman antiquity, or it may occupy a chronological space between the historical subdivisions of 'archaic' and 'Hellenistic'. In this latter sense, 'classical' has implications for what comes before and what comes after – at least, it does so in the hands of historians who like to impose upon the past the vegetable metaphor of growth, efflorescence and decay. The analogy itself has a long history: for our purposes, it is sufficient to notice its prevalence among certain influential intellectual figures in eighteenth- and nineteenth-century Europe. For example, in his pioneering survey of ancient art, published in 1763, the German antiquarian J. J. Winckelmann outlined a scheme whereby Greek art, from its 'seeds' in the archaic age, matured into a 'grand or high style' that is epitomized in the mid-fifth century BC by the work of Pheidias; relaxed into 'more grace and complaisance' during the fourth century BC, and thereafter went into 'decline' and 'fall' under the 'imitators'.

Winckelmann, writing from the vantage of the modern Enlightenment, saw liberty as key to the 'flowering of the arts'. It followed, therefore, that as the democratic city-states of Greece – notably Athens – yielded to rule by Macedonian autocrats, this flower must wilt: 'Art which received its life, as it were, from freedom, must necessarily decline and fall with loss of freedom.' So, while Macedonian governors may have been generous with their patronage, this compromised the quality of the art produced. For Winckelmann, 'prodigal flattery worked to the detriment of truth and industry in art'. In retrospect, his censure seems overstated: himself the beneficiary of patrons first in Saxony, then at the Vatican, did he not see how artists had flourished, for instance, under the Medici rulers of Renaissance Florence? But the sense that the Hellenistic age was one of decline would linger on.

The term 'Hellenistic' was invented by Winckelmann's compatriot J. G. Droysen in the 1830s. As a scholar, Droysen is credited with developing the 'great man' style of history, exemplified by his youthful biography of Alexander the Great. When Droysen proceeded to the sequel of Alexander's Successors, however, he resorted to a more generalized mode of defining an epoch – the epoch extending from Alexander's 'manhood' (336 BC), through the Successors as dynasts, and ending with the death of Cleopatra, last of the Ptolemies, in 30 BC (though Droysen, a firm Lutheran, allowed a terminus with the birth of Christ). Adopting the word *Hellenistes* from its New Testament usage – there used to denote Jewish individuals or communities for whom Greek was the daily language of convenience – Droysen identified Alexander's key legacy as one of cultural 'fusion' (*Verschmelzung*) between Greece and Asia. So the emphatic difference between 'Hellenic' and 'Hellenistic' is that 'Hellenic' is synonymous with 'Greek', while 'Hellenistic' means something like 'in Greek style'.*

---

* When Philip and Alexander embarked upon their conquests, there was no nation of Greece, but something like a thousand dispersed independent Greek city-states.

Droysen's ultimate purpose may have been to explain a remarkable phenomenon: how a strange cult launched from the shores of Lake Galilee became a major world religion. Yet Droysen, like all of us, occupies an intellectual context. As a student in Berlin, he absorbed the lessons of G. W. F. Hegel, who for his system of 'Aesthetics' (historical, generic and encompassing music and poetry as well as the fine arts) began with the premise that 'the inner production of art' was related to a set of 'world-outlooks' that could be grouped by time and place. It was typical of the Hegelian approach to history that a period could be defined by a consequent *Zeitgeist*, or 'spirit of the age'. Such generalizing approaches remained dominant throughout the nineteenth century. In Britain, George Grote (one of the founders of the University of London) published a twelve-volume *History of Greece* that championed Athenian democracy – piloted by its 'prime minister' Perikles – as the great legacy of the classical age: for Grote, the history of Greece ended with Alexander. And from his professorial eminence at Basel, the cultural historian Jakob Burckhardt confirmed the picture of decadence setting in with the rise of Macedon. In Burckhardt's account, the 'true pursuit of fame' that epitomizes the classical age gave way to 'chasing after cheap celebrity' in the Hellenistic epoch.

But even as Burckhardt went to press (in 1872) with that sentiment, discoveries were being made in Asia Minor that would challenge the historical consensus.

• • •

It was not a German professor but rather a road and railway engineer from the Ruhr, Carl Humann, who put Pergamon on the archaeological map. He was surveying in the Troad area of north-western Anatolia in late 1864 when he noticed that on one particular hillside local builders were using unearthed pieces of marble as a source of lime cement. Seeing that these were carefully carved pieces of marble, Humann intervened to halt the destruction and began planning to excavate. Two decades later, one of the most striking monuments of ancient sculpture was being reassembled in Berlin: the Great Altar of Zeus, from the city of Pergamon. Had Winckelmann been alive to see it, he would surely have recognized the vigour and virtuosity of craftsmanship here – rooted in the classical period, but with a ripeness and maturity that set it apart: as Humann exclaimed, 'a whole new epoch in art'.

Excavations have continued for over a century, revealing that the Great Altar, though exceptional, was part of a highly impressive architectural whole. The location accentuates its conspicuous effect: a natural eminence some 400 metres above sea level dominating the plain of the river Caicus, it offered an obvious acropolis ('high city'). Its theatre, seating some 10,000 spectators, is the most steeply banked structure of its type. The city would seem to be the capital of an expansive territory.

The impression is somewhat misleading. Pergamon's territory, as annexed after the death of Alexander (see page 186), was relatively modest in extent, compared with the regions secured by Seleucus, who had fought with Alexander in Asia. Like Alexander, Seleucus married a Bactrian girl; but this did not inhibit him from adding a Macedonian wife – a move that signalled his geopolitical 'double identity'. Seleucus first created a capital in Mesopotamia – Seleucia on the Tigris, not far south of modern Baghdad – then, just over a decade later, another capital to serve his rule in Syria, at Antioch on the Orontes (forerunner of Antakya, on Turkey's south-west border). Both cities were served by navigable rivers (at Seleucia, the Tigris was connected to the Euphrates by a canal), and well placed to serve east–west trade. An 'open-door' policy to incomers, predominantly Greeks, Macedonians and Jews, ensured that both cities – and indeed a number of others founded by Seleucus, many of them in his name or that of Antiochus (the name of his father, and a son who succeeded him) – prospered. Daphne, a recreational suburb of Antioch, became a byword for luxurious, even decadent, living. Archaeologically, however, the remains of these great Seleucid cities hardly compare with those of Pergamon. Partly this is due to the fortunes of historical survival, but it also indicates that Pergamon was a special place even in antiquity.

By domain, and in terms of populace, Pergamon was distinctly one of the smaller Hellenistic kingdoms. The site was part of the region of Mysia, known for its fertility, pine forests and mineral deposits. Pergamon's success, however, was historically due to good fortune – or rather to the opportunism of certain Macedonian deputies who happened to be in the right place at the right time when Alexander died.

Alexander famously amassed great quantities of bullion during his Persian campaigns. His immediate successors duly quarrelled over it. At the battle of Ipsus in 301 BC, Lysimachus, ruling in Thrace, contested its possession with Antigonus, fighting in Phrygia (in west-central Anatolia) for his dominions there. Supported by Seleucus, Lysimachus prevailed. Much of the treasure he took to Thrace, but a portion he left in Asia Minor, to be guarded by an administrator – one

Philetairos, son of a Macedonian general called Attalos. This portion was 9,000 talents, the value of which may be impressionistically conveyed by reminding ourselves that all the gold on the Athena Parthenos statue amounted to a mere 44 talents. The place chosen for its safekeeping was Pergamon. A circuit of fortification walls would be added, but this was a natural stronghold.

Philetairos may have been primed from an early age to become a 'manager' of court funds – depending on whether he became a eunuch by accident or parental design. His portrait on coins shows a thickset, resolute individual. In any case, he proved a shrewd custodian, and his lack of a son did not frustrate schemes of inheritance. The treasure was intact when Lysimachus died, and Philetairos kept hold of it when the erstwhile ally of Lysimachus, Seleucus, was assassinated in 281 BC. Eventually there was dynastic confusion about the ownership of Pergamon and its precious contents. Since Philetairos had taken precautions to arrange suitable defences, he might claim that Alexander's bequest was safer with him than with anyone else. Pergamon was nominally under Seleucid supervision, but when Philetairos died in 263 BC, his nephew Eumenes succeeded to his post. Over the following two decades, this Eumenes effectively made Pergamon independent, and though he never actually assumed kingly title, we know him as 'Eumenes I', the first of the Attalid dynasty.

It was the successor to Eumenes who styled himself *basileos* ('king') – Attalos I. He tried to look like Alexander, at least in his official portrait. But Pergamon as a city was not Macedonian in aspect. Cults of Athena were instituted; a local version of the Panathenaic festival was devised; and in the library, stocked with such Athenian 'classics' as the tirades of

Demosthenes against Philip, a marble evocation of the Athena Parthenos presided. Schools of philosophy, in particular the Stoics, gathered at Pergamon; and so, too, did textual critics, geographers, geometricians, sculptors and others. The precedent, of course, was Ptolemaic Alexandria – but the model, ostentatiously, was Periklean Athens.

Pergamon lay beyond the military reach of the Ptolemies. Rivalry between the two cities was expressed by oblique confrontations – including mutual scorn between the opposing scholars: the Alexandrians fastidious about lexical detail to the point of absurdity, the Pergamenes deplorably disposed to lateral thinking. To check the growth of the library at Pergamon, Alexandria spitefully blocked the export of papyrus – the writing surface that was provided by a plant native to Egypt. The effect of this was that the scribes at Pergamon developed their own material for manuscripts – animal skin (calf, goat or sheep) stretched and dried to form what we call parchment.*

Attalid Pergamon, like Periklean Athens, considered itself the urban embodiment of civilized values. As with Athens, articulating what it meant to be civilized entailed some contrast with hostile outsiders. But the Attalids were, nonetheless, autocrats – and the Athens of Perikles was of course famously democratic. It is true that democracy as a system was not lauded so much in antiquity as it was in the pages of later admirers such as George Grote. Still, there was opprobrium attached to tyranny; a city which boasted its possession of the authentic words of Demosthenes must have been

---

* The term derives from a Latin word that refers to the origin of the material, *pergamentum*.

sensitive to this. How could the Attalids redeem themselves as despots? Almost providentially, it seems, hostile outsiders materialized. They came not from the east, as the Persians had done, but from Europe.

To refer to them as 'Gauls' may be misleading. *Galati* is strictly how we should style them – Celts who, around 300 BC, began to migrate down the course of the Danube and through the Balkan peninsula, crossing the Hellespont in 278 BC. Eventually they would settle in the area of central Anatolia that became known as Galatia. They are recorded as having attacked the sanctuary of Delphi en route; though their aggression might be harnessed by hiring them as mercenaries, these Gauls troubled several of the Hellenistic kingdoms throughout much of the third and second centuries BC. It was around 240 BC when Attalos I met them in battle by the Caicus. Whether this was a full-scale engagement, or else a buy-off that persuaded the Gauls to move on eastwards, we do not know. Historians suspect the latter, partly on the grounds that Pergamon (presumably) never possessed the citizen manpower to field a formidable army. Whatever the reality, it was commemorated as a great victory on the Pergamene acropolis, specifically in the sanctuary of Athena Nike, where a statue group comprising at least three life-size bronze figures was set up. The composition was pyramidal, with an apex formed by the figure of a long-haired, broad-shouldered Gaul averting his head while plunging his own sword towards his heart via a point above his clavicle. Hanging limply from his other arm is the body of a woman, her lifeblood oozing: she is taken to be the warrior's own wife, killed by him for the same reason he is now killing himself – so as not to be captured alive. Nearby is the body of a battlefield victim, fatally wounded in the chest and stripped of everything except the gold torc, or neck-bracelet, characteristic of the Celts. He is twisting himself into a position that might facilitate a few last intakes of breath. His armour is gone – seized by the enemy – but a circular battle trumpet lies by him.

Marble versions of these figures may be seen in museums in Rome. 'The Dying Gaul' has been well known since its discovery in the early seventeenth century. 'Dying Gladiator' was its early title, and it was apostrophized thus by Lord Byron – as showing some unfortunate prisoner of war, 'butcher'd to make a Roman holiday'. Winckelmann, for his part, was led into a strained reinterpretation. The carving of the figure of this 'Dying Gladiator', and its heroizing effect, he considered very fine: therefore it must come from the absolutely admirable classical period. But gladiatorial games did not exist then. So the statue (Winckelmann argued) must represent an Olympic herald killed in battle. Modern scholars take it to be a Roman commission, based upon the victory group at Pergamon, but perhaps with a fresh motive: one attractive suggestion is that the statue decorated the estate of Julius Caesar, who came to have his own reasons for feeling satisfied to see the image of a vanquished Gaul (see page 243).

The Gauls who harried Pergamon were known by repute in Alexandria. In one of his poems Callimachus derides them not only as barbarians – a 'senseless tribe' – but as 'latter-day Titans', launching crazed assaults upon divine order. A later Greek writer notes the Gallic custom of washing their hair in liquid lime, making it dense and tousled, so that they looked like satyrs, or even Pan. The commemorative group created for Attalos I succeeds in capturing these stereotypical aspects of the Celtic marauders, without demeaning them as an enemy. Here, then, is a victory monument without the victors: what we see are the images of physically formidable opponents who have a certain pride in their own identity – and show the same reluctance to surrender, the same dignity in defeat, that Roman writers would later admire in the Celts of Germany. The achievement of Attalos in overcoming such spirited foes is heightened: he can therefore, like Ptolemy, claim the title of 'Saviour'. But the likeness of the Gauls to chaotic Titans also invites the Pergamene partisan to reflect on the divine alliance between Attalos and the Olympian deities: a special relationship that would be fully publicized by the next Attalid, Eumenes II.

• • •

The rule of Eumenes II lasted from 197 to 160/159 BC, when his brother and eventual successor became co-regent. It was a period of extensive development within the citadel. Careful stewardship of their funds did not inhibit the Attalids from grand projects. Eumenes built the library and pursued the acquisition of prestigious texts with enthusiasm; he added the vertiginous theatre, which largely survives, and a gymnasium. And it was probably under his sponsorship, sometime after 168 or 166 BC, that the Great Altar of Zeus was raised. On his death, Eumenes was deified, and it seems (from later epigraphic evidence) that the altar was consecrated, perhaps around 150 BC, in honour of all twelve Olympians, plus the divine Eumenes.

Altars were traditionally modest structures – solid tables placed to the fore of a temple entrance. Their elaboration under Hellenistic royal patronage was spectacular, in both size and decoration. At Syracuse, the third-century BC tyrant Hiero II sponsored a massive podium that could accommodate the slaughter of some 450 oxen at once. At Pergamon, the altar itself was inconspicuous; but the surrounds were quite literally palatial – a colonnade all around, with projecting wings. The main frieze, over 100 metres in length (about three-quarters of which survives), was not only visible, on the exterior wall of the altar podium, but immediately comprehensible. A glance is enough to recognize that it represents the primal battle between the Gods and the Giants. Since this was mythically the establishment of supremacy by Zeus and his fellow Olympians over the earth's aboriginal inhabitants – of heavenly power over the 'earth-born ones' – it might be considered an eminently suitable subject to decorate a site where the Olympians were worshipped.

Impressionistically the frieze represents a tumult, with action so violent that it spills onto the entrance steps. Yet this is a tumult in which the faces of the Olympians are invariably calm, and those of the Giants all contorted, or paralysed by fear. The 'Gigantomachy' is a great battle; yet it is a contest in which the superiority of one side over the other is absolute. How far the ancient viewer was supposed to read the images as emblematic of Attalid victory over the Gauls we can only guess – but that message seems symbolically intended.

The heroical and divine dynastic origins of the Attalids were outlined by the interior frieze located within the inner courtyard of the altar. Sure enough, there we find Herakles: son of Zeus, father of Telephos (by Auge of Tegea), and therefore progenitor of the Attalids. The frieze is far from complete in its excavated state, and again we are without direct access to the epic that was surely concocted at royal behest. Still we can see that it was, in its quiet way, no less adventurous artistically: the transitions of time and place are smoothly managed, with a controlled urgency that compresses the story while staying true to its heroic scope. Of the various narrative strands, perhaps the most significant is the involvement of Telephos in the Trojan saga, where he figures alternately as an opponent and then as an ally of the Greeks. Such mythical equivocation suited the Attalids very well, because their philhellene cultural affinities had to be increasingly balanced with a foreign policy oriented towards Rome. As the Romans were tracing their own origins from the Trojan side of the Trojan War, it was opportune for the Attalids, whose kingdom after all encompassed Troy and the Troad region, to align themselves as neighbours of old.

Pro-Roman entente was furthered by Attalos II (160–138 BC), who planted two new cities in Asia (one, on the coast of Pamphylia, was Attaleia – today's Antalya). But still the Athenian connection was maintained. It was Attalos II who endowed Athens with a new stoa along the east side of the Agora, around 150 BC (reconstructed in 1956): a discreet token of eastern influence was signalled by the 'Pergamene' capitals of this colonnade, using Asiatic palm-leaf designs. To this generous bequest we should add mention of the Pergamene donation once to be seen on the south-west wall of the Athenian Acropolis. This consisted of a multitude of statues, probably bronze, commemorating several distinct but symbolically connected battles: of the Gods against the Giants; of the Athenians against the Amazons; of the Athenians against the Persians at Marathon; and of the Pergamenes against the Gauls in Mysia. Each group seems to have included dead or dying figures; triumphant types, some on horseback, and others pathetically kneeling, cowering from blows. It was as if each victory were sanctioned by the same universal moral justification. The Giants threatened proto-divine order in an excess of hubris: they were put down. The Amazons threatened prehistoric Athens: they were repulsed. The Persians threatened historic Athens: they too were beaten back. Finally, the Gauls threatened Pergamon, the Athens of the east, and, thanks to the Attalids, they suffered the same fate as their evil predecessors. This Lesser Gaul Group (as it is known, to distinguish it from the earlier monument of Attalos I) was clearly programmed by someone who had studied patterns of symbolism in classical Athens.

A sense of the mythical past prefiguring the present also emanates from the Laocoon group – a sculpture that sent Winckelmann into rhapsodies of praise for its expressive equilibrium of passionate emotion and dignified control of emotion. Excavated in Rome in 1506, this statue was immediately recognized as a marble ensemble saluted by Pliny the Elder in superlative terms.* Michelangelo, allegedly present at the excavation, was part of the process whereby the group was enshrined as an antique masterpiece in the Vatican. Laocoon's story was well known but variously told. Greek sources, including Sophocles, related that he was a maverick priest at Troy, who offended Apollo by certain acts of impiety – for one, fathering a pair of sons when he was supposed to be celibate. For Roman writers, notably Virgil, Laocoon was the insightful Trojan who warned his fellow citizens not to

---

* Whether the Laocoon we see in the Vatican is indeed the same statue group as known to Pliny is a matter of some debate.

accept the 'gift' of a huge Wooden Horse left by Greek warriors as they (apparently) abandoned their decade-long siege of Troy ('I fear the Greeks, even when bearing gifts'). Either way, Laocoon met his death by the wrath of Apollo, who sent two giant serpents to attack the priest and his sons – and this is the painful moment envisaged by the statue.

Was it morally or aesthetically wholesome to contemplate this event as 'realistically' imagined? In the late eighteenth century, Winckelmann's enthusiasm for the statue caused a debate about the relative values of visualizing horror in two or three dimensions, instead of suggesting it with words. That debate goes on, albeit now transferred to issues of computer games and virtual reality. Meanwhile, the scholarly consensus is that a Laocoon group made of marble and found in Rome is probably not an original. Stylistically, the statue belongs to Pergamon – and was very likely made there, in bronze, in the third or second century BC.

Why would the story of Laocoon appeal to Pergamon? Perhaps, as one hypothesis goes, because the Attalid dynasty saw some historical symmetry between the fates of Troy and Pergamon, as cities. Attalos III acceded to power in 138 BC, but a greater power was already at large in the eastern Mediterranean. His predecessors, as noted, had endeavoured to maintain some kind of alliance with Rome. Opposition clearly risked a drastic end: in 146 BC the ancient city of Corinth had been entirely destroyed by order of the Roman general Mummius. Childless, and reportedly more interested in zoology than dynastic politics, Attalos drafted a will instructing that Pergamon and all its possessions – including the nucleus of the treasures once entrusted to Philetairos – be bequeathed to Rome.

We have no documentary proof that Attalos III commissioned a statue showing the violent end of Laocoon. Only when rationalized in retrospect does it seem like Pergamon's swan-song. As noted above (page 4), 'Pergamos' was one name for Troy. With a fatal gesture of defiance, Laocoon had attempted to save his city. It might be said that Attalos, by his death, sought to save Pergamon. A bequest was less dramatic – though it seems to have come as an utter surprise to its beneficiaries – and yet, as it turned out, a good deal more effective as a means of saving a city from destruction.

The gesture also played nicely upon the logic of mythical destiny. Troy was doomed to fall: Laocoon was proved right by events. However, as the towers of Troy blazed and Greek warriors ransacked the palace of Priam, one Trojan hero made his way out of the city, with his small son by his side and his father clinging to his shoulders. By divine instruction, the threesome were heading westwards, to create a new city. They did not known exactly where in the west it would be. But the hero, called Aeneas, had the premonition, and determination, that this new city of theirs would grow to exceed all others in its power. So he could promise, as he cast a parting glance at Troy: 'We will be back.'

VIII
ROME

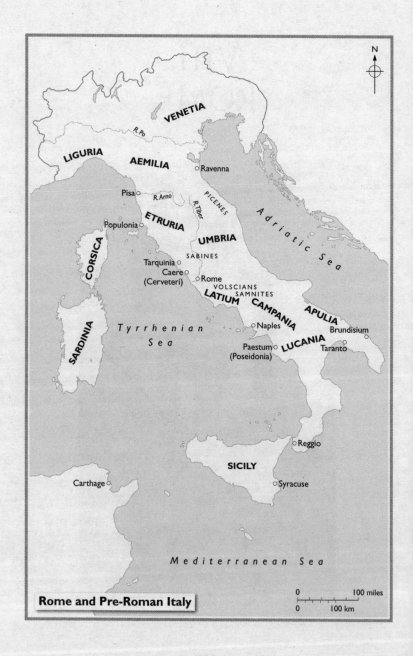

N

R. Po

VENETIA

LIGURIA

AEMILIA

Ravenna

Pisa

R. Arno

R. Tiber

PICENES

Adriatic Sea

Populonia

ETRURIA

UMBRIA

SABINES

CORSICA

Tarquinia

Caere
(Cerveteri)

Rome

VOLSCIANS

SAMNITES

LATIUM

CAMPANIA

APULIA

SARDINIA

Tyrrhenian
Sea

Naples

Brundisium

Paestum
(Poseidonia)

LUCANIA

Taranto

Reggio

SICILY

Carthage

Syracuse

Mediterranean Sea

Rome and Pre-Roman Italy

0		100 miles
0		100 km

A visitor to Rome in the eighth century BC would have found a pastoral scene – that is to say, the place was home to a community of shepherds (*pastores*, in Latin), occupying oval huts constructed of wattle and daub around timber posts, with roofs of thatch. Family enclosures, including livestock, were spread over a series of hills and knolls rising above a trough carved slowly but steeply through volcanic stone by the river Tiber. Proximity to a river crossing, combined with the advantages of hill-top habitation, was the obvious motive for settlement. Pastures may have been richer elsewhere, depending on the season, but such a natural ford is not to be found downstream, nor upstream for a long way. So the shepherds stayed upon the hills (conventionally, though inaccurately and inconsistently, numbered as seven).

In archaeological parlance, the period of Rome's original settlement is known as the Early Iron Age. A few burial sites of this period have been explored within the city: compared to those of the Etruscans to the north, they show sparse signs of actual or imminent splendour. A fuller picture of Early Iron Age society in this part of central Italy is yielded by excavations in the Alban hills east of Rome – at Palestrina, for example, and Osteria dell'Osa (near Gabii). But visitors to modern Rome could be forgiven for being unaware of the profound obscurity of the city's origins. Strolling through the

Forum, with its arches and columns, we readily accept a civic space that symbolizes what Rome became: the centre of an empire extending from the Atlantic to the Euphrates, from the Danube to the Sahara.

Yet the guidebooks tell us that here was the very abode of Rome's founder. An oval pattern of post-holes may indeed be inspected on the Palatine Hill. It is plausible that these are the traces of an Early Iron Age dwelling, or at least pertain to a structure erected in that archaic mode. The signpost *'Capanna di Romulo'* ('Hut of Romulus') is tolerable – so long as we keep the inverted commas in the title. For there was a time when structures and places associated with the origins of Rome were visible, or made visible. By the time of Rome's most famous orator, Marcus Tullius Cicero, in the mid-first century BC, a reed-built hovel claimed to be the home of Romulus, Rome's first king, was on public display. Rome's first emperor, Augustus, chose to erect his own residence close by (in due time, the Palatine Hill became so congested with grand houses that its name transferred to any such 'palatial' home or 'palace'). And if the primitive house of Romulus was signposted, why not other elements of the Romulus story? The fig tree where twin boys were washed ashore in the shallows of the Tiber, for instance? Or the cave where the boys were suckled by a she-wolf?

Those elements, in summary, seem rather as if they follow a worldwide, cross-cultural pattern. A king (Numitor), of Alba Longa,* is overthrown by a younger brother (Amulius). He, fearing rivals, makes his sister (Rhea Silvia) a priestess

---

* The place now better known as Castel Gandolfo, the pope's summer residence in the Alban hills.

sworn to celibacy (as one of the Vestal Virgins). She is seized in amorous rapture by a deity (Mars – the Roman Ares, god of strife), and gives birth to twins (Romulus and Remus). Her uncle orders the infants to be thrown into the Tiber, but they are borne by the river to the site of Rome. A mother-wolf takes them into her den and rears them with her cubs. Discovered by a shepherd, the boys grow to avenge their grandfather and to create their own joint kingdom at Rome. Fraternal unity then disintegrates, as each brother builds a wall around his own domain. Remus scorns Romulus by jumping over his wall (around the Palatine). Romulus kills Remus – and goes on to rule Rome for four decades, before being assumed to divine honours.

So there are echoes of other stories here – of Moses, of Oedipus, of Cain and Abel, and such like. Nonetheless the tale gained credence. By Roman tradition Romulus became king sixteen generations after the Trojan War, in the year equivalent to 753 BC, and was succeeded by Numa Pompilius. Five further royal rulers followed, before the revolution that created the Roman republic in the late sixth century BC. How the kings succeeded each other, and how they managed to reign for so long (apparently), remains mysterious. Mysterious, too, is the legendary twist whereby Aeneas, a refugee from the fall of Troy, comes to Italy with a mission to establish a city that will one day both avenge and exceed Troy. Aeneas leaves Troy carrying his father Anchises on his back, and with his small son Ascanius by his side. When eventually Aeneas reaches Italy, his host will be Evander, an old friend of his father's (though Anchises has died en route). Evander had created a settlement or shrine upon the Palatine Hill; Herakles was said to have paid him a visit and obliged him by dispatching a monstrous cattle-thief called Cacus. This tale was reconciled tenuously with that of Romulus by making Ascanius (also known as Iulus) the first king of Alba Longa. But even ancient writers realized that the story of Aeneas and the story of Romulus were rather like rival explanations of Rome's origins. Was either, in any case, really the stuff of history?

• • •

Archaeology can only go so far in redressing the folksy tales of Rome's foundation and early regal period. Accepting as much, there was a celebrated attempt in nineteenth-century Britain to reproduce the tone and tenor of lost Latin verses that once relayed such stirring stories as that of Horatius Cocles, the hero who single-handedly held off an army of Etruscans attempting to invade Rome. Thomas Macaulay, author of these sympathetic *Lays of Ancient Rome*, imagined how such fireside ballads eventually entered into the ancestral chronicles of Rome's oldest families, transforming 'poetical truth' into 'historical truth' – and succeeded with his English verses in capturing a credible sense of rhythmic patriotism. Macaulay's 'Horatius', notionally set in the fourth century BC, starts by conjuring up a determined enemy:

> *Lars Porsenna of Clusium*
> *By the Nine Gods he swore*
> *That the great house of Tarquin*
> *Should suffer wrong no more…*
>
> *Shame on the false Etruscan*
> *Who lingers in his home,*

When Porsenna of Clusium
Is on the march for Rome.

The Etruscans, descending from the north (from their city of
Clusium – Chiusi, in modern Tuscany), are in formidable
array. But if a wooden bridge can be demolished in time, their
access to Rome will be blocked. So Horatius and two companions volunteer to hold back the Etruscan advance while the
demolition is done. The 'dauntless Three' fight splendidly;
Etruscan corpses form a pile. As the bridge behind them
starts to crack, two of the threesome just make it across to
safety. Then Horatius, to the amazement and admiration of
the enemy throng, leaps into the foaming Tiber, which has
already carried away the timbers of the bridge – and swims
over to the bank, to a glorious reception:

With weeping and with laughter
Still is the story told,
How well Horatius kept the bridge
In the brave old days of old.

Such 'brave old days' were chronicled more prosaically, we
suppose, by the writers and annalists who in the late fourth
century BC began to construct Rome's archaic development.
Emigré Greek intellectuals, notably Polybius, subsequently
contributed their research (how a shepherds' village by the
Tiber had come to conquer all Greece and more was naturally a question of considerable interest). By the late first
century BC it was possible for the Padua-born historian Livy
to embark upon an account of Rome 'from the founding of
the city' (*ab urbe condita*) that would extend to 142 volumes.

Only thirty-five books of his great project survive, but among the survivors are accounts of the regal period at Rome. Livy can do little to bridge the gap between Aeneas and Romulus, and the immediate successors to Romulus are left more or less in a state of quaint uncertainty. Patriotic as he is, however, Livy cannot disguise the truth that Rome as an urban entity was not created by Romans.

For about a century – the sixth century BC – Etruscan kings ruled at Rome. The name of the ruling dynasty was the Tarquins; though given a Greek (Corinthian) origin by some historians, the surname suggests a connection with the Etruscan city now known as Tarquinia, on the Tyrrhenian coast, some sixty miles north of Rome. There is nothing in the records to imply that these Etruscans encroached by force. The first Tarquin, indeed, enjoys a generally benign place in Roman memory as one who wrought monumental improvements within the urban landscape. Archaeology confirms the tradition. Under the rule of this 'old Tarquin' (traditionally Tarquinius Priscus, fifth king of Rome, 616–578 BC), the area of the Forum was drained and paved; a large temple to Jupiter was raised on the Capitoline Hill; and the first substantial residences were laid out on the slopes of the Palatine.

Subsequent members of the family did not add lustre to it. The epithet of a prominent successor says enough: as Tarquinius Superbus – Tarquin the Proud – he evidently ruled in a tyrannical fashion. It was his son Sextus, however, who brought an abrupt end to the regime. This princeling was party to a session of all-male banter about wifely virtue, which led to impromptu espionage upon the lady, Lucretia by name, whose husband had proclaimed her matchless. At the sight of her, diligently attending to her loom when other women might have been ready for some diversion from their chores, Sextus determined to make a conquest. Choosing an opportunity when her husband and other menfolk might be absent, he invited himself to Lucretia's house and stole into her quarters at night. He held a dagger to her throat, threatening not only to kill her but also to place beside her the body of a naked slave, as if some squalid affair had ended in mutual suicide. He had his way and departed. Lucretia's husband and her father, each accompanied by a friend, came home to find the victim distraught yet resolute. She would not be tested on her innocence. Urging the men to ensure justice, she plunged a knife into her body.

Such is the tale of the 'Rape of Lucretia': a tragic scene with far-reaching political ramifications, for the Tarquins were consequently expelled from Rome. Instrumental to their expulsion was Lucius Junius Brutus. One of the witnesses to Lucretia's grief, his name became associated with a rigorously anti-monarchical ideology. When it happened that his two sons were implicated in a plot to restore the Tarquins, this Brutus did not flinch from having them executed. And centuries later, when the prospect of autocratic rule at Rome reappeared, a similarly motivated scion of the Junian line, Marcus Brutus, put his ideals before personal friendship to commit an act of tyrannicide.

The Tarquins were driven into exile in 509 BC – a year suspiciously close, as readers may note, to the date given for the downfall of the tyrannical Peisistratids at Athens. At Rome, however, the new constitution was not billed as *demokratia*. It was based upon the concept of the *res publica*, literally 'public thing'. What exactly comprised the republic, and how to ensure its integrity, were problems that would exercise Roman politicians and orators for several centuries. Meanwhile, two chief magistrates were elected, each to serve for a year. In time these officials would be known as 'consuls'; theoretically their powers were shared and equal, and in the first instance Brutus and Lucretia's husband Collatinus took the dual office.

Was it such a radical change of constitution? The question arises because, lodged awkwardly within the story of the Etruscan episode at Rome, we encounter one Servius Tullius, to whom Roman tradition attaches a series of important political reforms. Servius, seemingly known to the Etruscans by the name of Mastarna, may have been a usurper – perhaps, as his Latin name suggests, of servile birth. In any case, his rule in the mid-sixth century (578–535 BC) is credited with measures that appear to prepare a way for some kind of commonwealth (including the taking of a census, which led to the office of *censor* – extending to the control of 'public morals'). The essential motive may well have been military. Rome organized its fighting force by units of 100 men ('centuries'). Centuries were raised from kinship groups, known as *curiae*, and the archaic right to bear arms is likely to have carried some property qualification. The consequent problem can be crudely stated: if the Roman army was to be enlarged, Rome required more citizens. Servius, instituting the first census, divided Rome's populace into several classes, recognizing a hierarchy of wealth and property; at the same time, it seems, he multiplied the numbers of the various ranks and enfranchised more of the city's inhabitants. At the top were those available to serve as cavalry – 'horsemen' (*equites*); then came the infantry, armed heavy or light according to their worth in land and assets; and then the skirmishers and non-combatants (field cooks, bugle-blowers, and so on).

The Roman republic never disowned this militaristic cast throughout its social and political vicissitudes. Up until the end of the Roman empire, in fact, the nomenclature was retained: an 'equestrian order' might change in its composition and powers, but it was still composed of *equites*. And it remains an important aspect of Rome's early development for those wishing to understand the transformation from shepherds' village to world power. Roman history brims with instances of what we might describe as 'class struggle', involving plebeians (commoners) on one side and patricians (aristocrats) on the other. The story of Lucretia offered historians such as Livy a dramatic moment of change, but the transition from elective monarchy to republic may have been rather gradual, and it was not long after the republic's foundation that the plebeians staged a series of formal 'secessions' from the city – withholding their labour in order to gain access to civic offices and rights of political representation through their own delegates (tribunes).

The social tensions persistent in the early republic are illustrated by another tragical story we find in Livy – that of Coriolanus. Born Gaius Marcius within a patrician family, he lost his father at an early age, and by way of response to the loss trained himself to become an outstanding soldier. There was no shortage of opportunity to prove his bravery: in the early fifth century BC, Rome was periodically at war with her neighbours to the east, the Volscians. It was during an attack upon the Volscian town of Corioli that Marcius found himself so far in the vanguard that for a while he was isolated within the town walls, a one-man fighting machine. The title 'Coriolanus' was awarded in recognition of his valour, and he was nominated for election as consul by his patrician peers. But support from the plebeians was still necessary. By custom, a warrior-hero such as Coriolanus would make a public display of the wounds he had received in the front line. Whether from modesty or pride, or some potent amalgam of both, Coriolanus declined to make such an exhibition of his martial scars – to have his 'nothings monstered'. The tribunes accused him of aristocratic conceit and had him banished from the city.

An embittered Coriolanus walks away – to join his former enemies. He takes command of the Volscian forces and is on the brink of leading them to a vengeful assault upon Rome when his mother, wife and children come out in supplication. Tellingly, it is not so much with desertion of family that they reproach the renegade, but rather with betrayal of Rome, his 'nurse'. Coriolanus allows them to prevail – in the sad knowledge that this means his own disgrace and end.

• • •

The process whereby Rome extended her dominion over not just the Volscians but 'all Italy' (*tota Italia*) deserves analysis. It began with apparently minor and localized moves to secure access along the Tiber. Downstream were salt-pans at Ficana, and the potential for a seaport that would become Ostia. Upstream the river bordered the fertile contours of the Sabine Hills. Legend told that Romulus himself established a Roman crossing of the Tiber northwards at Fidenae – and, notoriously, presided over an impudent scheme to increase Rome's manpower, when he invited the Sabine tribe en masse to a festival and then abducted the women for obligatory wedlock. A battle by Lake Regillus, dated around 496 BC, traditionally marks the occasion when Rome gained ascendancy over neighbouring Latins. There were various other inland 'Italic' communities to reckon with, but the principal opponents of Roman expansion were the Samnites to the south, and the Etruscans, whose territory not only occupied much of the 'green heart' of the Italian peninsula, but also stretched across the Apennines to parts of the Adriatic coast, and for some while included parts of Campania too.

The Etruscans, as noted earlier (page 113), were rich and well connected with the wider Mediterranean. Their custom of elaborate funerals and burials has yielded plentiful evidence of a developed taste for luxury goods from the Orient and Greece; Etruscan aristocrats gained a reputation for extravagant lifestyle and clearly enjoyed the social formality known to the Greeks as the symposium, or 'drinking-together'. Greek observers were alarmed to note that Etruscan wives participated equally in such parties, but that scruple did not prevent Greek traders from supplying the Etruscans with thousands upon thousands of the painted clay vessels required – wine-jars, jugs and cups. Carefully deposited in underground tombs, as if to sustain their owners in the afterlife, these vases, produced mainly in Corinth and Athens, survive in museum collections around the world – and challenge us to wonder how much of the painted decoration, often mythical in subject, made sense in Etruscan terms.

Something like half a million Etruscan tombs riddle the volcanic landscape of central Italy – a numerous community of the dead. But how coherent was the society of the living? Eventually, the Romans came to recognize 'Etruria' as a regional identity. Yet the cities of the Etruscans, while comprising a federation, appear never to have been firmly united; the political organization of these dozen or so leading cities seems to have been uniformly oligarchic or monarchical. Power rested in the hands of certain families, who controlled magistracies and priesthoods; beyond them extended an underclass largely deprived of rights and property. This, at least, is how some Roman historians came to characterize the Etruscans, claiming that a tendency to internal discord made Etruscan cities readily susceptible to conquest. Whether the Romans preyed upon the grievances of oppressed serfs, or preferred to 'Romanize' an existing elite, we cannot now determine. The Etruscan story of how Etruria succumbed is lost and unlikely ever to be recovered.

Though not of an Indo-European tongue, Etruscan inscriptions can generally be construed. Etruscan literature, however, has not survived, so any account of how Rome conquered Etruria derives, beyond the archaeological record, from Roman historians. They report that the first Etruscan city to fall was Veii. Like most Etruscan centres, Veii was situated upon a plateau and naturally well protected. Substantial walls and fortified gateways were added in the fifth century BC. But these were not enough to withstand a persistent Roman siege, to which Veii capitulated in 396 BC. And in taking the city, Rome gained not only riches stored within its walls (among them, reportedly, many golden statues), but also a productive hinterland, irrigated by extensive systems of underground channels. Rome's next move was to make use of that agricultural resource.

Etymology, once again, gives us an essential clue to following the course of history. Our words 'colony' and 'colonist' derive directly from Latin terms that in turn relate to the verb *colere*, 'to cultivate', and the noun *colonus*, 'one who tills the land'. At the core of Rome's mission to expand was the intent of planting settlements for her own soldiers and populace. If an individual's right to bear arms – and his duty to be called up for military service – was founded upon the principle of an agricultural smallholding, then such soldier-farmers needed land.

This system was destined either to cause or to yield to various social and economic problems. Its topographical effect, in any case, was considerable, thanks to the methodical Roman practice of allotting land to colonists by the process of 'centuriation'. We think of a colony as an urban unit, and so it was – in part: a town (*urbs*) where a market, shops, temples, and places of political and administrative activity, such as the basilica (a covered public hall), were located. The layout of these structures was articulated according to a basic intersection of streets aligned orthogonally. A principal east–west axis, the *decumanus maximus*, was established, along with a main north–south axis, the *cardo maximus*; then parallel roads were laid out, subdivided regularly to create a network of squared areas extending into the countryside. It is this rural extension that reveals the core activity of Roman surveyors (usually known as *agrimensores*, 'field-measurers'). Dimensions were variable, but in principle derived from the basic unit of the *iugerum* – the area of land that could be tilled in a day by a ploughman and team of two oxen (a little over 2,500 square metres, or half an acre and more).

Grid-patterns of centuriation may still be observed today across broad tracts of the Po Valley, colonized during the third century BC. Here the Romans had a particular score to settle, for in 390 BC Rome itself was attacked by an army recruited from the Celtic tribes occupying these parts; the Roman term for the region was 'Gallia Cisalpina' ('Gaul this side of the Alps'). As Etruscan cities were subdued, or allied themselves with Rome, so the Romans were able to advance northwards. The colony of Ariminum (Rimini), planted in 268 BC, made a bridgehead for taking Celtic territory and the area occupied by the Veneti people. Integral to the centuriation process, of course, was a system of straight roads: so, for example, the Via Flaminia was constructed to connect Rome to Rimini and the Adriatic, taking its name from Gaius Flaminius, who organized the 217-mile (321 km) project while censor at Rome during the 220s BC.

In 326 BC the Greek city of Neapolis – today's Naples – allied itself with Rome against the Samnites. Within three decades the Samnites were 'pacified': the citizens of Neapolis could feel grateful that they had opted for the winning side. Their counterparts in the city of Tarentum (Taranto), on the eastern seaboard, were not so prescient. Challenging Rome over a naval treaty, the Tarentines summoned assistance from Epirus, in the north-west of Greece. Pyrrhus, king of Epirus and an able commander, enjoyed initial success after his arrival in 280 BC. But, as he famously remarked after one of these battles, 'another success like that and I am undone'. Casualties on both sides were heavy, but the Romans could more readily call up fresh troops. Pyrrhus was defeated in 275 BC at a place called Maleventum, 'bad event'. The site was immediately renamed Beneventum ('good event') by the Romans, and 'Pyrrhic victory' came to signify any success obtained at too much expense.

Pyrrhus, following the example of Alexander, deployed elephants in combat. Strategically it is debatable how effective the animals were: their impact lay perhaps in creating more panic than actual damage in the enemy ranks. But the logistics of bringing pachyderms to the battlefield fascinated the Roman historical imagination – at least as evident in the accounts by Livy and Polybius of the most ambitious transcontinental attempt to contain Rome's burgeoning power. This was the invasion of Italy by Hannibal.

• • •

Hannibal took his own life, exiled in Asia, aged in his mid-sixties. If he ever composed his memoirs, they have not survived, so we depend for his story upon Roman sources. These are not overtly prejudiced – indeed, a sentiment of steady admiration for the Carthaginian general prevails – yet a sense of Hannibal's motivation is hard to recover. His father was Hamilcar Barca, said to be descended from the brother of Dido: the legend was that as a small boy, Hannibal was obliged by his father solemnly to swear that he should always be hostile to Rome. (The Romans liked to portray the Barca family as if it were working out an ancient vendetta against Aeneas.) Hamilcar was a leading protagonist in the so-called 'First Punic War' (264–241 BC), and this was a conflict that would credibly have left his three sons – Hannibal, Hasdrubal and Mago – feeling that there was a score to settle. Its causes, however, lay lodged in older times.

The Phoenicians, as noted above (page 111), were explorers of the western Mediterranean in more or less the same period as that of Greek colonization. Beyond their 'New City' (Qart-Hadash, or Carthage) on the shores of North Africa, founded around 800 BC, they established settlements and trading posts in Sicily, Sardinia, Corsica and the Iberian peninsula. At the time of their greatest rivalry with the Greeks, in the late sixth and early fifth centuries BC, the Phoenicians found allies in first the Etruscans, then the Romans, to whom their ethnic identity was known as 'Punic'. But the Roman advance through mainland Italy was bound to challenge the Punic (Carthaginian) sphere of interest.

There ensued three Punic wars. The first mostly comprised naval encounters and ended with the enforced expulsion of Carthaginians from Sicily. Rome subsequently demanded the concession of Sardinia and Corsica. It must have seemed clear, in the view from Carthage, that if trade routes to Europe were to be maintained, the Punic presence in Spain had to be strengthened. This indeed became Hamilcar's policy: from his base at Gades (Cadiz), he advanced Punic control as far as Alicante on the east coast. And Hannibal, who accompanied his father on this expedition, pressed the strategy further. It was Hannibal who in 219 BC laid siege to the city of Saguntum, a little to the north of Valencia. Saguntum was allied by treaty to Rome: the siege – successful after eight months – was a direct provocation. So the Second Punic War was announced.

The Carthaginian fleet had suffered badly in the first war: this partly explains Hannibal's decision to attack Italy by land. With a force totalling perhaps 100,000 men (including some 12,000 cavalry, and thirty or more elephants), he might feel confident of victory. But by the same token this would be a slow-moving army – and there were, obviously, major topographical obstacles en route, not least the broad flow of the lower Rhône. How Hannibal steered his column across the Alps is a topic that generates passionate discussion to this day;

it was no less fascinating in antiquity – there were perennial debates about the practicalities of passage (for example, splitting great rocks by heating them, then drenching them with vinegar) and it provided exercises for schoolboys in persuasive rhetoric. Pupils should sympathetically imagine the vertiginous challenge, the ice and cold, the weary baggage trains, the harassment from local tribes... If they were Hannibal, what would they say to encourage their men?

By the time Hannibal had made the crossing – achieved in a fortnight, probably in late October – his invasion force may have been substantially depleted. And how far the Gauls of the region cooperated with Hannibal's declared intention to 'liberate' them from Rome is not clear; a sizeable contingent seems to have joined the Carthaginians when they traversed the Apennines in 217 BC. Nonetheless, it appears that the Romans had underestimated both Hannibal's determination and his capacity. Engagements in the Ticino valley and then by the river Trebbia were decided in favour of Carthage. A Roman plan to attack in North Africa was hurriedly cancelled. Further legions were mobilized to block Hannibal in central Italy: concealing his army in the hills above Lake Trasimene, Hannibal ambushed and massacred a force of some 25,000 led by Gaius Flaminius.

That Hannibal had his sights upon taking the city of Rome is generally doubted. His hope (it is assumed) was to win support from regions and factions within Italy apparently oppressed or threatened by Roman expansion, and thereby to restore a balance of power in the western Mediterranean by compelling Rome to withdraw from her recent gains in Sicily, Sardinia and elsewhere. As it happened, he gave one further display of his strategic genius at the site of Cannae, in

Apulia, in 216 BC: outflanking a numerically superior force of Romans and their allies, his army inflicted terrible carnage (Roman casualties were tallied at 50,000). Ancient sources register surprise that he did not march upon Rome forthwith. Thereafter, the tide of events changed. The Romans recognized that a strategy already tried by one of their commanders, the phlegmatic Fabius Maximus, nicknamed 'Cunctator' ('Delayer'), was most effective in this situation. A 'Fabian' campaign of wearing down the Carthaginian invaders by gradual attrition instead of open battle duly resulted in stalemate. For several years Hannibal operated, officially unbeaten but never fully engaged, in the south of Italy. Meanwhile Spain, which he had left garrisoned by his brother Hasdrubal, yielded to Roman forces led by father and son of the Scipio family. It was the son, Publius Cornelius, a survivor from Cannae, who then advanced across to Africa (earning him, eventually, the title of Scipio Africanus). Hannibal was obliged to return to his homeland, where at a battle near Zama, on the coast of Tunisia, he conceded in 202 BC, having lost many of his most loyal and experienced troops. Carthage had no choice but to accept the aggressive peace terms subsequently imposed.

• • •

Delenda est Carthago: 'Carthage must be destroyed.' The phrase is associated with one of the Roman republic's most characteristic politicians, Cato 'the Censor'. The title of censor carried considerable power, and not only in scrutinizing potential politicians (who, if deemed eligible, wore a symbolically white toga – *candidatus*, 'whitened', whence our 'candidate'). Censors were also responsible for raising taxes and for public spending projects. Cato came to the office (and others, including consul) having first distinguished himself as a military tribune. His origins were more rustic than aristocratic: he was the archetypal republican insofar as he defined himself by farming and fighting – and kept that identity to the fore, although he was also a sharp lawyer. His best-known contribution to Latin literature was true to his political stance: a handbook of practical farming advice, issued in staccato sentences of carefully 'unpolished' Latin.

It was perhaps due to his agricultural wisdom that Cato, visiting Carthage as part of a delegation in 153 BC, concluded that Rome's enemy in North Africa must be utterly destroyed. Carthaginian power had been pruned, as it were: it would only grow back even stronger. On one occasion, to prove his point, Cato came to the Senate at Rome carrying a basket of newly picked figs: 'Look how fresh these figs are', he announced, 'and they come from Carthage: that is how close our mortal enemy lies.' Within a few years, Cato had his way. A pretext for war – thus the Third Punic War – was found, and surrender deemed insufficient: in 146 BC the city was comprehensively 'taken out' by Roman troops.

Similar destruction was visited upon the city of Corinth in the same year – punishment for the Corinthians assuming a lead role in an anti-Roman alliance of Greek cities (the Achaean League). Lucius Mummius, the general who conducted the action, is reported to have been somewhat careless about the fate of the many statues and objets d'art ransacked from Corinth's sanctuaries. However, a number of Corinthian cemeteries were raided – not for any military reason, but because an antiquarian market existed back in

Rome for the jewels, vases and other collectible treasures to be found in old Greek tombs.

Here we apprehend that the process of conquest was causing something of an identity crisis among the Romans. According to Livy, the crisis began with the sack of Syracuse in 211 BC, by Marcellus. This not only marked the end of independent Greek city-states in Sicily, but also signalled a shift in Roman 'taste'. For Syracuse the prosperous *megalopolis* was replete with rich pickings – not only numerous works of art in various media, but also scientific instruments and other valuable items of intellectual property (for instance, a geographical globe). So although the eminent scientist Archimedes himself did not survive their siege, the Romans may be said to have captured his knowledge. Back at Rome, the tradition was to stage a 'triumph': originally this occasion served to 'demilitarize' a returning general, who was obliged to exchange his arms for civilian garb on the boundary of the city and to preside, from a mobile throne, over a victory parade that ended in the Forum. Enemy spoils (*spolia*) and captives were a conspicuous part of the procession, and the Roman public came to expect that some of this booty would become 'urban decoration' (*ornamenta urbis*). So Rome became a showcase for masterpieces of Greek sculpture, a museum of exotic curiosities, and a repository of 'alien wisdom'. Some republicans, notably Cato, grieved vehemently at the resultant loss of pristine Roman simplicity. As the poet Horace put it, 'captive Greece captivated her brutal conqueror'.

However, beyond the developing penchant for the sophistications of Greek art, rhetoric, science and philosophy, there lay a more substantial cause for republican concern. With each victorious battle, with every successful siege, came the human trophies – a quantity of slaves. Men, women, children: regardless of their age or social station, these were the victor's due. Their definition (by Aristotle) as 'two-legged animals' seems particularly inadequate when we remember that many highly educated individuals (including Greek philosophers such as Epictetus the Stoic: see page 163) could find themselves slaves as a result of Roman conquest. The little Cycladic island of Delos, occupied by Roman 'businessmen' (*negotiatores*) in the late third century BC, became a central place for the bargaining and distribution of this human traffic, reportedly capable of processing up to 10,000 slaves per day. The ready supply of such cheap labour to the Italian peninsula did not square with the ethos of a republic built around citizen-farmers. The self-sufficiency of smallholdings characterized by 'Mediterranean polyculture' – mixed crops, some livestock, plus fruit, nuts and vegetables: 'a little of everything' – gave way to the so-called *latifundia*, industrial 'big farms' dependent upon slave gangs and managed by stewards on behalf of absentee landlords.

This, at least, was the scene evoked by the Gracchi brothers, Tiberius and Gaius, when serving as tribunes in the second half of the second century BC. But their land reforms, launched around 133 BC with the aim of restoring a rural population of tenant smallholders (and a yeomanry for the Roman army), did not bring an end to the problem.

• • •

'Social war'; civil wars; wars with enemies in the east, in particular with the Persian-descended dynasty of Mithridates and his successors in the Black Sea area known to the Romans as Pontus: these conflicts not only dominate the middle to late republic, but interact with each other. A broad résumé of the period tells of class discord leading to the rise of a populist leader and general, Marius; the recruitment of professional armies whose victories overseas would enrich generals such as Marius, and assure loyalty from the troops to a particular general, rather than to Rome, and consequently the rise of rivals from opposing factions. In the case of Marius, his chief rival was Sulla: a patrician whose military prowess enabled a certain political daring that led to the award (from himself and aristocratic friends) of the title *dictator* at Rome in 81 BC.

Dictator means 'he who says': it invites the object, 'what must be done'. It was an extraordinary office built into the republican constitution essentially as a means of investing one magistrate with 'emergency powers' – to lead an army, quash a rebellion, or confront some other kind of crisis at home or abroad. It had been called upon when Hannibal threatened. Now Sulla revived the title as a way of making constitutional changes and conducting 'proscriptions' against his political enemies. A *proscriptio* was basically a list – originally an inventory of property to be sold as a result of bankruptcy or unpaid debt. Under Sulla it became a mode of public condemnation, naming certain 'proscribed' individuals as enemies of the state and allowing at least the confiscation of their property – and at most their immediate execution.

Sulla stood down a year before his death in 78 BC. Inadvertently he had shown how the republic would fail. The next generation of ambitious leaders included Caesar, Crassus and Pompey – those who would form the first 'triumvirate', or 'three-man rule', in 60 BC. Their alliance was for the sake of passing convenience. Crassus came to grief on an expedition with Roman forces against the Parthians, a semi-nomadic people whose territory, since Seleucid times, extended from the Euphrates to the Indus: at the battle of Carrhae, in northern Mesopotamia, in 53 BC, legionary standards were lost in a rare event – a Roman military disaster. Pompey had more success in the east, defeating Mithridates. But the most secure, and lucrative, campaign was that of Julius Caesar in Gaul (58–51 BC). An ancient estimate of casualties during the course of this war numbers a million Gauls dead and two million captured. But its history is dominated by Caesar's own account – which features no such statistics, nor any attendant remorse.

If the style equates to the man, then Caesar's character may readily be measured. His narratives of campaigns, whether against Gallic tribes or fellow Romans, couched in the third person ('Caesar commanded that…'), are models of patient and unemotional prose. The subject is war: not the pity of war, rather its relentless prosecution. *Caesar exposito exercitu et loco castris idoneo capto*: 'Caesar the army having been landed and a place suitable for camp having been taken'… generations of Latin-learners have come to beware the general's predilection for a certain trick of syntax (the 'ablative absolute', whereby a noun and part of a verb join to express a 'done deed'); yet the methodical pace of his writing reflects how Caesar prevailed over Vercingetorix the Gallic chieftain, Pompey, and other opponents. He will pick out individuals for acts of conspicuous heroism – such as the standard-bearer who jumped overboard to lead the amphibious raid upon Britain in 54 BC – but more often it is a story of steady preparation and collective resolve.

The Celtic battle-cry – *Cecos ac Caesar,* or *Merde à César* – needs no further translation. Caesar's image of the Britons who mustered to confront him is one of a disorderly rabble – terrifyingly wild in appearance, but easily overcome by superior tactics, training and military hardware. But the narrative of extending Rome's boundaries, and the narrator's self-effacing style, are equally deceptive. Caesar's quest for power (*imperium*) was primarily on his own behalf. When his opponents back at Rome, including Pompey, persuaded the Senate to rescind his right to command, Caesar abruptly turned the force of his legions from north-west Europe to his native Italy.

He crossed the Rubicon – the river marking the boundary of Italy with Cisalpine Gaul – early in 49 BC. *Alea iacta est,* 'the die is cast', proverbially associated with this move by Caesar, implies a gamble. And so it was, both politically and militarily: for Pompey not only had supporters at Rome, but powerful forces and allies abroad. Pompey and his senatorial comrades decamped to Greece as Caesar marched upon Rome. A series of battles ensued around the Mediterranean. Pompey was roundly defeated at Pharsalus in Thessaly in 48 BC, and subsequently knifed to death while seeking asylum in Egypt; his offspring were seen off at Munda in Spain. In Asia Minor, the son of Mithridates, Pharnaces, attempted an opportunistic rebellion. It was after Caesar's swift and effective reaction to this threat that he resorted to the first person with a laconic communiqué (to a friend): *veni, vidi, vici* – 'I came, I saw, I won.'

Did victory go to his head? Coins with the image of Caesar began to appear in 45 BC, and he claimed the office of *dictator* for life. He declined the title of king (*rex*), but for some Romans he had already gone too far. Marcus Brutus and

Gaius Cassius were leaders of an assassination plot carried out in the Forum on 15 March (the Ides of March) 44 BC. The ominous prognostication of an Etruscan soothsayer – 'Beware the Ides of March' – was, like most astrological predictions, too enigmatic to be of any use. Caesar's dying words are popularly known as *et tu, Brute?* – 'And you, Brutus?' – querying the involvement of one whom he considered a friend. Another report makes the three words Greek: *kai su, teknon?* – 'And you, son?' – which, in conjunction with the rumours that Caesar had an affair with Servilia, mother of Brutus, may be taken literally.

Officially Caesar left no son of his own. His will, famously divulged by one of his former staff, Marcus Antonius (Mark Antony), bequeathed a cash sum to every citizen of Rome. Antony was not, however, the designated successor: for it also transpired from the will that Caesar had adopted as heir a great-nephew, who would take the name Gaius Julius Caesar Octavianus (Octavian). Young as he was – just nineteen – Octavian sensed the opportunity to challenge Antony. But first he had to avenge Caesar's murder, and he needed Antony's military experience for that end. Co-opting Lepidus, an aristocrat who had cause to be grateful to Caesar, Octavian and Antony formed another triumvirate.

Of the twenty or so senators who joined in the assassination, perhaps the majority were motivated by envy of Caesar's power, leaving Brutus isolated in his hope for a return to the republic, as founded in the late sixth century BC (and involving his ancestor). In any case, the mood in Rome was unsympathetic, in particular among Caesar's legions. Brutus and Cassius found themselves abroad, raising an army in the eastern Mediterranean. They met the forces of the triumvirate, led by Antony, at Philippi, in Macedonia. A protracted battle took place in October 42 BC. In defeat, both Brutus and Cassius committed suicide.

Mark Antony was a successful, confident general; popular with the rank and file, he was also an athletic, hard-drinking, effusive character who liked to play the part of the *miles gloriosus* ('victorious soldier'). His antics – swaggering bare-chested in the Forum, harnessing a team of lions to a chariot, vomiting over the bride at a society wedding, and so on – were among the causes of intense disapproval from certain quarters (Cicero, for instance, loathed Antony, and eloquently so). Lepidus, mild and indecisive, was never going to be a rival. But in Octavian there was a true alternative type: he seemed to embody two maxims associated with the god Apollo – 'Know yourself' and 'Nothing in excess'. In due time, Octavian would make explicit his personal affinity with Apollo; meanwhile, it was easy enough to polarize Mark Antony as a debauched Dionysiac type, for Antony had become amorously involved with Cleopatra VII, daughter of Ptolemy XII. In itself this dalliance, conducted as something of a public spectacle, would have been enough to generate rumours at Rome of Antony's plans to create a centre of power in Ptolemaic Alexandria. The scandal was compounded, however, by the fact that Antony was then married to Octavian's sister, Octavia.

Relations between Octavian and Antony had been tested when Antony's brother Lucius led a revolt spread across several Italian cities. The uprising essentially represented a protest against the settlement of veterans from Caesar's army, who were being rewarded with holdings in prime agricultural territory. Justifiable as such local complaints might have been,

Octavian took the opportunity to gather many of his enemies among those he punished by an act of mass execution at Perugia, in the central Italian region of Umbria. The triumvirate allowed each of its members a certain 'hit list' of proscriptions: so, in turn, Octavian was powerless to save his most eminent supporter, Cicero, from Antony's revenge.

Octavian was astute in winning favour from the legions, but he had little aptitude for generalship in the field. Fortunately, a friend from boyhood, Marcus Vipsanius Agrippa, proved not only a tough soldier, but also dependably subordinate. The portrait of Agrippa shows a stolid, lantern-jawed type, of whom it is readily believed that, when given the task of renovating Rome's sewerage system, he demonstrated the effluent hygiene of the city's main drain, the Cloaca Maxima, by paddling its length in a canoe. Under his command, in 36 BC, Octavian's navy successfully confronted a rogue fleet operating from Sicily under Pompey's youngest son, Sextus. A showdown between Octavian and Antony became inevitable – though it suited Octavian, when issuing a declaration of war in 32 BC, to identify Cleopatra as the enemy (this was not, therefore, *civil* war).

Opposing seaborne and land-based forces were marshalled the following year at a promontory of north-west Greece. What eventually happened in the waters off this promontory, called Actium, remains obscure – as we peer through the gloss of wondrous victory later concocted by poets and partisans. Antony was slightly disadvantaged by his opponents' refusal to fight on land; Octavian's tactic seems to have been to cut off Antony's army by a naval blockade. The rival fleets were well matched, with Antony's flotilla supplemented by Ptolemaic ships. However, in the midst of a battle to break through the blockade, on 2 September 31 BC, Cleopatra and her vessels turned away from the engagement and headed back to Egypt. Was it 'all for love' that Antony chose to follow her? One report tells of formerly faithful legionaries refusing to fight for Antony. In any case, he sailed with Cleopatra to Alexandria, effectively deserting the main body of his troops.

Those troops did not immediately surrender: Octavian spent a week or so negotiating terms with them, doubtless expensive to himself. A settlement established, he spent some months in Greece before extending the pursuit. Accepting defections of their troops, depriving them of allies abroad, Octavian had Antony and Cleopatra trapped in Alexandria. His forces arrived at the city by the summer of 30 BC, and Antony rallied for a final battle. At a desperate moment in the fighting Antony was given the message that his queen was dead. He asked his valet, Eros, to dispatch him; Eros refused, stabbing himself instead. Antony did likewise – learning, too late, that Cleopatra was still alive. He died in her arms.

It was (as Shakespeare, following Plutarch, realized) the stuff of tragedy – and it was not quite complete. Cleopatra, by then almost forty, may have thought to seduce the young conqueror, as she had charmed his great-uncle Julius. For his part, Octavian had eyes upon the reserves of Ptolemaic royal treasure she possessed, and indeed her entire kingdom. If the queen made any advances, they were resisted. Eventually Cleopatra did as Octavian wished, and committed suicide.

For some decades Rome had been viewing the kingdom of Egypt with predatory intent: the country offered rich pickings from its productive economy, and in particular a copious grain supply. There were stories that Ptolemy XI had signed a will, concealed by his successors, donating Egypt to Rome as Attalos III had bequeathed Pergamon. Octavian removed Cleopatra's offspring by Antony from the scene, and had her teenage son by Julius Caesar assassinated (Caesarion, or 'Little Caesar', as the boy was called, had been touted by Antony to become the next Ptolemy). So the dynasty was exterminated. Octavian seized control of its treasuries and took upon himself the divine role of pharaoh. Henceforth Egypt was under Roman rule; but unlike any other province, it remained the personal property of the emperor. A prefect of non-senatorial rank was the emperor's delegate; Alexandria was granted no elected assembly; and so long as this private domain of Egypt was the 'bread basket of Rome', the emperor could personally keep the populace of Rome supplied – or not, as he pleased.

• • •

It was during the years immediately after Actium that young Octavian transformed himself into the venerable 'Augustus'. Caesar had been deified, so his adoptive heir was therefore entitled 'son of a god' (*divi filius*). This sacred status would be bolstered by the assumption of an office made vacant by the death of Lepidus around 12 BC – that of the republic's 'Chief Priest', or *pontifex maximus*. *Pontifex* literally translates as 'bridge-builder'. The bridge here was the metaphysical connection between mortals and gods. It seemed appropriate that Octavian, taking on the associated duties of state ritual, temple maintenance and so on, should become 'worshipful' by name.

He reportedly considered calling himself Romulus, but there were reasons why that name carried associations (including fratricide) unsuitable to a leader or 'first one' (*princeps*), however earnestly he sought to recover the original ideals of Rome as a city. Cicero had seen in the young Octavian one who would rescue the republic. In effect, the mature Augustus did quite the opposite: making his uncle's name generic, and extending the military sense of 'he who gives the orders', he established a system of autocratic rule whose incumbent was both a 'Caesar' and *imperator*. But Augustus studiously disguised this constitutional revolution. His own statement of the political transformation reads as follows:

> In my sixth and seventh consulships [28–27 BC], after I had put an end to civil wars, although by everyone's agreement I had power over everything, I transferred the state from my power into the control of the Roman senate and people... After this time I excelled everyone in authority, but I had no more power than the others who were my colleagues in each magistracy.

Where 'authority' (*auctoritas*) ended and 'power' (*potestas*) began, we may wonder – but the paradox of being 'first among equals', *primus inter pares*, was germane to such ambiguities.

Not only were all the offices of the republic upheld (albeit that they were filled by one man and his close associates), but archaic priestly orders and ancient rituals were also revived; an antiquarian concern for the past was validated by the sense that a new era, fostered by 'Augustan peace' (*pax Augusta*), was really a return to the prehistoric innocence of the 'age of Saturn'. Saturn's cosmic reign was a time when no one had yet thought of turning trees into timbers for ships or fences, and metals were not extracted to make weaponry; animals came freely to be milked, crops grew in superabundance, and the seasons favoured flowers and fruit. Visual evocations of this happy epoch were included in public monuments, such as the Ara Pacis ('Altar of Peace'), commissioned in 13 BC, with its frieze of acanthus at once riotous and symmetrical; also on small-scale objects, and in private spaces, such as the dining-room attached to a villa north of Rome belonging to Augustus' wife Livia. The paintings from this room, relatively well preserved, are among the loveliest pictures from antiquity – at least in their cumulative effect: they create a vista that seems like an earthly paradise. Only when we peer closer do we notice a strange level of biodiversity here. Flowers that bloom in the spring, such as blue periwinkles, appear with fruits that mature in autumn, such as quince. Birds – quails, thrushes, orioles, nightingales – animate the foliage, regardless of their migratory habits. Such is the marvel of the Golden Age created by Augustus.

Augustus regularized the production of a new gold coin, the *aureus*: an early issue shows him seated on a consul's chair, flourishing scrolls, with the message that he had restored the laws and rights of the Roman people. The conjunction of message and medium is telling, for much of the political success of Augustus may be imputed to his own spending power. In the autobiographical inscription he left, the *Res Gestae* ('Things Done'), Augustus states that he donated no less than six hundred million *denarii* to public causes – including the settlement of discharged soldiers.* He raised

* The sum is put into proportion when we learn that the annual pay of a legionary soldier was about 225 *denarii*.

funds from his subjects, of course ('And it came to pass in those days, that there went out a decree from Caesar Augustus, that all the world should be taxed…'). However, as a principle of provincial administration, Augustus introduced the regular payment of salaries to Roman officials. A *salarium* was originally the allowance granted to a soldier for his purchase of salt. Now it became the term for remuneration of governors and others serving the emperor abroad, obliging them to him and making them less inclined, in theory, to extort money from their local subjects.

Agrippa set up for public display at Rome a calibrated 'Map of the World' (*Mappa Mundi*), emphasizing how much of it belonged to Rome. A statue of Augustus showed the emperor barefooted but dressed in a military cuirass; picked out in relief on this corselet was a symbolic celebration of a 'bloodless' victory in 20 BC, when the Parthians had been persuaded to yield up not only over a hundred Roman military standards, but also thousands of Roman prisoners: so the power of Augustus made itself felt even where Roman armies had failed.

At home, Augustus prided himself that he had transformed the capital from a sprawl of buildings in mud-brick and volcanic stone into a city that looked like Athens or Pergamon – a city complete with gleaming colonnades. Great sculptures from Greece, obelisks from Egypt, variegated marbles from North Africa became part of the urban fabric. The Campus Martius was one area of the city conspicuously transformed: called the 'Field of Mars' because it had served for military exercises in the early republic, this would be where the Altar of Peace was installed. Here, too, an old ship was displayed, said to be the boat that brought Aeneas from

Troy. Of two obelisks brought (by specially constructed vessels) from Egypt's Heliopolis in 10 BC, one was set up to serve as a giant sundial: on the emperor's birthday, which was the autumnal equinox (23 September), its shadow touched the Altar. Augustus also arranged for his own monumental tomb in the vicinity – a vast 'Mausoleum', surmounted by a statue of himself. Meanwhile Agrippa endowed public baths and a temple dedicated to 'all the gods', the Pantheon. Because it burned down and was eventually rebuilt by an emperor who had some architectural flair (Hadrian), we cannot be sure how far its existing design corresponds to the original. From the front, a Corinthian portico gives the impression of a standard Greek temple. Once inside, there is nothing 'standard Greek' about a coffered concrete dome or rotunda spanning 43 metres (142 ft), and equally high.

So Rome became grandiose. Yet it is at this time that the pleasures and virtues of 'country living' first find expression in Western art and literature. Previously, poets at the Alexandrian court had developed the genre of pastoral or bucolic verse. The Latins, with their republican tradition of thrifty connectedness to agricultural independence, added not only a certain element of authenticity, but also moral purpose – and rich symbolic implications.

As befitted a nation conscious both of its pastoral origins and of the republican ideal of farmer-soldiers, there was a tradition of agricultural lore in Latin. Cato had led with his brusquely didactic manual on farm management; a more polished account of stock-breeding and other topics was produced in the first century BC by the learned Varro. Archaeologists of rural Italian sites – patiently collecting carbonized remains, separating them by a flotation process and scrutinizing the botanical traces – have corroborated the pattern of agricultural effort outlined by these Latin sources. Wheat, barley and oats were regular crops, supplemented by fava beans and lentils; sheep, cow and pig were the prime domesticated animals, and game, such as red deer, was regularly on the table.

Distinguished Latin families could identify their 'roots' in such habits of subsistence – for instance, 'Fabius' from *faba* (broad bean), 'Cicero' from *cicer* (chick-pea). Self-sufficiency was a virtue: to keep a productive garden (*hortus*) was a point of pride with householders across a wide social range. We see this at Pompeii, where actual gardens have been partially reconstructed from organic remains, and a distinct genre of wall-painting looks like the beginning of a Western visual tradition of still life. A bowl of apples or eggs, a bundle of asparagus: these were tokens of hospitality, given or received, and signs of *rus in urbe* – 'the country in the town'. Artists in Roman employ began to produce scenes of 'landscape' – fields, forests, streams and so on – apparently for its own sake, not just as a backdrop for some mythical episode. And poets took up the rustic theme.

Among the close associates of Augustus was a comfortable aristocrat of Etruscan descent called Maecenas. He created his own leafy estate upon Rome's Esquiline Hill, complete with a heated swimming pool and a tower overlooking the city; it is within this area that a small building was discovered in 1874 and immediately entitled the 'Auditorium of Maecenas'. Once exquisitely decorated with garden scenes, it seems to have been an enclosed ambience for convivial gatherings and poetic recitals. Was this where the literary heroes of the Augustan age – including Virgil, Horace and

Propertius – first aired their compositions? The period generally is recognized as a showcase of 'Golden Latin artistry' – a
series of technical devices (word order, metre and more)
capitalizing upon the flexibilities of an inflected language. But
style was not the only form of virtuoso expression. Momentum
swelled with thematic purpose – a distinct 'spirit of the age',
extending also to writers of prose (notably Livy) and philosophy in verse (Lucretius: see page 166).

How far Augustus himself intervened to ensure that the
poets were 'singing from the same hymn sheet' is not clear:
part of his mature political genius lay in not appearing dicta-
torial. The case of Ovid, arguably the Roman poet whose
influence has been most extensive over the centuries, is
instructive. Ovid's *Metamorphoses*, an ingenious weaving
together of mythical 'transformations', continues to appeal to
modern readers – as does his love poetry, which, like that of
his predecessor Catullus, strikes a confessional, sensual tone.
Ovid followed literary convention when turning his hand to
the so-called *paraclausithyron* – the 'lament by a [closed]
door', a poetic set-piece in which an ardent and tormented
lover implores his mistress to open up to him. More inven-
tively, Ovid teased the establishment when he suggested that
the fine marble colonnades now adorning Rome were perfect
places for casual encounters with foreign girls (Augustus
passed legislation to penalize adultery, and also tried to
encourage inter-Italian marriage). At some point, however,
the poet went too far. His mistake may have been no more
than to have witnessed some misbehaviour by a female
member of the imperial family. In any case, in AD 8, Ovid was
removed, by order of Augustus, to a settlement called Tomus
in the Black Sea region. From here the poet, often described

as 'urbane', lamented his fate insistently, pleading for pardon – to no avail.

There was no office of poet laureate as such: had there been, its obvious incumbent was Virgil. His early work, the *Eclogues*, was composed in conscious emulation of Theocritus. 'Charming' is the word one might apply to these poems, with a nuance of damnation – though beneath the artifice of shepherds' idle musing Virgil also lodged a protest about the effect of settling military veterans in Italy (at least around his own area of Mantua). A more authentic voice resounds in his 'agricultural manual', the *Georgics*. This sequence can hardly have been addressed to those who actually worked the land: Virgil, however well informed he seems, had nothing to teach them. But it amounts to more than a handbook on how to run a mixed arable and dairy farm (with detailed supplementary notes on pruning vines and keeping bees). The *Georgics* is a love song to Italy's landscape as created and curated by the country's farmers. Implicitly, the poet calls upon city-based villa-owners to be involved with the husbandry of their estates. Explicitly, he thanks Octavian for providing the necessary peaceful conditions to do so.

The commission to compose an epic about Rome's arch-founder Aeneas was, we are told, reluctantly undertaken by Virgil. He worked upon it for a decade, licking its lines into shape (as he put it) as a mother bear would tend her cubs. He died, in 19 BC, without finishing it to his satisfaction, and asked his friends to burn the manuscript. Fortunately for us, those friends disobeyed the poet's wishes. The *Aeneid* survives as proof not only that epic could be written, after Homer, but also that epic could grow, in moral scope, beyond Homer. In the Preface to this book we noted the concept of *humanitas Romana* – not quite equivalent to humanitarianism in the modern sense, but certainly a prefiguring of certain gentle virtues. With Virgil, the epic tradition resonates with concerns of justice and sympathy, earning him the critical accolade of writing 'civilized poetry'. His capacity 'to harmonize the sadness of the universe' – the dictum approved by scholar-poet A. E. Housman as poetry's purpose – has endeared Virgil to pessimists down the ages; in his time, however, Virgil articulated a vision of Roman identity that made the construction of empire a mission of laborious benevolence. The family tree connecting Augustus to Aeneas may have been less than robust. But Virgil created in Aeneas a hero sufficiently driven by patriotic purpose for the kinship to be at least poetically credible.

Virgil's friend and fellow recipient of favour from Maecenas was Horace, who had fought at Philippi on the side of Brutus and Cassius, but was able to transfer allegiance with evident conviction. Horace enjoyed a relaxed rapport with Augustus, and from Maecenas he was granted an estate in the Sabine Hills, which gave him the chance to play at being a farmer. In his poet's role, Horace likened himself to a bee, making forays to innumerable small sources of sweetness. The categorical titles of his works – Epistles, Satires, Sermons – sound more forbidding than they are, threaded through by gentle mockery and moralizing. It is for his Odes, however, that Horace is best known, and it is from that he is often quoted (for instance, *carpe diem* – 'Seize the day'). These *Carmina*, 'Songs', adapting Greek lyric metre to Latin expression, are mostly brief in length, and more or less Epicurean in sentiment, yet they are chiselled into sharp lines and nice angles, with a carpentry of words satisfying even in translation: each poem 'clicks into place', the result of hour upon hour of patient craft ('the labour of the file', as Horace called it). The world evoked by an Horatian Ode is one where wars and alarms do happen, beyond frontiers or overseas, duties call, love has its seasons, and a single night awaits everyone; but honest work, and contentment with moderate pleasures, bring happiness.

• • •

Pax Augusta did not prevail everywhere. In AD 9, a rebel German leader called Arminius (subsequently rendered as 'Hermann') organized an ambush and massacre of a Roman army led east of the Rhine by Quinctilius Varus. To this day Bavarian beer-drinkers raise their tankards triumphantly to the *Varusschlacht*, the 'Varus battle' that took place in the Teutoburg Forest, destroying three legions and their auxiliaries. Further east, the Parthians remained a rival superpower. Nevertheless, Virgil and Horace could with sincerity salute an epoch of fruition and regeneration at Rome. The title *pater patriae*, 'Father of the Fatherland', voted by the Senate for Augustus in 2 BC, had been given several times before (originally it belonged to Romulus), and subsequently would be conferred perhaps too readily upon the emperors. With Augustus the honour seemed appropriate: he was the progenitor of a new state.

Though his portraits remained youthful, Augustus ruled until a peaceful death in his late seventies. So long was one essential problem of the new constitution postponed: who would succeed? Enough of republican sentiment survived in the Roman Senate to prohibit an overtly dynastic procedure;

yet there was no elective mechanism instead. An emperor must either produce an heir regarded as worthy and capable, or else identify such a figure beyond immediate family and make him a son by adoption.

Virgil, Horace, Agrippa, Maecenas: all these preceded Augustus to the 'single night awaiting everyone' – and, alas, so did several young men intended to inherit power from Augustus. The conjunction of two families, the Julians and the Claudians, eventually yielded a successor in the person of Tiberius, his stepson by Livia. That Tiberius suffered some sort of inferiority complex from the process of reluctant adoption is credible. In any case, the ensuing sequence of Julio-Claudians is so stained with infamy that we have little hope of making an objective judgement. Historians of a later age – notably Suetonius, composing his biographies of the *Twelve Caesars* in the early second century AD – could not resist dramatizing the post-Augustan epoch with a parade of monsters: Tiberius (AD 14–37), distrustful and distrusted; Caligula (AD 37–41), a psychopath; Claudius (AD 41–54), an imbecile; and Nero (AD 54–68), after a promising start, the histrionic lead player in a period known for gastronomic excess, gratuitous violence and general debauchery.

Crisis of succession came to a head after Nero's suicide: AD 69 is known as the 'year of the four emperors', in which several generals contested power. The victor was a bull-necked Sabine called Vespasian, whose portrait seems to confirm the no-nonsense style of rule he brought to Rome. For a few decades a new dynasty prevailed: the Flavians, who courted popularity by erecting an amphitheatre where a colossal statue of Nero had once stood (hence it was known as the 'Colosseum'). Vespasian, Titus, Domitian: the trio of father and two sons ended unhappily, with Domitian subject, as Nero had been, to a *damnatio memoriae* ('erasure of memory') after his death in AD 96.* Some sort of political solution was reached with the accession of Nerva (AD 96–8), then Trajan (AD 98–117): it lay not so much in the uncertain business of arranging marriages and hoping for heirs as in the *princeps* allowing senators to choose from among their number.

It is typical of the incisive style of Suetonius that he can characterize Domitian with a single vignette of the emperor alone for hours in a room of his palace, impaling flies upon the end of his writing stylus. Again there is little hope of redressing the historical picture – especially since Domitian also became notorious in the Satires of Juvenal. Satire (literally meaning a 'medley') was a Roman literary invention, allowing for all sorts of mockery and incorporating a republican tradition of 'free speech', but when it came to satirizing emperors, it was wise to wait until they were dead and disowned by their successors. (Juvenal seems to have been writing in the time of Trajan and Hadrian – but discreetly makes no reference to them.)

One of Juvenal's most entertainingly indignant pieces (Satire III) is a declamation about the horrors of living in Rome. A leading complaint is that the city is full of foreigners. The satirist gleefully trades upon simple xenophobia. But there was of course a positive aspect of Rome's 'open door' policy. It is shown by the partial record of a speech made by the emperor Claudius to the Roman Senate in AD 48. The text of the speech was inscribed on bronze tablets set up in a

---

* *Damnatio memoriae* was the senatorial go-ahead for vilification of someone deemed an enemy of the state: citizens might take hammers to associated statues and inscriptions.

sanctuary near the Roman capital of Gallia Narbonensis, Lugdunum (modern Lyons). Claudius had connections with the city – it was his birthplace – and the people of Lugdunum had reason to be thankful to Claudius, for it was as a result of this proposal that they became eligible as Roman senators (provided they met qualifications of personal wealth). Whether Claudius delivered the speech with a natural speech impediment, or hammed it up as a mumbling scholar, we cannot tell. (He may have suffered from cerebral palsy, and then only pretended to act the fool.) But what survives of the transcription seems in part like a recondite lecture upon early Roman history, with the emperor divulging his researches into the ancestral origins of some of Rome's semi-legendary kings. The tablet even includes an interjection from the audience, telling Claudius to get on with it and come to the point. Yet he has already made his case – and another record of the speech, by the historian Tacitus, confirms its effective message. The crux was this: since the time of Romulus, Rome was built on the principle of granting citizenship even to its former enemies. Sabines, Etruscans, Samnites and others were already among the ancestry of Rome's ruling class: why not extend the ethnic range? True, Claudius observes, other cities were never so open: Athens, for instance, never altered its policy of refusing citizenship to all foreigners. But where was Athens now?

• • •

Italy was chosen by the divine inspiration of the gods... to unite scattered empires, to make customs more gentle, and through the sharing of a common language, to draw together in conversation the discordant and untutored tongues of so many nations, to bestow civilization upon the human race – in short, to become a single homeland for all peoples throughout the world.

These visionary ecumenical words come not from an emperor, but from one of the empire's functionaries, Pliny the Elder. Pliny was a friend of Vespasian; it was to Vespasian's son Titus that Pliny dedicated, in AD 77, a remarkable book called the *Naturalis historia*. Scientifically it is undistinguished: Pliny's military and administrative career gave him little time for his own enquiries into 'natural history', even if he had been inclined to that sort of Aristotelian research. A nephew – another Pliny, and so known as Pliny the Younger – left an affectionate account of how scholarly pursuits combined with his uncle's busy public life. While eating, bathing and travelling, the older Pliny found time to collect information. Indeed, he was probably still doing so when he died, in August AD 79, asphyxiated by fumes from the eruption of Vesuvius. (He was commanding a naval rescue mission, but seems to have lingered out of curiosity to witness the volcanic spectacle.) His *Natural History*, containing some 20,000 useful facts culled from 2,000 volumes (the estimate is Pliny's own), was not his only work, but it is the only survivor. Copyists were presumably drawn to the thirty-seven volumes because of the apparent comprehensive scope of the project. Our term 'encyclopedia' comes from a Greek phrase, *enkyklios paideia*, 'all-round education', but Pliny lays the chief claim to have produced an ancient encyclopedia. Information in the *Natural History* may not always be lodged where the modern reader expects it to be – Pliny's reports on Greek sculptors and architects, for example, are inserted into sections dealing with various metals and stones – and criteria for distinguishing facts from hearsay are not very evident. Beyond offering answers to questions of general intellectual curiosity, however – how *do* hedgehogs perform sexual intercourse? – the *Natural History* gives us a particular insight into Roman imperialism.

Partly this comes from the obvious nexus between war, conquest and knowledge: what Pliny knows about elephants, for example (including the unproven 'fact' that they are scared of mice), clearly comes from Roman experience of elephants in war, and Roman control over territories where elephants are found (and can be transported to Rome for public shows). But there is a palpable tension between pride of possession and shame of affluence. Pliny wants Rome to dominate the natural resources of the world; yet he deplores the vanities and luxuries arising from access to such bounty. So, while dedicating the book to Titus, he says he wants it to be read by Italy's farmers. Do they especially need to know about hedgehogs and elephants? No: but this is Pliny's way of tracking the historical process recounted here. Rome was once a community of frugal smallholders by the Tiber; now it dominates the world. By itemizing what can be known of this Rome-dominated world, Pliny's implicit message is one of austere congratulation: Romans, regard the fruit of your labours – but remember who you are by simple origin.

IX
EPHESUS

Many Romans settled at Ephesus on the coast of Asia Minor, one of Rome's most prosperous provinces. Formerly a Greek settlement, then handsomely rebuilt in Hellenistic times, the city was part of the Attalid bequest to Rome. But it 'belonged' to Rome also by mythological ratification. Ephesus lay within the region known as the Troad – the territory supposed once to have been the ancient realm of Troy. During the epic fall of Troy, Aeneas had left with the promise of return. And so it became fashionable for Romans to do just that – to relocate to the land of their distant forebears. The discovery of a block of houses terraced into a hillside at Ephesus shows in what grand style they here created their 'home from home'.

Thousands of visitors to Ephesus regularly disembark from ships at the Turkish port of Kushadasi and are transferred by bus to the site – once itself a port city, but like other sites along this coast moved inland by river silt. The presence of a daily throng – served, or tolled, by local traders – animates the ruins. The impression of a 'living' city is furthered by the partial reconstruction of some of those ruins: most strikingly, a two-storey library dating to the early second century AD, whose colonnaded façade includes niches for statues of personifications appropriate to studious pursuit of the reading matter within (some 12,000 scrolls are estimated to have been kept here).

The Roman Empire

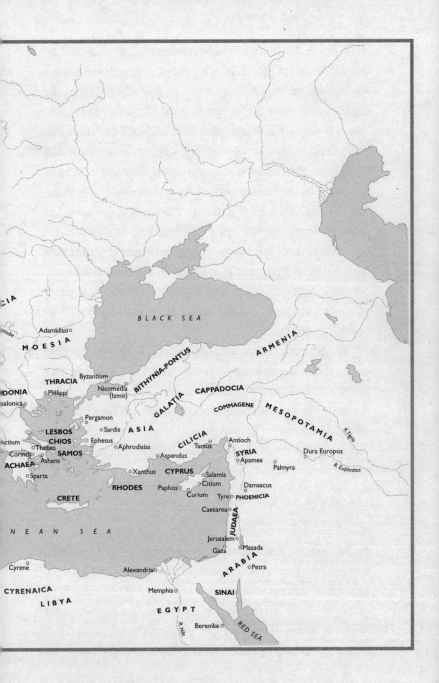

Wisdom, Virtue and Understanding are represented by three decorously robed female figures. A fourth symbolizes Knowledge or Expertise as it was possessed by Celsus, the individual sponsor of this building (which is also his tomb). This Celsus, a Roman senator and regional administrator, evidently provided funds sufficient not only to construct the library, but also to continue its operation; an inscription adds, for example, the requirement that the statues are to be regularly adorned with fresh garlands. How much was added in financial terms by the son of Celsus, responsible for this commemorative project, is not clear; but in any case the benefaction was, as it remains, prominent in the urban experience. Set on a right-angle turn of the city's main street, it either offered an island of calm or made reading, like shopping, part of the daily routine.

The Romans took some justifiable pride in their tradition here: Julius Caesar, it was said, had planned a public library for Rome, and the first was established a decade or so after his death by Asinius Pollio. Known as the Atrium Libertatis, 'Hall of Freedom', this was funded by the spoils of war, yet consciously devoted to peaceful pursuits, and above all it was accessible and wide-ranging – it is possible, for example, that the poet Ovid was here able to read the Book of Genesis in its Greek (Septuagint) version. Texts and documents had been stored in democratic Athens and in the Hellenistic courts, but the ideology of general availability belongs to late republican Rome. Unrestricted access may be doubted, but at least the location of a Roman library was typically not recondite. The emperor Trajan placed one in the midst of his eponymous forum in Rome – imaginatively reconstructed, it looks rather like a grandiose nineteenth-century reading room; his successor Hadrian gave Athens, 'city of culture' par excellence, a library that stood conspicuously within view of the temples on the Acropolis; while at Thamugadi (Timgad) in the highlands of Algeria the library endowed by one Rogatianus occupied an entire block (*insula*) of a gridded colonial city – remote, but by no means cut off from the world of learning.

So the Library of Celsus at Ephesus makes a statement of civic identity. At the same time it honours an individual. What connects the two functions is the custom of euergetism or 'doing good'. The origins of this custom may lie with an archaic aristocratic or monarchical virtue of liberal munificence, but it was during the third century BC that it developed into an overtly civic institution, especially in the eastern Mediterranean. A well-to-do citizen, male or female, contributed cash or services in kind to some project that would embellish the city, or in some way enhance the lives of its citizens, thus earning the title of *euergetes*, 'benefactor'. A statue, set upon a base inscribed with grateful sentiment and placed in some public venue, was the standard acknowledgement of such generosity.

In many cities, occasional endowments were evident immediately upon entry, as some monumental arch or gateway was set up, often to mark an imperial sojourn (Trajan and Hadrian, in particular, were 'on tour' for much of their time as emperors). At Ephesus, the coincidence of local initiative and blessing from Rome is made apparent throughout the city. The details of one obvious example, signposted on the main thoroughfare as the Nymphaeum or Fountain of Trajan, are instructive. 'Nymphaeum', a 'place of nymphs', though perhaps appropriate to its ornamental decoration

– including a statue of Aphrodite holding a shell – makes the structure sound rather frivolous: it would otherwise be more prosaically known as a *hydragogeion*, a 'water terminal'. Though not the first such public fountain in Ephesus, it was doubtless a welcome addition to the range of urban amenities (or, as we might judge, utilities) in a site where no rain falls throughout the summer months. And at first sight, it must certainly have seemed 'of Trajan', for a colossal statue of the emperor once dominated the scene (a single foot remains). But an inscription partially preserved on the two-tier façade leaves onlookers with no doubt that it was not the emperor but his delegate in Asia, one Claudius Aristion, who with his wife Julia Laterane funded this project *ek ton idion*, implying 'from personal funds': not only the 'fountain', but also an aqueduct bringing water from the Lesser Meander river some 20 miles (32 km) away. The couple, who both held priestly offices, dedicated their benefaction jointly to Artemis, goddess of Ephesus, to Trajan, and to 'the fatherland'. So the nexus of local, imperial and cosmic order was confirmed.

· · ·

From Ephesus to the Highlands of Scotland is, to put it gently, a change of scene. Both were part of the same empire: but no Roman legions were ever garrisoned at Ephesus, or indeed along coastal Asia Minor generally, while Scotland under the Romans offers a landscape of forts, marching camps and a barrier made of stone and turf. The Roman name for the indigenous Celtic inhabitants was Picti, 'the painted (or tattooed) ones'; it was in the mid-second century AD that the so-called Antonine Wall was constructed west–east between two deep inlets (the Firth of Clyde and the Firth of Forth) in order to keep these Picts or Caledonians confined to the mountainous north. The emperor giving his name to this defensive policy was Antoninus Pius, adoptive successor to the more flamboyant Hadrian; no doubt he was attempting to signal a territorial advance upon Hadrian's Wall, created just two decades earlier as a frontier of 73 miles (117 km) and consisting not only of a high stone wall and ramparts, but also of a defensive ditch and a system of gates and watch-towers. It may have been in this part of the empire that the Ninth Legion disappeared, perhaps lured into a wholesale massacre. The excavation of hundreds of wooden writing tablets from the frontier fort of Vindolanda, however, yields only information about the more humdrum details of maintaining guard: turns of duty, ordering supplies and so on. Some soldiers seem to have been stationed at Hadrian's Wall with their families; others had to write home with requests for extra layers of clothing.

It happened that one of the governors of Britain in the late first century AD, Agricola, was the father-in-law of one of Rome's most distinguished writers and historians, Cornelius Tacitus. Tacitus is best known for his accounts of the imperial court at Rome from the death of Augustus until the Flavian dynasty – the *Histories* and *Annals*, written in a critical spirit and a highly distinctive compressed Latin style. Tacitus writes with a gravitas we do not find in Suetonius, but like Suetonius he presents a sequence of more or less damnable characters at the centre of power: the slippery Tiberius, the unhinged Caligula, the bumbling Claudius, and so on; Augustus appears only tolerable by comparison. Two short works by Tacitus, by contrast, look out to the periphery of empire. One is the *Germania*, an ethnological study of Celtic tribes to the north of the Rhine and Danube. Though tending towards stereotype, this picture of the 'Germans' – tough, forest-dwelling, hard-drinking, belligerent, proud – has served various phases of modern German nationalism.

The other is the *Agricola*, ostensibly an essay in family biography. Agricola as subject remains enigmatic, and his campaign to make the whole of Britain secure as a Roman possession enjoyed no lasting success; yet a particular battle in the Grampian Mountains gave Tacitus an irresistible opportunity to imagine Roman imperialism as viewed by indigenous peoples – in this case, an alliance of northern tribes formed to resist not only Agricola's legions but also the Roman fleet, which had apparently extended its navigational reach to the Shetland Islands (already known as Ultima Thule). The speech crafted by Tacitus on behalf of the local leader is a resounding call to arms; at its core is the following summary of Rome's menace:

> Global predators, having stripped the land with their pillage, now they ransack the sea. If their enemy is rich, their motive is greed; if poor, sheer lust for power. East, west, nothing satisfies them: they must be the only people who covet wealth and poverty alike. They plunder, slaughter and steal, all in the name of empire: they create a desert and they call it peace.

These urgent words lead us to a topic of radical debate about the nature of the Roman empire. Broadly, it turns on the question: were the Romans motivated by the acquisition of raw materials, slaves and taxable subjects – or did they act upon a vision of 'civilization' extended across continents for mutual benefit? To the well-known phrase of modern comedy, 'What have the Romans done for us?', we may add the oft-cited lines of Virgil's *Aeneid*: 'Roman, called to rule over others, remember that this is your craft: to impose custom upon peace, bring justice to your subjects, and disarm the tyrant.' It is debatable whether this vocation gave licence for the sort of local government prevailing at places like Ephesus by the first century BC, with tax-farmers ('publicans', or *publicani*) purchasing the right, by five-year lease, to gather dues on all sorts of activities. Archaeologically, however, there can be little doubt on the matter. Wherever they went, the Romans invested in infrastructure. True, such infrastructure facilitated military operations. But roads were not only, nor even primarily, for troop movements; when it came to building aqueducts, or laying out a system of urban drainage, the Romans were proudly conscious that such 'civil engineering' was part of their national identity. Observed by Greek writers within the empire (notably Strabo and Polybius), it became something of a truism.

The sentiment is nowhere better expressed than in the prelude to one of the least readable of surviving Latin texts, the treatise *De aquis* ('Of Water[works]'), by Julius Frontinus, appointed *curator aquarum*, 'water overseer', by Trajan's predecessor Nerva in AD 97. A former governor of Britain, Frontinus seems to have taken his responsibilities for Rome's water supply very seriously, informing himself of copious technical details involved in hydraulic engineering – gauges, settling tanks, and so on – and priding himself on rising to the administrative task. Prior to collating the details, however, he cannot resist eulogizing the glorious combination of *splendor* and *utilitas* embodied in a Roman aqueduct – and comparing it to the huge yet peculiarly 'pointless' pyramids of Egypt, or the many much admired 'masterpieces' created by the Greeks. He hardly needs to extend the appeal to commonsense approval. Given the choice of a pretty marble statue or a ready supply of fresh drinking water, who would hesitate?

• • •

Thirsty pedestrians at Ephesus did not need to make the choice: fresh water and elegant statuary came together. Elsewhere in the empire, the connection between Romans and water can be significant in other ways. A good example is the site of Aquae Sulis in Roman Britain. Its modern name, Bath, is enough to indicate a reason for Romans establishing a temple there. Hot springs – geologically unique in Britain – were an obvious attraction. Indigenous Celts are thought to have kept some kind of shrine at the springs. However, the monumental development of facilities for 'taking the waters' was Roman, and took place within a few decades of the Roman conquest of Britain in AD 43. In the east of the country there was violent revolt led by Boadicea (or Boudicca), queen of the Iceni tribe. In the west, sufficient accord between Romans and locals allowed the creation of Aquae Sulis as a spa sanctuary where two deities enjoyed joint veneration. One was Minerva, the Etrusco-Roman version of Athena; the other was the Celtic goddess Sulis. A small temple in the Corinthian order was erected, and sculptors brought over from north-east Gaul added decoration in local sandstone – rough by classical standards, but done with a certain vigour and symbolic insight – including, for example, an owl for Minerva.

'Sulis' is Celtic for 'eye': as well as being a genius of the place, the goddess Sulis may have been worshipped as all-seeing, to judge by a number of objects recovered from the reservoir at the site. These are 'curse tablets' – pieces of lead inscribed with denunciations of some crime against person or property. Petty theft is the most common complaint, but pleas are made for dire and bloody revenge. Though Latin is the usual language of the curse, Sulis is the deity to whom the appeal for justice is made. So the site was host to a sort of ethnic and religious fusion.

'Syncretism' is the proper term for such mixed cult practice, and it occurred elsewhere. In Gaul, for example, the Romans added formal architecture to a sanctuary in honour of Sequana, who presided over the springs that were sources of the river Seine, rising to the north of Dijon, in Burgundy. Large quantities of votive sculptures, mostly in wood and stone, and many representing human body parts, indicate that this was a place of pilgrimage for the physically afflicted. It flourished as such for some five centuries – before closure by a Christian emperor.

Further south in Gaul, a spring was originally one of the natural features that gave its identity to the Roman colony of Nemausus (Nîmes). But this local source was inadequate for the town's development, so an aqueduct was constructed that brought water from mountains some 30 miles (over 50 km) to the north. The gradient sustained over the distance was remarkably subtle – and certainly not discernible to the eyes of anyone gazing at the best-known monument of this aqueduct, as it crosses a river on three tiers of arches: the Pont du Gard.

Trajan's wife Plotina came from Nîmes. The region was simply known as 'Provincia nostra', 'our province' (whence, eventually, 'Provence'). Roman-controlled territory was never so expansive as it was at the time of Trajan's death, in AD 117. Trajan personally vouchsafed a policy of accommodation between Roman rule and local customs. But was such a 'relaxed' attitude enough to hold an empire spread over several continents?

• • •

Imperial territories as 'stabilized' in the mid-second century AD were demarcated by a combination of natural and artificial limits. Schoolroom maps tend to create a misleadingly neat overview of this geography, arguably remote from Roman ideals of an *imperium sine fine*, an 'unlimited empire'. Still, boundaries were necessary, if only for the practicalities of jurisdiction and taxation. To the west, the entire Iberian peninsula (Hispania) was kept by a single legionary fort. Gaul (Gallia) required no military presence (Asterix and his friends remain a comic-strip fantasy). As noted, Britain (Britannia) was not much 'Romanized' beyond its southern parts; Ireland (Hibernia) lay entirely without. Central Europe was divided by a heavily fortified frontier along the rivers Rhine and Danube, including a masonry wall that extended 342 miles (550 km). Vienna (Vindobona) was one of the frontier camps of a province named Pannonia, stretching southwards to the Balkans. Beyond the Danube, the Carpathian Mountains helped to protect the Roman presence in Dacia. The shores of the Black Sea were surely not so 'barbarous' as Ovid pathetically presented them in his poems of exile: on the Asian side, the region of Bithynia came firmly under Roman control, as indeed did Asia Minor as far as the river Euphrates. Beyond lay the territory of the Parthians, extending as far as the Indus Valley. This was always difficult country for the Romans: a garrison city, Dura-Europos, was installed above the Euphrates in the second century AD; it would not hold, a century or so later, against resurgent Persians. Meanwhile the Middle East – allowing this to comprise, in mixed modern and ancient terms, Syria, Lebanon, Judaea, Jordan and Arabia – was peaceful so long as local populations paid requisite fiscal and religious dues (a difficult condition, predictably). The site of Petra embodies an efficient compromise: capital of the Nabataean kingdom in Arabia, it lay within Rome's empire, yet enjoyed virtual autonomy as a channel of commerce and caravan transit. The signs of its prosperity as a 'client state' are carved into the pink sandstone of Petra's cliff-cut gorge – including a theatre.

There was no canal linking the Arabian Gulf and the Mediterranean, but the Red Sea port of Berenike, established by the Ptolemies, served to connect Rome with India. Roman control of the Nile extended upstream as far as Meroe in the Sudan, between the river's fifth and sixth cataracts. Westwards to Libya, the former Greek colony of Cyrene became capital of the Roman province of Cyrenaica. With spots of habitable land dispersed against a background of parched desert, North Africa was likened to a leopard's skin. The nomadic Berbers plied age-old trade routes across the arid regions, but the Romans promoted olive cultivation where possible. The Libyan coastline they knew as Tripolitania became an area of intensive farming, defended at the Sahara's northern edge by forts along the contours of the Gebel escarpment. Military headquarters in North Africa were at Lambaesis in Algeria, where barriers were constructed to connect with the natural defence line of the Atlas Mountains. Finally, control of Tingis (Tangiers) in Morocco sealed Roman control of the Mediterranean. They would refer to it as 'Mare nostrum' – 'Our Sea'.

It was Trajan's successor Hadrian who affirmed a policy of concentrating forces at the frontiers of the empire. The flaw in the policy may be obvious: if Rome's barbarian enemies were once able to breach the overstretched defences, they found an interior more or less unprotected and easy to raid. But for the best part of a century there was security, during the age of the Antonines – when, according to one influential opinion, 'the empire of Rome comprehended the fairest part of the earth, and the most civilized portion of mankind'.*

• • •

Pax Romana – the beneficent peace that Rome, in Virgil's vision, was destined to impose – still has its apologists. But of course the story varies, and not only according to the teller. Regional differences are quite enough to dapple our panorama of the Roman empire; perhaps it does not surprise the modern reader to learn that one area never 'pacified' was that part of the Middle East known (to the ancient Greeks and others) as Palestine.

Rome – led by Pompey – intervened among disputing claimants of the Hasmonean (or Hashmon) monarchy in 63 BC (the so-called 'Maccabean Revolt' against Seleucid rule

---

* The voice is that of Edward Gibbon, of whom we shall have more to say in the next chapter.

in the second century BC established not only a new priestly class, the Pharisees, but also a local dynasty). With Roman support (first from Mark Antony, then from Augustus), a certain Herod was declared 'King of the Jews'. Herod was able to maintain pro-Roman rule for three decades, and the Romans had their own name for his kingdom (Judaea). His building programme included not only 'Italianate' palaces and fortresses for himself, but the handsome Mediterranean port of Caesarea and a substantial reconstruction of Solomon's temple in Jerusalem. If this endowment to the central place of Jewish worship was intended to win Herod favour among the Jews, it failed. Herod's 'classical' sympathies – he was also a generous benefactor to the Olympic Games – were too much by way of compromise. Whether he ordered a massacre of baby boys at Bethlehem, for fear of a rival, is not attested beyond the New Testament Gospel of St Matthew. But Herod ('the Great') was a murderous type, and left an uneasy succession on his death in 4 BC. The problem of Jewish resentment of even 'indirect' Roman rule persisted. Matthew's Gospel also records how a group of Pharisees tested one potential rebel in the region with the question of whether resistance to taxes was justified. The response from this rebel – Jesus, from Nazareth in the district of Galilee – was to call for a Roman coin, ask (rhetorically) whose image and name were inscribed upon it, and recommend that everyone render unto Caesar that which was Caesar's: an elegantly evasive retort.

Jesus was put to death by order of the Roman procurator, or provincial governor, Pontius Pilatus, around AD 30. Although chronologically imprecise, the biblical accounts of this event are sensitive to the awkward distribution of power between local dynasty (another Herod) and Roman imperial delegate. Which of them should deal with this mysteriously inoffensive rebel, nominated in some quarters as a would-be King of the Jews?

Before long, during the time of Claudius, the Romans dismissed their Herodian client kings. But provincial governors fared no better alone. Beyond three existing Jewish factions in Roman Judaea – Pharisees, Sadducees and Essenes – a fourth developed, a sect of religious extremists that became known simply as the Zealots. By AD 66, the Zealots were engaged in active confrontation with the Romans. Our main source for the history of this movement is an unusual author within the classical canon, Flavius Josephus. A Pharisee, Josephus was one of the local Jewish authorities in Galilee when the Zealots' revolt broke out. Surviving its vicissitudes, he later became resident in Rome, where he wrote (in Aramaic, then in Greek) his histories, culminating in a compendious volume of *Jewish Antiquities*.

Josephus does not report a concerted and sustained 'grand strategy' on the part of the Romans: this appears only in retrospect, as wishful thinking among latter-day historians in search of synthesis. But one recurrent element of Roman imperial policy, as Josephus and others knew, was that of punitive vengeance. Not for nothing was the Roman god of war customarily hailed as Mars Ultor – Mars the Avenger. In Judaea the avenging principle had already been demonstrated when Titus, commanding the Roman army sent to crush the Zealots' uprising, captured Jerusalem in AD 70, and allowed or presided over the looting and destruction of the Great Temple. The action can hardly have been an accident, nor even spontaneous: huge quantities of timber must have been locally gathered to fuel such a holocaust. Nor, seemingly, was Titus at all ashamed of it: his triumphal funerary arch erected on the slopes of the Palatine Hill shows the Menorah, the seven-pronged golden candelabrum precious to Hebrew identity since the time of Moses, being carried shoulder-high as booty.

But for full expression of Roman vindictiveness there is nothing to match what happened afterwards. Many Jews were expelled from their homeland. But a relatively small contingent of Zealots – numbering 960 by the account of Josephus, if women and children were included – retreated to the Judaean desert. Their refuge was Masada, an outcrop by the Dead Sea, fortified a century earlier by Herod the Great and once used by the Romans as a minor garrison. The site was almost impregnable, yet so isolated as to present hardly any threat to the Roman administration of Judaea. Nonetheless, the Roman governor Flavius Silva decided to make an example of Masada. He marched across the desert with an entire legion (the Tenth) and set up a series of camps around the lofty fortress. Thousands of Jewish prisoners of war were put to work alongside auxiliary troops in establishing a supply line. Then, in clear view of the Zealots above, the legionaries commenced their labours of laying a siege. First they threw a wall and ditch around the site: no one was going to escape. Then they set about constructing their means of access to the top. Ladders and siege-towers would never work. So the Romans more or less moved a mountain: that is, they heaped a massive ramp of soil and rocks against Masada's western cliff.

There were of course no bulldozers. The task took the best part of three years. In the meantime, the Zealots confined on the plateau summit could do little but observe a laborious feat of engineering. Thanks to a covering of fertile soil and Herod's provision of ingenious conduits and cisterns to collect such rainwater as might fall, they were able to sustain themselves. But their doom was all too obvious. The acoustics of the site made it possible for the Romans to announce, day by day and without shouting, what fate had in store – as if there were any doubt.

Josephus, with undisguised admiration, transmits what took place among the rebels as the end approached, in AD 74. Their leader, Eleazer ben Ya'ir, spoke of the absolute need to astonish the Romans. There were (he reasoned) fates worse than death: the degradations of slavery and rape. So he exhorted members of the community to make their own end. The men must kill their wives and children, then draw lots for the killing of each other. The last man left was to set fire to the site and run himself through.

Two old women, along with a few children, stayed hidden in an underground recess while the mutual slaughter took place. These few survivors eventually gave Josephus the basis for his account: for otherwise the Romans, battering their way into the stronghold, found only a charred pile of bodies – and were duly amazed, even saddened, by the sight.

The site of Masada remains a peculiarly raw archaeological experience: the historical record of what happened there seems written in the sand and stone. Following an excavation in the 1960s led by Yigael Yadin, variously a distinguished Israeli army commander, politician and university professor, the fastness and its surrounds appear to corroborate all that Josephus reports (though human remains discovered so far do not tally to anything like 900). And as an obstinate bastion ringed around by hostile encampments, Masada has become somewhat emblematic of Israel as a modern state; oaths of allegiance are sworn there by young citizens called up for national service.

But why did the Romans spend so much time, effort and military expertise upon Masada? It can hardly have been because – as Yigael Yadin supposed – these Zealot families constituted a serious threat to provincial law and order. The place was too remote and disconnected. The strategic motive reduces, then, to one of exemplary punishment. By leaving 'no stone unturned' in pursuit of these discontents in Judaea, the Romans intended to issue a warning to would-be rebels across the empire: even the desert gave no place of escape.

• • •

A similar message is visually relayed by the spiral narrative carved on Trajan's Column in the centre of Rome. Rising almost 40 metres (130 ft) high, the monument – with an inner stairwell – seems to have been intended, when first raised in AD 113, to provide a vantage point for an overview of the levelling involved in the construction of Trajan's Forum nearby. Its base then became the tomb of Trajan, who died in Cilicia, on his way home from an ambitious attempt to extend the empire's eastern frontier. 'Ambitious' means that Trajan's policy of attacking the Parthians is thought, at least with hindsight, ill-judged. All the same he was an outstanding emperor, *optimus princeps*, in the eyes of the Senate, and to be venerated accordingly. Possibly it was thanks to his imaginative successor Hadrian that the exterior of the column became a decorated scroll, showing how Trajan had secured the region of Dacia for Rome. A visual record of that process would surely have been made by artists 'embedded' with Trajan's army, and worked up into paintings to be displayed at the occasion of triumph back in Rome: deposited in archives, such paintings may have been the source for the bas-reliefs of the column. Trajan himself wrote an account of the Dacian Wars – it has not survived, but was probably modelled on Julius Caesar's Gallic *Commentaries*. In any case, the frieze – which would extend about 200 metres if 'unrolled' – has been hailed as a masterpiece of 'continuous narrative'. Its sculptors remain anonymous. Yet they knew, whoever they were, that the Roman empire was essentially not built upon winning battles. Iconographic tallies testify as much: of the 155 scenes identified within this narrative of war, just eighteen show outright hostilities.

Historical background is assumed. Dacia, roughly equivalent to the territory of modern Romania, had been a troublesome region for Domitian, whose attempts towards 'pacification' in the late 80s AD had brought to prominence a redoubtable local leader who took the name of Decebalus. The Romans guardedly acknowledged Decebalus as a client king, but he evidently resented such subordinate status. In the spring of AD 101, Trajan – having become emperor in AD 98 after a distinguished military career – launched the first of his campaigns to assert Roman authority over an increasingly independent Dacia.

The story as told upon Trajan's Column begins along the river Danube, where we see there is a Romanized city prepared for Dacian attack, with piles of wood and straw ready to light beacons of alarm. The sense of impending danger is immediately set. However, the Roman army, led by

Trajan, is mobilized and about to begin its offensive by crossing the river. A pontoon bridge of boats has been constructed, and standard-bearers are stepping across, leading files of Praetorian guards and legionaries. The soldiers carry, rather than wear, their helmets for the march. Soon we will see them establishing a marching camp, unloading tents from a baggage train, fetching water, and so on. So the rhythm of the sculpture proceeds. It is of course a partisan monument: the fighting will happen, and the Romans will win. Nevertheless Trajan's Column shows the Roman army as convincingly invincible, as much on account of its logistical preparation as by dint of valour in battle. One important detail is shown early on – that is, at a height where any groundling viewer may absorb its importance. An engagement has taken place, and the Romans have sustained casualties: we see the wounded being brought to a field dressing station, and their injuries tended. Close by is the emperor; though he is shown about to deal with a Dacian captive, there is no doubt that as *imperator* he has already taken care to provide hospitals for his own troops.

Trajan appears sixty-odd times on the reliefs, usually flanked by two deputies. He will not be shown leading a cavalry charge, nor glamorized as if a second Alexander: dressed in the same basic garb as a legionary, his features and physique are distinctly unexceptional. Yet his presence is pervasive, and his ubiquity significant. Whether conducting sacrifice, addressing the ranks, receiving embassies or inspecting communication forts behind the front line, Trajan is completely involved and pivotal to the success of the war.

Viewers with an eye for detail will notice how much of the fighting is delegated to auxiliaries – Syrian archers, for example

– and again, as Romans, feel grateful to Trajan for the implied value he puts on preserving the lives of legionaries (always distinctively attired in the *lorica segmentata* – a cuirass with overlapping metal pieces). With some visual effort, viewers might also observe that there is a 'pause' in the narrative approximately halfway up the column. This marks a truce agreed after two years of fighting, whereby Decebalus was allowed to continue as king, but with his powers limited and a tribute payable. The terms of the pact were soon broken, so Trajan was obliged to resume operations in AD 105. This time he set out for conquest: the destruction of the Dacian capital, Sarmizegethusa, and capture of Decebalus.

Decebalus shared at least one determination with the Zealots at Masada: he would not be taken prisoner and exhibited, grovelling for mercy, at Rome. A scene close to the top of the column shows Roman cavalry closing upon the Dacian leader in a forest, just too late to prevent him from cutting his own throat. The sequel lies beyond the column's helical scope. Dacia is annexed as a province, and Trajan gains not only a very rich hoard of gold and silver treasure amassed by Decebalus, but access to exploit rich mineral seams in the Transylvanian mountains. Decebalus survives as a Romanian national hero, his bearded features now carved on a colossal scale in cliffs above the Danube near Orshova. There is no doubting, however, the primary message of Trajan's Column.

• • •

It was as well that Dacia yielded riches, for Trajan had committed himself to some expensive public projects at home, most notably the enlargement of Rome's maritime gateway near Ostia in the Tiber delta. Known simply as Portus ('Harbour'), this was transformed into a hexagonal docking area over thirty-two hectares in extent (the size of an average Roman city), complete with ship-sheds, canals and enormous storage facilities for the consumer goods and raw materials brought to Rome from the Mediterranean. The scale of the project (initiated by Claudius) is captured by Aelius Aristides, a Greek orator from Asia Minor:

> Around [the Mediterranean] lie the continents far and wide, pouring an endless flow of goods to you [Rome]. Delivered from every land and sea comes whatever is brought forth by the seasons and is produced by all countries, rivers, lakes, and the skills of Greeks and foreigners... So many ships arrive here with cargoes from all over, throughout the year, and with each return of the harvest, that the city seems like a communal warehouse of the world.

Most of the goods were perishable by nature and have left no traces; yet archaeology confirms that this eulogy of Rome's worldwide commercial network was not exaggerated.*

The city's population in the early second century AD would have been about a million. An army of about 400,000 men also had to be maintained, of course: some thirty legions, comprising about 165,000 citizen soldiers, were deployed around the empire, along with an even greater number of auxiliaries (who were given citizenship upon

---

* The project's unique geometric design and its sheer scale are best assessed if approaching Rome (on a clear day) in an aeroplane bound for Fiumicino airport.

discharge). Some idea of the logistical scale of operations can be glimpsed from surviving supply structures at (for example) the naval base at Misenum, not far from Naples. But perhaps the clearest view of Rome's imperial 'reach' comes from a celebrated semi-private residence: Hadrian's so-called Villa at Tivoli.

Located at a discreet distance along the Anio river, north-east of Rome – perhaps so the emperor, unlike Nero, might not seem to have annexed prime residential real estate within the city – the villa precincts extend some eighty hectares, with buildings so large they can hardly be absorbed all at once. At least some of the structures may have been designed by Hadrian himself: as a young man he had tried his hand at architecture, only to be scornfully told by Trajan's official architect, Apollodorus, that his plans looked like pumpkins. Inevitably, Apollodorus did not survive the transition from Trajan to Hadrian, and at Tivoli Hadrian was able to indulge some fantasy. Work began in AD 118, just a year after his succession; much was completed within a decade, but builders were busy there up until the emperor's death in AD 138.

The family of Hadrian's wife Sabina appear to have been landowners in the district, which – despite its sulphurous fumes – was considered a healthy resort for well-to-do Romans. Yet Hadrian's intention here can never have been just a retreat – a place of leisure (*otium*) distinct from business (*negotium*) or 'not-leisure' (*nec-otium*). The villa indeed includes a vast colonnaded courtyard, for long philosophical walks; a 'maritime theatre', where dinner might be taken with a view of waterborne entertainment; and several elaborate follies evocative of imperial travels in Greece, the Middle East and Egypt, such as a reconstruction of the canal connecting

Alexandria to Canopus in the Nile Delta, and a replica of the temple (and statue) of Aphrodite at Knidos. But there were also substantial reception areas, offices, barracks and store-rooms. These suggest that the emperor did not remove himself from duties in Rome; rather, his 'administration', up to 1,000 strong, came with him to Tivoli. A half-day's journey from the capital, it may have seemed a world away. There was not so much as a perimeter fence by way of enclosure. But the impression of picturesque isolation, furthered by Romantic experience of the site, is deceptive. With Hadrian in residence, this was the centre of power.

The complex was slightly used by Hadrian's immediate successors – Antoninus, Marcus Aurelius, Commodus – but fell into disrepair thereafter. Much was robbed before a learned pope (Pius II) visited in 1461 and began a process of archaeological salvage that continues still. One twentieth-century scholar who became fascinated with the site and its creator was the French Academician Marguerite Yourcenar, whose empathy extended to her imaginative reconstruction of the *Memoirs of Hadrian*. Alas, just a few lines of elegiac verse survive from Hadrian's own hand, and we can only speculate as to his intentions and personality. 'Graeculus' ('Greekling') was his nickname, and his predilection for Greek culture extended unashamedly (it seems) to pederastic fondness for a boy called Antinous. This Antinous accompanied Hadrian on his official travels; it was on one such journey, sailing down the Nile in AD 130, that the young favourite drowned. It may have been an accident – though Hadrian's enemies did not think so; in any case, the emperor made a prodigal show of grief, founding a city in Egypt called Antinoöpolis and instituting cults of the deified Antinous across the empire. The legacy is a remarkable series of post-humous statues and portraits, now to be seen in museums around the world, commemorating youthful good looks that are both typically classical and yet particular. The 'bee-stung' lips of Antinous are invariably set in a pout, and his features are sometimes downcast as if he is aware of premature doom; too soft in form to pass as a champion athlete, he nevertheless assimilates to a type of Apollo and may even be dressed in the guise of another god.

• • •

At Tivoli Hadrian showed how an emperor might encap-sulate, in rustic Latium, the cosmopolitan grandeur of Roman power. He was not, however, complacent: he reacted swiftly, for example, to another Jewish rebellion, in AD 132–5 (the Bar Kochba revolt), slaughtering many thousands of insurgents and expelling the Jews from Jerusalem (which he renamed the Roman city of Aelia Capitolina). On his coins he claimed the title *Restitutor orbis terrarum*, 'Restorer of lands worldwide'. His Antonine successors might with some sincerity declare that Hadrian had left the empire confirmed in its wonderful magnitude. A temple dedicated to the Deified Hadrian – since absorbed into Rome's old stock exchange – featured a series of relief-carved plinths showing some twenty-five personified provinces: female figures in generally docile attitudes, including a subdued, seated Britannia, and Gallia folding her arms in placid contentment. It must then have seemed incon-ceivable that Rome herself could ever feel threatened.

Rome began with a simple palisade (or two); the city limits expanded as the empire grew, with various ways of marking its boundaries. The great brick-built defence walls visible today – particularly well preserved in their south-eastern section, by the exits of the Via Appia and Via Latina, and in the modern mind's eye still representative of Rome as a city – were erected in the AD 270s, in the time of the emperor Aurelian. Their dimensions (some 7 metres high and 3.5 metres thick, with regular projecting watch-towers) and extent (making a circuit of just over 12 miles, or almost 19 km) imply a huge public spending project, presumably giving employment to thousands of local labourers. The enclosure was also a means of raising revenues, since control of the gateways facilitated the levy of duties on goods coming in and out of the city. Aurelian tried, during his brief reign, to reverse the shortfalls in the imperial budget: he was not content, as some of his predecessors seem to have been, simply to reduce the amount of silver contained in a silver *denarius*. But defence of the imperial capital did indeed become necessary, as the potential flaw within Hadrian's defence policy duly materialized. Two major barbarian incursions into northern Italy during the mid-third century gave the people of Rome proper reason to fear a direct assault – the more so when troops were called away to deal with a revolt in the east led by the warrior-queen Zenobia (al-Zabba) of Palmyra. There Aurelian prevailed. Nevertheless Rome became one of a number of cities across the empire, including Antioch, Athens, Bordeaux, Thessaloniki and Verona, fortified or refortified during this period.

• • •

The story of the 'decline and fall of the Roman empire' awaits our final chapter. For some historians the necessary prelude to that story lies with the rise of Christianity: the threat to Rome essentially coming not from hordes of belligerent barbarians, but from recruits to an ostensibly eirenic sect. But in any case an episode recounted in the New Testament gives us reason to return to the city of Ephesus, where – in the course of his mission to spread the Christian message – we find the apostle Paul around AD 54. The Acts of the Apostles records that he spent about two years there, disputing with Greek philosophers, ministering to the sick, preaching the 'word of the Lord' to both Greeks and Jews locally – and organizing bonfires of their books.

Paul's activities, as might be expected, caused some controversy. The Jewish community at Ephesus, long established, expressly distanced itself from him. Among the Greeks was a craftsman called Demetrios, who specialized in making miniature silver shrines of Artemis. He convened an assembly of his fellow craftsmen, and pointed out the threat that this preacher was posing to their livelihoods. A part of Paul's message, Demetrios rightly saw, was that 'there are no gods which are made by hands': if this message gained popular acceptance, not only would local artisans and traders be out of business, but the goddess Artemis, worshipped in Asia and abroad, would be insulted. Ephesus was claimed as the very birthplace of the goddess. Demetrios succeeded in raising an uproar: rallying to the cry 'Great is Artemis of the Ephesians!', a crowd rushed into the theatre at Ephesus in what appears to be an attempt to lynch the missionary.

Partly by virtue of Paul's discretion in lying low and shortly afterwards slipping away to Macedonia, but mostly by the calming invocation of Roman law, the situation was defused. Paul was judged legally blameless of either 'temple robbery' or blasphemy. Anyone coming to this incident with a knowledge of Greek religion, however, will see why Demetrios and other Ephesians were provoked. Theological hostility towards the fabrication of sacred images would not only lead to the demise of an artistic tradition – and a lively trade – but also bring about the eclipse of a long-established deity. The local combination of Artemis with a 'Mistress' or 'Mother Goddess' of greater antiquity (perhaps to be associated with the Anatolian Cybele), and the likely veneration of Artemis as the guardian spirit of the city, can only have made the issue more explosive.

Paul himself presents an interesting case of shifting identity within the Roman empire. Born as a Jewish citizen of Tarsus in Cilicia (whose inhabitants had been granted citizenship by Julius Caesar), he was raised as a strict Pharisee before converting to Christianity. By Paul's own account, this happened while he was on his way to Damascus, in Syria, in search of Christians to arrest and present for trial at Jerusalem. He did not renounce his Roman citizenship on becoming a Christian. On the contrary, he invoked his legal rights as a Roman citizen when necessary (at Ephesus this resort saved his life). Yet by his mission he was at least implicitly challenging the imperial cult – and therefore the personal authority in whose name civil justice was dispensed.

How should the provincial governor respond to such an implicit challenge? The quandary is evoked in the text of a letter written to Trajan by Pliny the Younger around AD 112, while he was serving as senatorial legate in the region of Bithynia (now northern Turkey). Pliny begins by saying he needs the emperor's advice on a matter he has previously not encountered – *de Christianis*, 'about the Christians'. What, in short, was the procedure for dealing with them? Evidently a number of cases have already been brought before him; Pliny also mentions that a list containing names of local Christians has been anonymously published. His present policy is as follows. He asks the suspects if they are indeed Christians. Those confessing to be so are further interrogated, with threat of punishment; if they remain staunch to their belief, Pliny orders them 'to be led away' – whether to prison or worse is not clear. If the accused are Roman citizens, they have to be dealt with by Rome. But evidently this policy is not working, for these Christians seem to be multiplying. In the case of those denying the charge, he has a series of simple tests: he obliges them to pray to the gods in his presence; to worship the emperor's image, and other statues of deities, with libations of wine and incense; and also 'to speak ill of Christ, which they say no true Christian can be forced to do'. Delivering such proofs of innocence, anyone denounced as a Christian may go free. But Pliny's enquiries into the nature of Christian practices have evidently left him puzzled. Beyond non-adherence to the imperial cult, what crimes have they committed? Their custom is to rise early in order to sing hymns *Christo quasi deo*, 'to Christ as if god'. They take vows not to cheat, steal, commit fraud or adultery; they will honour their debts; and when they assemble, they partake only of food that is 'harmless and ordinary'. The most suspicious aspect of their behaviour is that mere serving girls get to offi-ciate as 'ministers'. Pliny summarizes it all as a 'depraved and unrestrained superstition' – yet one that is spreading.

Trajan's reply is brief, firm and dignified. The governor should not start a campaign of persecution. If unrepentant Christians are brought before him, let him punish them according to the laws. But he must ignore anything like surreptitious denunciations: 'such things do not belong to the spirit of our age.'

With hindsight, the emperor's attitude may be seen as dangerously complacent. Perhaps one of his predecessors (Nero, if stories about him can be believed) persecuted Christians; certainly one of his successors (Diocletian) did so. Trajan, while stopping short of condoning outright tolerance, appears not to have registered the sect as a threat to state religion. He did not foresee the time when these Christians, seizing imperial power, would show no such equanimity towards practitioners of pagan cults.

X
CONSTANTINOPLE

The Pliny who encountered Christians in Bithynia was consul at Rome in AD 100 – a considerable achievement for a man of bourgeois family from the shores of Lake Como, even with the aid of his uncle's influence. One of his duties as consul was to give an official speech of praise to the emperor. Pliny's *Panegyric* survives, and is something of a masterclass in adulation, as the virtues of Trajan are cast into strong relief by comparison with one of his blameworthy predecessors (Domitian). Much of the content and tone is now rather nauseating to read, even if history vouches Trajan to have been one of Rome's 'good' emperors. One passage is worth quoting, however, for its nuances of obsequious respect:

> An open tribute to our emperor demands a new form…
> We should flatter him neither as a god, nor a divine being;
> we are not speaking about a tyrant, but a fellow citizen
> [*civis*], not our master but our parent. He is one of us, and
> his special virtue lies in thinking so; never forgetting that
> he is a man while also a ruler of men. Let us then appre-
> ciate our good fortune and prove our worth by our use of
> it, and at the same time remember that there can be no
> merit if greater deference is paid to rulers [*principes*] who
> delight in the servitude of their citizens than those who
> value their liberty.

An emperor's virtues, beyond remembering to be a fellow citizen, were not difficult to define. He should be inspirationally brave as a soldier. He should be sufficiently confident in his power to show mercy (*clementia*) when appropriate. He should know the meaning of justice. And he should embody and display piety – for although, as Pliny remarks, he was not among the gods, the emperor was considered to rule with divine sanction and to mediate with divine will on behalf of all citizens.

Upon his death, an emperor could be added to the list of those officially recognized, on account of their merit, by honours of state veneration. This recognition was effectively the opposite of 'memory damnation' (see page 260): it brought cult status (in the literal sense) that might last centuries. The award of such deification enables us to make a register of which emperors should be historically classed as 'good'. Augustus comes first (and always foremost); then Claudius; then Vespasian and Titus; then Nerva, Trajan, Hadrian, Antoninus Pius and Marcus Aurelius. The consecration of Claudius was lampooned in a work attributed to Seneca, imagining it as a 'pumpkinification'. 'Oh dear. I feel I'm becoming a god', Vespasian is reported to have joked upon his deathbed. But the selectivity of the list is significant. Marcus Aurelius was not the last recipient of the honour. Already we see, however, how delicate was the constitutional basis upon which Rome's empire depended. In retrospect, many historians wonder why this empire collapsed. But it is equally wondrous that it lasted as long as it did – given such uncertainty at the centre of power. This chapter is the story of how that centre could not hold physically, nor ideologically.

• • •

Marcus Aurelius was a Stoic (see page 164), with a reputation
for the wisdom of indifference. But he appears to have been
foolishly partial in pressing the cause of his elder son
Commodus as his successor. Commodus, portrayed as a
villain by ancient historians and in modern film (*Gladiator*),
ruled for over a decade (AD 180–92), and his violent death
precipitated another contest for power. The military unit
closest to the emperor, the so-called Praetorian Guard, first
supported and then dispatched a general called Pertinax.
Army commanders from several parts of the empire made
bids for power. The prize went to Septimius Severus, who at
the time was based in Pannonia – though his birthplace was
the colony of Lepcis, in North Africa (which he duly
aggrandized as a city). Emperor between AD 193 and 211,
Septimius was afterwards deified – a seal upon the
effectiveness, or military efficiency, of his reign. 'Enrich the
soldiers and scorn all other men' was allegedly his deathbed
advice to his sons; the elder, nicknamed Caracalla ('Cloak' –
after a habit of dress), seems to have taken this as a blessing
to have his brother murdered.

Caracalla was himself assassinated in AD 217, to be eventually followed by a young man from Syria with the name of
Heliogabalus (or Elagabalus). Through his mother
Heliogabalus was connected to the Severan family. Senior
members and supporters of the family at Rome may have
thought they could manipulate the youth, who was just fourteen when made emperor. But Heliogabalus had no intention
of being worshipped only posthumously. Born to a hereditary
priesthood of Helios the sun-god, he came to believe he was

that god, and as such demanded immediate and extravagant adoration. We need not enlarge upon his infamy as a teenage pervert; enough to cite his most notorious 'practical joke' – to shower a number of dinner guests with tons of rose petals, so that they suffocated under the cascade. Whether the decadence of Heliogabalus is exaggerated, his unsuitability as emperor was soon acknowledged: he was murdered, at eighteen, by the Praetorian Guard.

Caracalla, definitely not divine material, made one very important change to the empire. His motive for doing so may have been one of economic necessity – the need to bring in more taxes. Or he may have wanted to affirm unity across Rome's assorted territories. Either way, he issued an edict in AD 212 granting Roman citizenship to all free individuals throughout the empire. Already, as described above (page 261), citizenship could be awarded to non-Romans who showed themselves cooperative with Rome, so within the Senate, and therefore within the army command and regional administration, there were Greek, Celtic and Oriental names. Caracalla's edict now made citizenship indiscriminate. Theoretically, then, anyone (male and not a slave) might become emperor.

The key qualifying factor should be immediately added: so long as they were favoured by the army. All the same, emperors appeared in the third century AD from various ethnic and regional backgrounds, and in some cases from obscure and humble social origins. Maximinus (AD 235–8) was a burly peasant from Thrace; Philip (AD 244–9) an Arab; Aemilianus (AD 253) a Moor. These and many other names crowd the third century; some held power for only a few months, or less. We have already noted the action taken by a mid-third-century emperor, Aurelian (AD 270–5), in constructing a massive circuit of walls around Rome – a symptom, for some historians, that the empire was crumbling. Certainly it seemed ungovernable by a single emperor based in Rome. In AD 284 a soldier from Dalmatia, Diocletian, who had risen through the ranks, took charge, and he did not even visit the city until he had been in office for over a decade. It was Diocletian who in AD 293 constructed a system of tetrarchy – 'four-man rule'. The empire was bisected east and west, and two rulers assigned to each half. The ruling pairs each subdivided into a senior partner (taking the name Augustus) and a junior (taking the name Caesar). Marriages were arranged as a means of cementing loyalties, and it naturally transpired that the four partners maintained separate headquarters. Tellingly, these did not include Rome. In the west, the capitals tended to be Trier, on the Moselle, and Milan; in the east, Sirmium in Pannonia (Serbian Sremska Mitrovica), and Nicomedia (Turkish Izmit) in Asia Minor (it was here that Diocletian kept his court). The unifying factor overall was supposed to be Roman law, enshrined by Roman religion; enforcement of this principle was probably behind the pogrom of Christians in AD 303.

Diocletian himself retired in AD 305, to the palace he had created for himself on the Dalmatian coast, at Split; here, like a Roman of old, he took pride in growing vegetables. His system of having 'seconds-in-command' was presumably designed to facilitate non-hereditary succession. But without Diocletian's forthright presence, the strains of shared power soon showed. A well-known statue in Venice, of tetrarchs embracing each other, was meant to represent the solidarity of the four-man alliance: it is not difficult, however, to imagine each one stabbing another in the back.

Civil war duly ensued. It was the son of one of Diocletian's tetrachs, Constantius, who gained the ascendancy. Constantius had a concubine, Helena, sometimes crudely referred to as 'a barmaid from Albania', and the offspring of this union took a name similar to his father's. This was Constantine, eventually known as 'Constantine the Great'. Anyone gazing at the powerful features of Constantine as they are transmitted by portraits (including two colossal examples in Rome) will believe that concerns about illegitimate birth never clouded the career of this man. He was with his father at York, in AD 306, campaigning in northern Britain, when Constantius died: the troops immediately declared the son for their 'Augustus'. Within a decade, Constantine had reduced the foursome to two, with a famous victory over Maxentius, a rival in the west, by Rome's Milvian Bridge. Within another decade, he had eliminated his remaining colleague Licinius, and so, in AD 324, the empire reverted to a single ruler.

But it was hardly a return to old ways. Like Augustus, Constantine set out to 'refound' Rome. His Rome, however, was to be located in a completely different place – and it was to be the centre of a radically different empire.

• • •

The city of Constantinople was not founded with that name, and officially ceased to be known by it in 1924, when Turkish nationalists insisted upon 'Istanbul'. Once it was a Greek colony, Byzantium. Subject to Persian domination, then Gallic raids, its position on the Bosphorus, as the eastern outpost of continental Europe, gave it an enduring strategic importance. Throughout the Roman period Byzantium prospered, except in the late second century AD when it chose to support a rival to Septimius Severus. Its fortunes recovered when it gained the new identity intended by Constantine, becoming 'New Rome' (*Nea Roma*, in Greek) or 'Rome II' (*Secunda Roma*, in Latin).

Such was Constantine's denomination for the city as chosen by him in AD 324, and formally inaugurated in 330. At that stage it was constitutionally still inferior to the old Rome. Ten years on, it had a Senate and the attendant hierarchy, and institutional aspects modelled on Rome, such as a regular distribution of bread to citizens. Already by then, however, the citizens of New Rome were referring rather to Constantinopolis, 'Constantine's city'. That name persisted, even after conquest by Ottoman Turks in 1453.

The walls of Constantinople, erected in the early fifth century AD, still appear massive where they survive. Once a moat existed too – it is now planted up with salad and herbs – further testimony to a system of defences much tested over the centuries. Within their enclosure, however, the modern visitor has to use a good deal of imagination to conjure up Constantine's fourth-century creation. Scant traces remain of the great imperial palace, and only the shape of an adjacent hippodrome can be discerned. Within this outline there is a circular recess, containing all that survives of a trophy originally raised to commemorate the battle of Plataea (see page 86) – a bronze column formed of three entwined serpents, brought over from Delphi as if itself a trophy of the classical past. More impressive is the design genius manifest in the structure of Haghia Sophia, the church of 'Divine Wisdom' recreated in AD 537 for the emperor Justinian by two architects from Hellenized Asia Minor, Isidorus (from Miletus) and Anthemius (from Tralles). Nearby, and contemporary with the church, an enormous underground cistern, with the capacity for 100,000 tons of water, testifies to the centralized urban organization of the city.

'Byzantium' endures as a poetic reference – W. B. Yeats imagined the boom of the cathedral gong across the 'dolphin-torn' straits of the Bosphorus – and 'byzantine' as a byword for the complex bureaucracy of the 'Byzantine empire' that grew from Constantine's transplant of Rome. Conspicuously, to judge from literary accounts, the city bore resemblances not only to Rome, but to other cities of the Greek and Roman world, for the Delphi tripod was not an isolated item of urban decoration. Constantine and certain high-ranking Byzantine officials brought in numerous masterpieces of classical art, including the Aphrodite of Knidos by Praxiteles and the enormous enthroned Olympic Zeus by Pheidias. There is a theory that this latter statue influenced the image of Christ 'Pantocrator', 'Ruler of All', as it eventually appeared in Byzantine art. But there were some in Constantinople who deplored the presence of classical art in the city. Whether a statue of Zeus, Aphrodite or some naked athlete, such artworks were now categorized as 'pagan'.

The origins of that term are curious: *paganus* first denoted the inhabitant of rural territory beyond villages and municipalities (a *pagus* was the smallest unit of settlement in Italy and the Roman provinces). Later it came to define someone who stayed 'in the sticks', avoiding military recruitment. Later still, in Christian writers, the sense of rustic backwardness came to imply attachment to old-style, polytheistic religion – and anyone unwilling to join up as a 'soldier of Christ'.

'Onward, Christian Soldiers...' We cannot know if Constantine had a dream before his battle with Maxentius at the Milvian Bridge in AD 312, a vision in which an angel showed him the Christian symbol of the Cross and told him he would prevail with its potency: this was a medieval legend.* We do not know, in fact, whether Constantine was ever actually baptized as a Christian. He was buried as the thirteenth disciple in the Church of the Holy Apostles at Constantinople, so perhaps the formality was administered as a last rite. His mother Helena, later sanctified, appears to have been an overt believer: she is credited with making a pioneering pilgrimage to Jerusalem, to seek out evidence for Christ's final suffering and crucifixion (the 'Passion'); in her honour Constantine dedicated a church at Christ's birthplace, Bethlehem. If Constantine was not himself of the faith, however, he was practically sympathetic to those who were. One of his first actions upon entering Rome was to disband the Praetorian Guard and the imperial household cavalry (both fought on the side of Maxentius). The cavalry's parade ground in the Lateran area he reallocated to Christian clergy, to become a cathedral church (or basilica, adapting Latin terminology), a baptistery, and the residence of the bishop of Rome. Traditionally, the first bishop may be reckoned to have been Christ's own apostle Peter, who was put to death in Rome

---

* Early Christians tended to use as an emblem the Chi-Rho motif, made from the first two Greek letters of Christ's name (XP) superimposed; in Constantine's biography, written by his confidant Eusebius, it is claimed that troops daubed the symbol on their shields before the battle by the Milvian Bridge (*pons Milvius*).

probably during the time of Nero (St Paul was also martyred in Rome at about the same time, around AD 60). The process whereby the office of bishop of Rome became that of 'pope' – from the Latin *papa*, in turn from the Greek *pappas*, 'father' – remains historically obscure. What is clear is that documentary detail for the organization of the Christian Church at Rome appears only after Constantine and the papacy of St Sylvester (AD 314–35).

With his then co-ruler Licinius, Constantine issued the so-called 'Edict of Milan' in AD 313. Christians throughout the Roman empire were thereby granted freedom of religious practice. Repression under Diocletian had clearly been counterproductive. The unspoken consequence of granting official freedom of belief was stark nonetheless. As Pliny had discovered in Bithynia, the test of a true Christian was whether he or she put allegiance to Christ over allegiance to the emperor. Who was then in charge?

• • •

Ironically, that question also extended to the communities of Christians around the empire. The lack of leadership was tending to doctrinal chaos. At this time, we should remember, Christianity coexisted with a variety of faiths and practices. While it would present itself as deeply different from those other faiths, the very effort of stating its difference resulted in theological dispute. One obvious claim to difference lay in the assertion of a sole deity: contrary to the traditional Graeco-Roman acceptance of many gods, male and female in gender, Christians practised monotheism, and customarily, like the Jews, referred to their deity as 'Lord' (*kyrios* in Greek). So if this male deity engaged in reproduction with a mortal woman – like Zeus, if not so promiscuously – did that entail more than one deity?

One Christian cleric who agonized over this question was Arius of Alexandria, who resolved it by teaching that Christ, 'Son of God', was not of the same substance as his divine father. This did not settle the matter; for, as other senior Christians perceived, the status of Christ consequently risked being blurred with that of a prophet or an angel. Arius had stated what in the Greek philosophical tradition would be termed an *airesis*, a particular 'course of thought': this yielded to the pejorative concept of 'heresy' – a course deemed to be in the wrong direction. By the fourth century, the possibilities for further variations of Christian belief were multiplying (the Gnostics, for instance, were maintaining that Christ had only *pretended* to live and die).

Constantine took the initiative. In AD 325 he sponsored a gathering of over 300 bishops and attendant clergy from across his empire at Nicaea (Turkish Iznik). Pope Sylvester was too old to make the journey, but sent delegates. Arius and some of his senior supporters were present; the opposition consolidated around a young deacon called Athanasius. Constantine himself chaired proceedings, which were rather heated. The Athanasians prevailed, and the synod produced a statement that still forms part of Christian doctrine (the Nicene Creed). Christ was deemed 'begotten not created', therefore 'consubstantial' with his heavenly father. The statement was not final – it developed into a more sophisticated theology of the Holy Trinity (Father, Son and Holy Spirit) during the fourth century – nor did it prove sufficient to prevent the opening of a deep split between Christians in the east and Christians in the west. Yet Constantine scored a remarkable political victory. In effect, he made the emperor the temporal head of the Church. The bishops needed his power to reinforce orthodoxy; Constantine needed their support to run his empire. One of those bishops, Eusebius of Caesarea, became a close adviser.

It was perhaps at the suggestion of Eusebius that in the New Rome there were to be no new temples raised for deities of the Graeco-Roman pantheon. But Constantine did not outlaw 'pagan' worship. The imperial office of *pontifex maximus* still existed, and he held it – reserving a penchant for the worship of Sol Invictus, the 'Invincible Sun', aligned to the Indo-Iranian mystery cult of Mithras. Archaeology makes it clear that Mithraism was diffused across the empire, enjoying particular favour among soldiers. In AD 321 Constantine ordained that one day a week be made a public holiday – a 'Sun-day' (*dies Solis*). And since Christians did not know (or could not agree on) the time of year when Jesus was born, Constantine arranged that the celebration of Christ's nativity should coincide with the winter solstice – long observed as an occasion of pagan festivities – and share the date already fixed for the birth of Mithras, 25 December.

Much more could be said about the commingling of paganism and Christianity – for example, the development of a 'mother goddess' cult for Mary, the mother of Jesus (in parts of the Mediterranean, sanctuaries of Demeter, and Hera, and of Isis too, continued to operate very much as before, save for the change of name). Episodic iconoclasm occurred, but Christians were inconsistent in their attitudes towards idolatry. Particular stricture was, however, reserved for the customs of animal sacrifice. In Christian theology, there had been one definitive sacrifice, made on behalf of all mortals by Christ crucified. Just one of Constantine's successors, Julian ('the Apostate', AD 361–3), 'lapsed', and made an attempt to restore the pagan ways. But this seems to have been driven by motives related to a childhood trauma – in a crisis of succession after Constantine's death in AD 337, Christian militia murdered members of Julian's family – as much as by an education in classical philosophy. Thereafter, imposing monotheism was a steady trend, with a series of councils convened to clarify dogmatic issues. Emperor Theodosius I decreed from Thessalonica in AD 380 that Christianity, as expressed by the Nicene Creed, be established as the one and only lawful religion of the empire:

> We desire that all peoples who fall beneath the sway of our imperial clemency should profess the faith which we believe to have been communicated by the Apostle Peter to the Romans… We should believe in one deity, the sacred Trinity of Father, Son and Holy Spirit… And we require that those who follow this rule of faith should embrace the name of Catholic Christians, adjudging all others madmen and ordering them to be designated as heretics…

Subsequent edicts expressly prohibited practices of divination and augury, conducting sacrifice, and pouring libations. The oracle at Delphi ceased in AD 390. The final Olympic Games seem to have been staged just before or around AD 400; among the last recorded victors are an Armenian prince called Varazdates, and two young brothers from Athens, Eukarpides and Zopyros.

'Pagan wisdom' retained some intellectual energy. Two Greek philosophers in particular enjoyed revivals of their reputation in late antiquity, yielding Neopythagoreanism and Neoplatonism. The latter was densely articulated by Plotinus at Rome in the second half of the third century AD, and then by his pupil Porphyry. Porphyry's critical examination of Christian belief was consigned to flames by imperial order; yet Neoplatonism lingered into the Middle Ages. Because so much of its discourse was focused upon 'the One' – a supreme divine essence, understood both as 'God' and 'the Good' – its doctrines, while abstruse, were congenial to various Christian authors, including Augustine and Thomas Aquinas. But the formal dissolution of Plato's Academy at Athens is said to have occurred under Justinian, in AD 529. Upon scrutiny, the 'last days of the Academy' are far from definitive, and a shut-down may have been brought on by the institution's own weakness, or descent into pedantry; or by Justinian's desire to 'head-hunt' Athenian professors for employ at his own court. All the same, this event traditionally offers the mercy of a terminus for a journey through classical civilization. What happens thereafter is, by historical convention, reckoned as another story.

• • •

It would need another book, certainly, to tell how so many parts of classical civilization grew into aspects of the modern world, and not only through a process of survival or salvage in the West (certain works of Aristotle are known to us only because they were treasured by Arabic scholars). Here it is enough to note that one central element of classical civilization was never proscribed, nor marginalized. On the contrary: it was at Justinian's command that an enormous project was undertaken at Constantinople – that of compiling a codification or 'Digest' of Roman law.

The Latin word *ius* gives us 'justice': a concept that was lodged in the early history of Rome, and kept significantly apart from politics and religion throughout Rome's republican and imperial development. The basic principles were inscribed upon the 'Twelve Tables', set up in the Forum in the fifth century BC: principles of *ius* rooted in *mos*, 'custom'. Our word 'moral' derives from the plural *mores*, a derivation that may be slightly misleading. For Roman justice, while inseparable from custom, became a formal field of expertise that might even abstract itself from morality, or at least 'popular morality'.

Elements of the old Twelve Tables persist as judicial topics down the centuries. Law (iv) on Table II, for example, states: 'When anyone commits a theft by night, and having been caught in the act is killed, he is legally killed.' Of course there had been law codes in other places and previous times. But the elaboration of systematic justice at Rome was unique in antiquity. 'Laws' (*leges*: related to the verb *ligare*, 'to bind') were generated to regulate all sorts of private and public business, and international encounters. While the Twelve Tables maintained the sense of rooting laws in accepted precedence or 'normative wisdom', they were not so inflexible as to inhibit modification and growth. In short, a science of jurisprudence evolved. Already by the time of Augustus a 'law library' had been established; but it was under Septimius Severus, and indeed the villainous Caracalla, that legal theory truly flourished, particularly in the persons of Paulus and Ulpian. The treatises and case-books of these two 'priests of justice' (as Ulpian liked to characterize lawyers) formed a substantial part of the 2,000 or so volumes collated, revised and codified by Justinian's commission. Justinian gave the work a Christian frame, affirming the contents of the *Digest* as approved by himself as 'Regent under authority of God over our empire, which is given to us by His Heavenly Majesty'. At the same time, he acknowledged the ineradicable long-term influence of Virgil and Homer ('father of every virtue'). And because the project was discharged in Latin, and at a time when the Byzantine empire was strong in Italy (witness, for example, the mosaics at Ravenna), Roman law, codified in Byzantium, returned to the curriculum of schools in its homeland.

• • •

Readers will be aware that we have yet to confront the grand old historical debate about the 'end' of the Roman empire – its supposed 'decline and fall'. From what has so far been said of the New Rome at Constantinople, it may already be apparent that this author belongs to the camp of those inclined to deny that any catastrophe took place.* But it seems only fair to indicate the extent of historical debate around this topic.

It has been tartly observed that when intellectuals lament the decline of civilization, what this really means is that they now have to do their own washing-up, when previously it was

---

* This is a version of the so-called 'Pirenne thesis' – an argument from the Belgian historian Henri Pirenne, pitched in the mid-1930s, that there is an essential continuity between the Roman empire and the 'Holy Roman Empire' created by Charlemagne around AD 800.

done for them. Surveying the numerous engagements of international 'great minds' with the apparent collapse of classical civilization, it is tempting to suppose that a version of this syndrome applies. Personal fears and prejudices are loaded upon the past. In the early twentieth century, for example, an eminent American professor of classics, Tenney Frank, took his first walk down the Appian Way (the road leading eastwards out of Rome, lined with many funerary monuments) and was disturbed to notice how many tombstones carried names indicating foreign and servile extraction. He then spent much scholarly effort in calibrating the 'racial mixture' of Roman society in the imperial period – and concluded that the high proportion (83 per cent, by his calculation) of non-Romans and ex-slaves led to 'Roman disintegration'.

This is what Latin rhetoric would call a non sequitur: 'it does not follow'. For Rome took pride in itself as an 'open society' (see page 261). Non-Romans were encouraged to join the project of expanding Rome and consolidating the empire. As for slaves, their lot throughout antiquity was mostly unenviable, but at least within Roman society they were given the opportunities of making money, maintaining their own slaves (the slave of a slave was a *vicarius*, from which we take the term 'vicar'), and attaining freedom. There would have been snobbery, in certain circles, towards 'freedmen' who made good: the literary caricature of Trimalchio, in the *Satyricon* of Petronius, written in the mid-first century AD, is a sourcebook of such snobbery. But, as the example of Trimalchio also indicates, this potential for upward mobility was the dynamic motor of the Roman economy. Tenney Frank's supposition that emancipated slaves destroyed the integrity of Roman society may derive not so much from the ancient evidence, therefore, as from his own upbringing in racially segregated Missouri.

The running total of explanations offered for the 'end' of the Roman empire has been put at over 200. External or biological causes – for example, climate change, malaria, lead-poisoning – compete with theories of manpower shortage, overtaxation, barbarian invasions, and so on. The allure of concocting such explanations is unlikely to dwindle, so long as we harbour fears about the fragility of our own 'civilization', or believe in cyclical history. But when did the morbid fascination begin? In the Anglophone world, at least, the obvious answer lies in the late eighteenth century, with the portly figure of Edward Gibbon.

'I had not been endowed by art or nature with those happy gifts of confidence and address which unlock every door and every bosom.' So Gibbon, author of *The Decline and Fall of the Roman Empire* (1776–88), resigned himself to the solitary state of scholarly vocation. But his life's great work was not some impartial, dispassionate pursuit. Into his six-volume account of how classical civilization came to an end, Gibbon poured much of his own person. His soulmates were Cicero and Horace. He believed that humankind had never been happier than when ruled by Marcus Aurelius and his predecessors – Nerva, Trajan, Hadrian and Antoninus Pius. And, in company with other celebrated intellects of his age – the European Enlightenment – Gibbon came to regard religion as twin to barbarism.

Gibbon's own account of how his project came about may be overdramatized, but it is telling nonetheless. 'It was at Rome... as I sat musing amidst the ruins of the Capitol, while the barefooted friars were singing vespers in the temple of Jupiter, that the idea of writing the decline and fall of the city first started to my mind.' To this day, the ruins of the Roman Forum, surveyed from the Capitoline Hill, offer a satisfying prospect to those in search of fallen splendour. And yet, of course, the ruin is far from complete. From the same vantage point, but with a different attitude, one might well ask: why has so much been preserved? Or, with regard to Gibbon's situation (dated October 1764), remark: so when did the temple of Jupiter Capitolinus yield to a church (Santa Maria Aracoeli)? Gibbon implies that hearing the hymns of Franciscan friars would steer his principal explanation for the decline and fall of the Roman empire: that Christians brought it down. Yet by the same token, imperial Rome was not obliterated. It simply became Christian Rome – just as imperial Rome replaced republican Rome and republican Rome replaced the Rome of the kings.

Anti-clerical though he undoubtedly was, Gibbon was too intelligent to overlook the fiscal, social and political problems of the late empire. (And his applause for Marcus Aurelius is immediately followed by recognition that Commodus, as chosen successor, was disastrous.) A faith in absolute values, however, was firmly maintained. History presented a dappled landscape. As the torch of classical civilization had been kindled by the Greeks, then nurtured to its brightest glow by the Romans, so it must sputter and die – and darkness ensue. The Goths, the Vandals, the Huns: we almost feel Gibbon shuddering as he describes their coarse illiterate habits and their reckless descent from the forests and plains of northern and central Europe into Mediterranean territory. Gibbon had no time for any notion of the 'noble savage'. So when 'barbarism' triumphed, it meant the systemic collapse of all civilized institutions. Swine browsed and shambled through fallen colonnades. For Gibbon this was not picturesque, but the image of a terrible regress.

• • •

Countering the sonorous prose of Edward Gibbon is a stylistic challenge. But substantive objections to his case can be readily raised. For a start, when we say that the walls of Rome were breached by invaders from the north – most notoriously in AD 410, by Visigoths led by Alaric – we might bear in mind that Alaric had served as a senior officer under the emperor Theodosius, that he and most of his men were Christians, and that someone at Rome opened a gate and let the Visigoths in. Stories of the three-day occupation tell of slaughter and terror, but archaeological evidence for widespread damage on this occasion, and a subsequent seaborne intrusion upon Rome by the Vandals in AD 455, is not conspicuous.

Naturally, since the main imperial administration was transferred to Constantinople, dilapidation of public buildings took its effect. Most damage to edifices and urban embellishment was caused by the process of local recycling. Imperial Rome is estimated to have contained something like half a million statues, largely in bronze or marble. Bronze was easily melted down; marble, put into kilns, was a good source of lime for cement. A form of *damnatio memoriae* prevailed, as objects deemed 'pagan filth' could be cleared away with impunity. What 'declined and fell' was, however, selective.

'Take holy water and sprinkle it in these shrines, build altars and place relics in them. For if the shrines are well built, it is essential that they should be changed from the worship of devils to the worship of the true God.' These instructions, issued during the papacy of Gregory the Great (AD 590–604), explain why certain classical structures survive remarkably well – the Pantheon, for instance, consecrated around AD 609 as a church dedicated to 'the holy Mother of God and all the martyrs of Christ'. Though Constantine himself spent precious little time in old Rome, the city honoured his memory by specially preserving the triumphal arch erected to celebrate his victory over Maxentius. Nearby, the Colosseum became a shrine to martyrs; also nearby, the exquisite church of St Clemente was constructed above a subterranean temple of Mithras.

Were many Christians actually put to death in the Colosseum – or anywhere else in the Roman empire? 'Martyr' means 'witness'; 'the blood of the martyrs is the seed of the Church' goes the rallying cry of Tertullian, the Carthage-based lawyer who converted to Christianity in the late second century and became one of its most vehement fanatics. As the works of Tertullian and other 'martyrologists' show, if passionate witness was wanted, nothing could match the spectacle of a Christian believer, male or female, aristocrat or slave, being put to death as public entertainment. But it is likely that Roman governors were also aware of the evangel-ical potency of such courageous displays; of course the impresarios of the arena were looking for a good fight, not unilateral calm surrender. So, while there is no doubt that Christianity was a crime, and Christians consequently liable to be penalized, we may put much of early Christianity's polemical literature in the same category as heroic poetry – the stuff of fantasy. One Christian author, Origen, candidly wondered if the real tally of martyrs even reached double figures.

A scratched caricature from the walls of a slave school, or *pedagogium*, on the Palatine shows a crucified figure, with the head of a donkey or mule, and a youth nearby in an attitude of prayer, with the crude legend (in Greek): 'Alexamenos, worship [your] god.' Classical civilization was a 'world full of gods', and in legend terrible things could happen to divine figures (for example, Dionysus, Herakles, Orpheus). The story of a divinity styled as a 'suffering servant', and yielding to a death penalty reserved for the basest criminals, was nonetheless distinctive. That the Christian faith appealed particularly to the socially marginalized – though it would seem so – is not demonstrable: Romans of various social stations were buried in the 'catacombs' – the name given to Christian cemeteries along the roads leading out of Rome, and later used generically. St Paul's letters to Christian communities around the empire in the mid-first century AD – at Corinth, Ephesus, Thessalonica and elsewhere – suggest cryptic communities charged with the adrenalin of illegality and complete conviction that a faith cemented by 'unconditional love' (*agape*) will prevail. By the fourth century, 'coming out' had become widespread. One splendid example of early Christian art is the marble sarcophagus of Junius Bassus: he was Rome's urban prefect (rather like a mayor, but with considerable judicial powers too) in AD 359. Christianity offered resurrection to individuals – and to the community. As the centre of a military-political empire shifted, so Rome's inhabitants were drawn to reinventing and revitalizing their city as *civitas Dei* – 'the city of God'.

So was it a gradual transformation, rather than a decline

and fall? Some historians begrudge a roseate view of late antiquity, in which even the marauding warrior bands of the Huns, led from the Steppes into Europe by their notorious chieftain Attila in the fifth century AD, become mere economic migrants. What happened to the civilization of hot baths, fine pottery, libraries and luxury goods? The fact remains, however, that of the 'barbarian hordes' ranged in opposition to the 'Roman empire' – including Goths, Saxons, Lombards and Franks – Christian authorities eventually made not only Catholics, but *Roman* Catholics.

Not all Christian minds were like Tertullian's, raging against anything that did not belong to the Christian gospel. St Jerome, fourth-century scholar and translator of the Hebrew Old Testament and Greek New Testament – producing the so-called Vulgate, or 'Popular' Bible – may have lamented that he was 'more Ciceronian than Christian'. Still, Cicero survived: and not only as a model of Latin style. After all, the virtues of an individual living within civil society, as expounded by Cicero – the life of contemplation, of justice and doing good, conducted with courage, moderation and a sense of propriety: these were fundamentally compatible with Christian tenets. The same could be said for values of *humanitas Romana* as voiced by Virgil and others, and indeed much 'pagan wisdom', from Homer onwards. So texts of the 'classics' were cherished by monks. Eventually, even objects could be soulmates. When works of classical art began to be excavated in and around Rome, their first guardians were cardinals and popes.

How much of this would have happened without Constantine we can only speculate. He was the last emperor to be deified as a god; and the first to be worshipped as a saint.

EPILOGUE

Sometime in the evening of 2 November AD 182, an unfortunate accident happened in Roman Egypt. It was the twenty-third year of the emperor Marcus Aurelius. An eight-year-old slave-boy, Epaphroditus by name, heard some castanet-players in the street below the house where he served. He went to an upper-storey window to watch the women dancing. In his excitement he leaned out too far – and fell to his death.

Many 'events' are related in this book: the sad fate of little Epaphroditus ('Delightful' – a common name for slaves) does not rank with them in historical significance. We mention it here as a sample of urban micro-history gleaned from the rubbish tips of Oxyrhynchus, a Graeco-Roman city west of the Nile. Oxyrhynchus does not feature in the chronicles of antiquity: it was an 'ordinary' place. Only the extraordinary preservation of its regular spoil dumps, sealed under mounds of desert sand, gives it fame. Beginning in the late nineteenth century, two young Oxford scholars, Bernard Grenfell and Arthur Hunt, made their names by organizing the excavation of these heaps. Their principal interest lay in recovering papyrus fragments of the 'classics' – and they were partly rewarded, with poetry from Sappho and Sophocles, comedy from Menander, and so on. But as they and subsequent scholars worked through loads of inscribed detritus from Oxyrhynchus, it became clear that portions of literature were far outweighed by documents relating to the business of everyday existence. Petitions, wills, contracts, receipts, accounts, dinner invitations, prayers, instructions on wrestling holds: the official report on the accidental death of Epaphroditus, making arrangements for his funeral, joins a mass of material that is still being sorted by the experts ('papyrologists').

'Rubbish' is one way of designating all this; viewed another way, it symbolizes more or less everything we have omitted from our traverse of classical civilization. The stuff of history may be woven in many ways. This book has followed rather traditional patterns. But tradition is, after all, in the very nature of the 'classical'.

TIMELINE

BC

c. 1450	Collapse of Minoan civilization
c. 1250	Destruction of 'Troy VI'
c. 1200	Collapse of Mycenaean palaces
c. 1000	'Big Man' burial at Lefkandi
776	Traditional date of first Olympic Games
753	Traditional date of founding of Rome
c. 750	Introduction of the Greek alphabet
c. 750	Greeks begin to settle abroad
c. 750–700	'Homer' active as poet
7th–6th century	Traditional date for Lycurgus and the archaic Spartan constitution
c. 590	Solon's reforms in Athens
6th century	Etruscan rule at Rome
546–527	Pisistratus rules as tyrant of Athens
514	Harmodius and Aristogeiton assassinate Hipparchus in Athens
510	Traditonal date of expulsion of last king of Rome; foundation of Roman republic
508–507	Cleisthenes' political reorganisation of Athens

490	Invading Persians repelled at Marathon
480	Persian sack of Athens
479	Persians defeated at Salamis and Plataea
450–429	Perikles prominent in Athens
447	Work begins on the Parthenon
431–404	Peloponnesian War between Athens and Sparta
430–426	Plague in Athens
415–413	Athenian expedition to Sicily
399	Socrates condemned to death in Athens
396	Fall of the Etruscan city of Veii to Rome
371	Spartans defeated by Thebes at Leuctra
338	Philip II of Macedon defeats the Greek city-states at Chaeronea
336–323	Alexander the Great conquers the eastern Mediterranean and the Persian empire as far as India
323	Division of Alexander's empire between his Successors (*Diadochoi*)
c. 300	Ptolemy I founds the museum and library of Alexandria
264–241	First Punic War
218–201	Second Punic War (Hannibal's campaigns in Italy)
200–146	Roman conquest of Greece
149–146	Third Punic War
146	Sack of Carthage; Sack of Corinth
133	Proposed land reforms of Tiberius Gracchus

133	Pergamon 'bequeathed' to Rome
91–89	'Social War' in Italy
88–82	Civil war between Sulla and Marius
73–71	Slave revolt of Spartacus
50s	Julius Caesar's campaigns in Gaul
49–48	Caesar versus Pompey
44	Assassination of Caesar
43	Triumvirate of Octavian, Mark Antony, and Lepidus established
31	Octavian defeats Mark Antony and Cleopatra at Actium
27 BC–AD 14	Augustus emperor

AD

2	Augustus receives the title 'pater patriae'
c. 30	Jesus Christ executed in Judaea
41–54	Claudius emperor
43	Invasion of Britain
50s	Evangelism of St Peter and St Paul
54–68	Nero emperor
64	Great fire of Rome
69	'Year of the Four Emperors': Galba, Otho, Vitellius, Vespasian
70	Sack of Jerusalem
79	Eruption of Vesuvius: Pompeii and Herculaneum buried
98–117	Trajan emperor

117–138	Hadrian emperor
c. 122–126	Hadrian's Wall, Britain
161–180	Marcus Aurelius emperor
293	Diocletian establishes Tetrarchy
313	Constantine sanctions Christianity throughout the Roman empire (Edict of Milan)
330	Constantinople/'New Rome' founded
393	Theodosius orders closure of Olympia
395	Division of Roman empire between West and East
410	Sack of Rome by Alaric the Goth

FURTHER READING

What follows is partial in two senses of that word. The titles indicated thematically here as ways of deepening, expanding, refining and complicating topics broached by our survey, will not constitute a complete and 'up-to-date' library of Classical civilization; moreover, their selection has been guided by personal preference. Old favourites are included as such. In some cases – Google, perhaps, lightens the obligation upon an author to be fully comprehensive in this duty – the references simply supply the source for allusions in the text.

The *Oxford Classical Dictionary*, now in its 4th edition (ed. S. Hornblower, A. Spawforth & E. Eidinow; available online since 2012) has styled itself as 'the unrivalled one-volume reference work on the Graeco-Roman world' – a reasonable boast. Partiality dictates mention of a lesser, yet illustrated, survey: N. Spivey & M. Squire, *Panorama of the Classical World* (revised ed. 2008).

History

'Whoever has read Herodotus has, for philosophical purposes, read all the history they need.' Schopenhauer's dictum, applied strictly, would liberate miles of shelf-space; however, the *Histories* (literally, 'Inquiries') of Herodotus are the obvious primary text of Classical history, and are available in various English translations. Penguin versions past (by A. de Selincourt, 1954) and present (by T. Holland, 2013) both succeed in conveying readability, while *The Landmark Herodotus* (ed. R. Strassler, 2008) furnishes illustrated annotation. Commentary: F. Hartog, *The Mirror of Herodotus* (2009). As for Thucydides: perhaps he never aspired to 'readability' in the first place – but his notoriously difficult Greek is rendered with due respect in translations by R. Crawley (1874) and S. Lattimore (1998). Necessary qualifications upon Thucydides' claim to transmit 'an exact knowledge of the past' are entered in F.M. Cornford's *Thucydides Mythistoricus* (1907).

These two 'founding fathers' of Classical history gave rise to numerous descendants in the tradition. Some of these do not survive, except by report and fragments; others, even when their names are well known, come down to us only piecemeal. Of the survivors, a selection of names may be offered, along with a rough indication of subject-matter: most have been translated in the Loeb Classical Library – the bilingual series founded in 1911 by New York banker and philanthropist James Loeb 'to make the beauty and learning, the philosophy and wit of the great writers of ancient Greece and Rome once more accessible by means of translations that are in themselves real pieces of literature'. In alphabetical order: Arrian (for arguably the most reliable account of Alexander the Great); Diodorus Siculus (for the rise to power of Alexander's father Philip); Dionysius of Halicarnassus (for the early history of Rome); Josephus (for Rome's mid-first century AD wars with the Jews); Julius Caesar (for Rome's conquest of Gaul); Livy (for early Rome, and Hannibal's campaigns, including his crossing of the Alps); Polybius (for Rome's conquest of Greece); Suetonius (for colourful biographies of 'twelve Caesars', from Julius Caesar to Domitian); Tacitus (for a more measured, if mordant, account of the Julio-Claudians and Flavians).

Two ancient authors who also supply the materials of history cannot be classified as 'historians'. One is Cicero, for whom no generic title seems sufficient. Here it may be pardonable merely to note his cardinal role as a progenitor of *studia humanitatis* – the 'proto-Humanities', we might say, developed as such during the Renaissance, and encompassing history, rhetoric, philology (Greek and Latin), moral philosophy, and above all poetry. No work of Cicero's states this faith more clearly than his (relatively) brief oration *Pro Archia Poeta*: significantly, this was one of the texts discovered in the fourteenth century by Petrarch, a pioneer of 'humanism' in the Western tradition.

The second 'unclassifiable' author is Plutarch. Various essays and treatises on (broadly) 'moral matters' by Plutarch are gathered under the title *Moralia* – amounting to fourteen volumes in the Loeb series; otherwise it is for his [*Parallel*] *Lives* that Plutarch is best known. 'Biography' is not quite the right word here: beginning with Theseus and Romulus, Plutarch's project was to 'pair' eminent Greeks with eminent

Romans, and he did not demur from shaping his material accordingly. But his literary instinct for the telling anecdote, and his interest in character, make for an abiding appeal. So he served Shakespeare with more than just plotlines (see T.J.B. Spencer, *Shakepeare's Plutarch* [1964]); and no Classical author is quoted more often than Plutarch in the *Essays* of Montaigne. D.A. Russell, *Plutarch* (1972), provides a good introduction.

Of course many sound general historical surveys of Graeco-Roman antiquity are available, e.g. The *Oxford History of the Classical World*, eds. J. Boardman, J. Griffin, & O. Murray (1986); S. Price & P. Thonemann, *The Birth of Classical Europe: A History from Troy to Augustine* (2011): more detailed essays distributed through the twelve-volume series of the *Cambridge Ancient History (CAH)*. A good sense of how the topics and 'angles' of ancient history are subject to change may sometimes be gained by comparing the first and second editions of this series: see, for example, how perspectives on Alexander the Great have altered since the *CAH* volume *Macedon*, 401-301 *B.C.* (1927) was replaced by *The Fourth Century B.C.* (1994).

Geography

For reasons perhaps not purely dictated by intellectual interest, the Mediterranean as a region has attracted some grand scholarly surveys, a model being F. Braudel's *La Méditerranée et le monde méditerranéen à l'epoque de Philippe II* (1949). Focused more particularly upon Classical antiquity are P. Hordern & N. Purcell, *The Corrupting Sea* (2000), and C. Broodbank, *The Making of the Middle Sea* (2013).

See also R. Sallares, *Ecology of the Ancient Greek World* (1991); A.T Grove & O. Rackham, *The Nature of Mediterranean Europe: An Ecological History* (2001); and, for the topography of events, R.J.A. Talbert ed., *Atlas of Classical History* (1985).

On ancient modes of navigation (and much more of maritime interest): L. Casson, *Ships and Seamanship in the Ancient World* (1971).

On patterns of subsistence in the Greek countryside, R. Osborne, *Classical Landscape with Figures* (1987); C. Runnels and T. van Andel, *Beyond the Akropolis* (1987). A survey of Roman evidence: S. Dyson, *The Roman Countryside* (2006).

Art, Architecture, and Urbanism

Our view of ancient art is distorted by the fact that so little of large-scale painting survives, and none at all of that ascribed to Greek 'great masters' such as Apelles; accordingly we perhaps over-value what survives relatively well, in the form of painted pottery. See T. Rasmussen and N. Spivey eds., *Looking at Greek Vases* (1991), and F. Lissarrague, *Greek Vases* (2001). More widely: N. Spivey, *Greek Art* (1997); A. Stewart, *Art in the Hellenistic World* (2014); A. Ramage & N. Ramage, *Roman Art* (6th ed. 2014). A sober account of how the Classical architectural orders evolved is A.W. Lawrence, *Greek Architecture* (5th ed. 1996); equally sober account of methods and practice in J.J. Coulton, *Ancient Greek Architects at Work* (1987); more romantic flights in V. Scully, *The Earth, the Temple and the Gods* (Rev. ed. 1979). The nuances of Roman design are explored in M. Wilson Jones, *The Principles of Roman Architecture* (2003).

How private houses evolved: E. Walter-Karydi, *The Greek House* (1998). On particular cities: N. Cahill, *Household and City Organization at Olynthus* (2002); J. Berry, *The Complete Pompeii* (2007). More generally, J.B. Ward-Perkins, *Cities of Ancient Greece and Italy: Planning in Classical Antiquity* (1974); and E.J. Owens, *The City in the Greek and Roman World* (1991).

Education

We have said relatively little about ancient education in this book, except implicitly. The monumental modern account is W. Jaeger (translated by G. Highet), *Paideia: The Ideals of Greek Culture* (1939–44): however Jaeger, while a principled opponent of National Socialism, was inclined towards a racial and aristocratic idealization of 'the Greeks', and parts of his text have not dated well. Alternatives include K. Robb, *Literacy and Paideia in Ancient Greece* (1994). The centrality of rhetoric to Roman schooling should be emphasized: see S.F. Bonner, *Roman Declamation* (1949). Readers seeking a full explanation of ancient rhetorical terms and their deployment should consult H. Lausberg, *Handbook of Literary Rhetoric* (1998).

On literacy, and libraries: W.V. Harris, *Ancient Literacy* (1989); L. Canfora, *The Vanished Library* (1990); L. Casson, *Libraries in the Ancient World* (2002).

There are several studies of how Classics as an academic discipline has fared in modern times: see e.g. C. Stray, *Classics Transformed: Schools, Universities, and Society in England, 1830–1960* (1998); and by way of national comparison, S.L. Marchand, *Down from Olympus: Archaeology and Philhellenism in Germany, 1750–1970* (1996).

Literary Genres

Writing history was, of course, a literary genre; see further literary references elsewhere in this bibliography. Here, however, are signalled some particular suggestions regarding formal types of output: J.B. Hainsworth, *The Idea of Epic* (1991); D.A. Campbell, *The Golden Lyre: The Themes of the Greek Lyric Poets* (1983); C. Segal, *Interpreting Greek Tragedy* (1986); R. Scodel, *An Introduction to Greek Tragedy* (2010); N. Holzberg, *The Ancient Novel: An Introduction* (1995); G. Williams, *Tradition and Originality in Roman Poetry* (1968); M. Coffey, *Roman Satire* (2nd ed. 1989); A.J. Boyle, *Roman Tragedy* (2006). On the art of the 'word-picture' (*ekphrasis*), and various 'postmodern' ways of reading Latin literature, D. Fowler, *Roman Constructions* (2000).

Philosophy

For general surveys: it is hard not to enjoy the urbane style of Bertrand Russell's *History of Western Philosophy* (1946); there is similar journalistic flair in A. Gottlieb, *The Dream of Reason* (2001). Otherwise, J. Brunschwig & G.E.R. Lloyd, *Greek Thought: A Guide to Classical Knowledge* (2000). For the Pre-Socratics, J. Burnet, *Early Greek Philosophy* (3rd ed. 1920) captures their cryptic poetry. On subsequent individual philosophers and schools of philosophy: G. Vlastos, *Socrates* (1991); R. Kraut ed., *The Cambridge Companion to Plato* (1993); J. Barnes, *Aristotle* (1982); J. Rist, *Stoic Philosophy* (1969); A.A. Long & D.N. Sedley, *The Hellenistic Philosophers* (1987). For various ways in which codes of ancient ethics can be extracted from literary and philosophical evidence, see A.W.H. Adkins, *Merit and Responsibility. A Study in Greek Values* (1960); B. Williams, *Shame and Necessity* (2nd ed. 2008); M.Nussbaum, *The Fragility of Goodness* (2001). P. Zanker, *The Mask of Socrates* (1995) explores the charisma of ancient philosophers as expressed visually.

Science and Mathematics

See G.E.R. Lloyd, *Early Greek Science* (1970); *id.*, *Greek Science after Aristotle* (1973). An entertainingly critical summary of scholarship since may be found in T.E. Rihll, *Greek Science* (1999).

Allegedly comprehensible for non-specialists: B. Artmann, *Euclid:The Creation of Mathematics* (2001).

Technology and Engineering

For ancient texts in translation: J.W. Humphrey, J.P. Oleson & A.N. Sherwood eds, *Greek and Roman Technology: A Sourcebook* (1998). Exposition of theory and practice in J.G. Landels, *Engineering in the Ancient World* (1978), and K.D. White, *Greek and Roman Technology* (1984). On the marvels of Roman hydraulics, A.T. Hodge, *Roman Aqueducts and Water Supply* (2002).

Economics

A. Burford, *Craftsmen in Greek and Roman Society* (1972); M.I. Finley ed., *Slavery in Classical Antiquity* (1960); P. Garnsey, *Food and Society in Classical Antiquity* (1999); Part

Three of R.I. Curtis, *Ancient Food Technology* (2001). R Meiggs, *Trees and Timber in the Ancient Mediterranean World* (1982) shows what happens when a Classical scholar is drafted into wartime service for the Ministry of Supply, and eventually brings that experience to bear in his academic research.

Medicine

Accounts of Greek and Roman medicine traditionally tend to use of the opposition of rational/irrational, or 'clinical medicine' versus 'faith healing': the contrast is not always helpful to historical understanding. Perhaps the most approachable introduction to the subject is through the relevant sections of R. Porter, *The Greatest Benefit to Mankind: A Medical History of Humanity* (1999).

Religion and Mythology

Readers wishing to know more about the religious beliefs of Greeks and Romans might try E.R. Dodds, *The Greeks and the Irrational* (1951); H.W. Parke, *Greek Oracles* (1967); A. Spawforth, *The Complete Greek Temples* (2006); J. Scheid, *An Introduction to Roman Religion* (2003); M.K. Hopkins, *A World Full of Gods* (1999) – this latter a deliberately irritating enquiry into how and why Christianity eventually triumphed.

Despite its author's eccentric understanding of mythology, R. Graves, *The Greek Myths* (1955) remains perhaps the most readable assemblage. To sample different approaches about how myths served in antiquity, see R. Buxton, *Imaginary Greece: The Contexts of Mythology* (1994), and J-P. Vernant, *Myth and Society in Ancient Greece* (1982). P. Veyne, *Did the Greeks Believe their Myths?* (1988) asks an apparently crucial question: alas, the answer reduces imprecisely to variations tantamount to 'sort of'.

From the Bronze Age to Homer

Troia/Wilusa, the current site guide to Troy written by one of its most dedicated modern excavators, Mannfred Korfmann (who died in 2005), is worth seeking out; for a more complex, updated account of the site, C.B. Rose, *The Archaeology of Greek and Roman Troy* (2013). Heinrich Schliemann has himself become an object of study: a handy introduction to his achievements and misdemeanours is H. Duchêne, *The Golden Treasures of Troy: The Dream of Heinrich Schliemann* (1995). Further: W.A. McDonald & C.G. Thomas, *Progress into the Past: The Rediscovery of Mycenaean Civilization* (2nd ed. 1990); J.L Fitton, *The Discovery of the Greek Bronze Age* (1996); J. Chadwick, *The Mycenaean World* (1976); E. French, *Mycenae: Agamemnon's Capital* (2002); A. Robinson, *The Man Who Deciphered Linear B: The Story of Michael Ventris* (2002). For Homer, the epic tradition, and hero-cult, the bibliography is fittingly grand: by way of introduction, see R. Rutherford, *Homer* (1996); also I. Morris & B. Powell eds, *A New Companion to Homer* (1997); R. Fowler ed., *The Cambridge Companion to Homer* (2004); advancing perhaps to J. Griffin, *Homer on Life and Death* (1980); G. Nagy, *The Best of the Achaeans* (1998), and by the same author, *Homer the Classic* (1995) – tracing the development of Homer's canonical status.

On the emergence from the 'Dark Age': A. Snodgrass, *Archaic Greece: An Age of Experiment* (1980). A bold account of how the Greeks became literate is B. Powell, *Homer and the Origins of the Greek Alphabet* (1991).

The quote from Simone Weil comes from her essay *L'Iliade ou le poème de la force*, first published (under a *nom de plume*) in *Les Cahiers du Sud* 1940–1; see J.P. Holoka, *Simone Weil's the* Iliad *or the Poem of Force* (2005).

Athens and Sparta

Freud's strange (or familiar) experience on the Acropolis is related in a letter he wrote to Romain Rolland in 1936: it is included in A. Phillips ed., *The Penguin Freud Reader* (2006), 68–76. Assorted Athenian suggestions: V. Ehrenberg, *From Solon to Socrates* (2nd ed. 1973); P.J. Rhodes, *A History of the Classical Greek World* 478-323 BC (2006); J.M. Camp, *The Archaeology of Athens* (2004); C. Berard ed., *A City of Images* (1989); J. B. Connelly, *The Parthenon Enigma* (2014); K. Dover, *Greek Homosexuality* (1978); J. Davidson, *Courtesans and Fishcakes: The Consuming Passions of Classical Athens* (1997); A.W. Pickard-Cambridge, *The Dramatic Festivals of Athens* (1953); S. Goldhill, *Reading Greek Tragedy* (1986); G. Herman, *Morality and Behaviour in Democratic Athens* (2006); O. Taplin, *Comic Angels* (1993).

Arnold Toynbee's definition of Sparta as an 'arrested civilization' (along with some other culprits, including 'Polynesians' and 'Eskimos'), comes early in his 10-volume *A Study of History* (1946) – best approached in its abridgement by D.C. Somervell, Vol. I (1987), 178–80. Also: W.G. Forrest, *A History of Sparta* (1980); E. Rawson, *The Spartan Tradition in European Thought* (1969); A. Powell & S. Hodkinson eds, *The Shadow of Sparta* (1994); G.E.M. de Ste Croix, *The Origins of the Peloponnesian War* (1972).

Greek Colonization

J. Boardman, *The Greeks Overseas* (4th ed. 1999) has been a stalwart account of the colonizing phenomenon (viewed archaeologically) since first published in 1964. A further handsome assemblage of archaeological data regarding Magna Grecia is G.P. Caratelli ed., *The Western Greeks* (1996). On the Euboean pioneers, see D. Ridgway, *The First Western Greeks* (1992). An important theoretical approach remains F. de Polignac, *Cults, Territory and the Origins of the Greek City-State* (1995). J.C. Carter, *Discovering the Greek Countryside at Metaponto* (2006) divulges results of one of the most thorough archaeological explorations of a Greek colony and its hinterland.

Greek Warfare and Greek Sport

There are reasons for grouping these topics: see N. Spivey, *The Ancient Olympics* (2nd ed. 2012). Further: M. Golden, *Sport and Society in Ancient Greece* (1998); V. Davis Hanson, *The Western Way of War* (1989); J. Rich & G. Shipley eds, *War and Society in the Greek World* (1993).

Alexander and the Macedonian Empire

E. Borza, *In the Shadow of Olympus: The Emergence of Macedon* (1990); W. Heckel and L. Tritle eds, *Alexander the Great: A New History* (2009); R. Lane Fox ed., *Brill's Companion to Ancient Macedon* (2011). R. Waterfield, *Dividing the Spoils* (2011) tells the story of the wars among Alexander's successors.

The Hellenistic Age

For some while it was unfashionable to study the period: that has changed, as evident from D. Ogden ed., *The Hellenistic World: New Perspectives* (2002), and G.R. Burgh ed., *The Cambridge Companion to the Hellenistic World* (2006). T.B.L. Webster, *Hellenistic Poetry and Art* (1964) remains, however, a useful survey.

Rome

For expert guidance around Rome's ruins: either A. Claridge, *Rome: An Oxford Archaeological Guide* (2nd ed. 2010), or F. Coarelli, *Rome and Environs* (Updated ed., 2014). On early Rome – an archaeological and historical 'minefield', as may be judged from T. P. Wiseman, *Unwritten Rome* (2009) – perhaps it is safest to start with T.J. Cornell, *The Beginnings of Rome* (1995). On the republican period, E.S. Gruen, *Culture and National Identity in Republican Rome* (1992). R. Syme, *The Roman Revolution* (1939), portrays Octavian-Augustus as a proto-Fascist. But history continues to regard the Augustan age as benevolent. Idiosyncratic selections from the vast bibliography around its visual and literary culture may be offered: G.K. Galinsky, *Augustan Culture* (1996); B. Otis, *Virgil: A Study in Civilized Poetry* (1964); W.F.J. Knight, *Roman Vergil* (1944); A. Noyes, *Portrait of Horace* (1947); E. Fantham, *Ovid's Metamorphoses* (2004); L.P. Wilkinson, *Golden Latin Artistry* (1963); P. Zanker, *The Power of Images in the Age of Augustus* (1988).

The Roman Empire

M. Beard, *The Roman Triumph* (2007); F. Millar, *The Emperor in the Roman World* (1977); E.N. Lutterworth, *The Grand Strategy of the Roman Empire* (1981); Y. Yadin, *Masada: Herod's Fortress and the Zealots' Last Stand* (1966); G. Webster, *The Roman Army* (1998).

Decline and Fall?

Edward Gibbon overtly modelled his historical aims and timbre upon Tacitus: he remains, however, a creature of the Enlightenment, and a noble composer of English prose. These are all reasons why Gibbon's *Decline and Fall of the Roman Empire* (1776–88) is worth reading, even if most historians today prefer to speak of 'transformation' rather than 'decline and fall'. J.B. Bury's annotated seven-volume edition of 1909–14 is the standard full text: readers daunted by this might try one of the many abridgements, or perhaps approach by way of Gibbon's *Autobiography* – available in various editions.

The debate continues: its lively flavours may be sampled from G.W. Bowersock, P. Brown & O. Graber, *Late Antiquity: A Guide to the Postclassical World* (1999); J. Elsner, *From Imperial Rome to Christian Triumph* (1998); B. Ward-Perkins, *The Fall of Rome* (2005) – the latter putting the case that hot baths and other comforts of civilized existence really did disappear, for centuries, when Rome succumbed to 'barbarians' after AD 410.

Oxyrhynchus and papyrology: P. Parsons, *City of the Sharp-Nosed Fish* (2007).

Afterlife

As for the classical 'reception' and 'afterlife': G. Highet, *The Classical Tradition* (1949), traces the fortune and influence of Classical literature through the Middle Ages and beyond; for more modern views, A. Grafton, G. Most & S. Settis eds, *The Classical Tradition* (2012); or M. Silk, I. Gildenhard & R. Barrow, *The Classical Tradition: Art, Literature, Thought* (2014). How texts were transmitted: L.D. Reynolds & N.G. Wilson, *Scribes and Scholars* (1991). See also R. Weiss, *The Renaissance Discovery of Classical Antiquity* (1969). On the visual legacy, F. Haskell & N. Penny, *Taste and the Antique* (1981); M. Bull, *The Mirror of the Gods* (2005), and E.H. Gombrich, *Aby Warburg: An Intellectual Biography* (2nd ed. 1986); and more generally, S. Settis, *The Future of the Classical* (2006).

Illustrations

Frontispiece: Image of a writer (possibly the poet Sappho). Detail of a painting from a house in the Insula Occidentale, Pompeii (Archaeological Museum, Naples).

I Detail of an imaginary portrait of Homer, probably from a Roman villa; first-second century AD, after an original type created *c.* 300 BC (Capitoline Museums, Rome).

II Southern view of the Acropolis, Athens. Photograph taken *c.* 1870.

III 'Young Spartans Exercising' by Edgar Degas, 1860 (National Gallery, London).

IV View of the theatre at Syracuse.

V Painting of Socrates, from a Roman house at Ephesus, 1st century AD (Selçuk, Ephesus Museum).

VI Silver tetradrachm with the image of Alexander the Great as Herakles (wearing the scalp of the Nemean Lion), after *c.* 330 BC.

VII Detail of the frieze showing the battle between Gods and Giants on the Great of Zeus from Pergamon (Pergamon Museum, Berlin).

VIII View of the ruins of the Temple of Venus Genetrix, late first century BC, in the Roman Forum.

IX View of the Library of Celsus, Ephesus.

X Adam and Eve: detail of the sarcophagus of Junius Bassus, fourth century AD (Vatican Museums).

INDEX

Aachaeans 6
Achilles 7, 20–21, 25
Acropolis 31–2, 47, 51, 64
Aegean 22–3
Aegisthus 17
Aeolians 23
Aeneas 15, 217, 223–4, 234,
    252, 256–7, 267
Aeneid 256, 275
Aeschylus 48, 50, 105
Agamemnon 3, 6–8, 25
Agesilaus 93–4
Agora 44, 51–2, 80, 162, 176
Agrigento 104, 116–17, 126,
    128, 140
Ajax 13
Alaric 320
Alcibiades 66, 90–91, 151, 152
Alexander the Great 156–7,
    160–61, 177–92, 204, 332,
    334, 343
  division of territory 186
  images 180–83, 185, 186
  military conquests 177–9,
    207
Alexandria 169–99, 248
altars 212–13
Amazons 34–5
Andromache 7–8
Antisthenes 161
Apelles 167–8, 181, 184

Aphrodite 5–6
Apollo 105, 106, 145, 189
Arcadia 119
Archias 99, 102–3, 105–8
Archimedes 193, 240
architecture 174, 290, 335
archon 37
Ares 5
Arethusa 102, 105
Argos 7
Ariadne 34
Aristides 289
Aristogeiton 40, 54, 59
Aristonothos 113–14
Aristophanes 48, 136
Aristotle 156–60, 175–6, 180,
    314
Artemis 81, 198, 272, 294–5
Asklepios 144, 146
  Asklepeion 147
Astyanax 7–8
Athena 5–6, 32, 38–9, 65–6,
    67–8
Athens 7, 31–69, 73, 81, 118,
    215, 341
  antagonism with Sparta 88
  democracy 33, 40, 42–8, 61,
    89, 205, 209
  Lyceum 157–8
  Stoa Poikile 162
athletics 119–26

Atlantis 23
Atlas 23
Attalids 209–15
Attalos I 210–12, 215
Attalos II 214
Attalos III 216–17
Attica 33–4, 36–7
Attila 323
autarkeia 137
Augustus (see also Octavian) 249–52, 258

basileus 36
Bath 276
Beazley, J.D. 52
Bithynia 278, 295, 301, 310
Boeotia 11, 17, 94, 110, 175
Boule 42
Bronze Age 18, 32, 35, 108, 120
Burckhardt, Jakob 205
Byzantium 306–8

Cadmus 11
Callimachus 194–5, 196, 198, 211
Calvert, Frank 15
Caracalla 303–4, 315
Carthage 116, 235–9
Caryatids 65
Cato 238–9, 253
Cavafy, C.P. 191
ceramics 52
Cecrops 32–3, 65–6
*censo*r 228, 238–9
Chaeronea, battle of 175
Chios 11
Christianity 294–7
Cicero 222, 247, 250, 323, 333
Claudius 260–61
Cleisthenes 41, 42, 44

Cleopatra 199, 248–9
Clytemnestra 16
Codrus 37
Colosseum 321
Constantine 306–13, 320, 323
Constantinople 299–323
Corinth 88–9, 99, 102–3
Coriolanus 229–30
Coubertin, Pierre de 124
Critobalus 151
Croesus 58, 106
Croton 100, 116, 122, 142–4
Cynics 160–62
Cyrus 58

Dacia 286–8
    Dacian Wars 286
Dardanus 5
Darius 58, 144, 177–8, 183
Dark Age 35, 36
Decebalus 286–8
Delian League 62–3, 68
Delphi 41, 92, 106–7, 119
democracy 41–2
Demosthenes 46, 175–6, 209
despotes 39
Deucalion 23–4
dictator 242
Diels, Hermann 138, 141
Dinocrates 188, 190, 197
Diocletian 305–6, 310
Diogenes 160–62
Dionysus 34, 48–9, 54
Discorides 146
Dorians 23
Draco 37
drama 48–9, 158–9
Droysen, J.G. 204–5

Ecclesiastes 194

Egypt 139, 140, 187–8, 192–3, 248–9
ekklesia 38
Empedocles 141
Ephesus 265–97
epic poetry 3, 10–11, 141, 155, 256–7, 337
Epictetus 163–4, 165, 241
Epicureanism 164–6
Epicurus 164–5
epinikian poetry 128
Erechtheus 32–3, 65, 67
Etruria 113
    Etruscans 113, 226, 231–2
Eumenes II 212
eunomia 73
Eupatridai 37
Euripedes 33, 48, 90–91
Europa 11
Evans, Arthur 18, 22
Ezekiel 111

Forster, E.M. 191
Frank, Tenney 317
Freud, Sigmund 31–2
Furtwängler, Adolf 15

Galen 147
Gauls 210–12, 237, 243
gerousia 77
Gibbon, Edward 318–20
Gilgamesh 10
Gorgias 150
Gortyn 47
Grote, George 205, 209

Haghia Sophia 308
Hadrian 271, 273, 280, 290–93
Hannibal 235–8, 333
Harmodius 40, 54, 59
Hecateus 14

Hector 7–8, 20–21
Hegel, G.W.F. 205
Helen 6
Helena 306, 309
Hellen 23
    Hellenes 23
Hephaestion 183, 185
Hephaistos 32
Hera 5–6
Heraclitus 141, 162
Herakles 5, 34, 121, 123, 188, 213, 223
Hermes 6
Herodotus 25–6, 55–8, 83, 112–13, 118, 144, 184, 198, 332
    Histories 25, 55
Hesiod 109–10, 192–3
hieroglyhics
    Cretan 18
    Egyptian 19
Hieron 128–9
Hipparchus 39, 40
Hippias 39, 40, 41, 58, 59
Hippocrates 144–5, 148
Hippodamus 118
Hippolyta 34
Hittite empire 4
Homer 3–15, 18–21, 27, 39, 141
    Iliad 3, 21, 37, 143, 193
    Odyssey 3, 114
    on maritime trade 109
Horace 257–8
Humann, Carl 205–6
Hygeia 144

Ionia 55, 114
Ionians 23, 115, 148
Iron Age 35, 221–2
Isocrates 92–3

isonomia 41
Ithaca 6, 15, 25

Jesus 281, 312
Josephus 282–4, 333
Julius Caesar 242–5, 333
Juvenal 260

Kallimachos 59–60
Kerameikos 52
Knossos 17–19, 22, 24
Kos 144, 147
Kranz, Walther 138, 141

Laocoon 215–17
Laomedon 5
Laurion 46
Lefkandi 36
Lelantine War 110
Leonidas 85
Leuctra, battle of 94
libraries 336
    Alexandria 192–4
    Athens 51, 270
    Ephesus 267, 270, 271
    Pergamon 209, 212
    Rome 270
    Thamugadi 271
Linear A 18, 22
Linear B 18–21, 24
literature 254–5
Livy 225–6, 229, 333
Loeb, James 332
Lucretia 226, 229
Lucretius 166
Lyceum 157–8, 159, 161,
    192–3
Lycurgus 76–80
Lysander 92
Lysias 45–6

Macaulay, Thomas
    Lays of Ancient Rome 224
Macedonians 93, 175, 186
Magna Graecia 104–5
Marathon, battle of 54–5,
    59–61, 162
Marcus Aurelius 147, 164, 302,
    325
Marius 242
Mark Antony 245–8
Masada 283–5
Maxentius 306, 309, 321
Medes 55
medicine 144–8, 158, 339
Menelaus 6, 13, 26
Messenia 35, 76
metoikoi 43
Milo 123, 143
Miltiades 59–60
Minoans 19, 22–5
Minos 22, 34
Minotaur 22, 34
Mnesikles 64–5
Muses 21, 192–3
museum 192–3
Mycenae 7, 14–18
Mycenaeans 19–22, 24–5

negotiatores 241
Neoplatonism 314
Neopythagoreanism 314
Nestor 11, 18, 38
Nichoria 35
Nike 68–9
Nikias 90–91
Nîmes 277–8

obelisks 252–3
Octavian (see also Augustus)
    245–50
Odysseus 6, 8–9, 12, 25

Olympia 13, 119–24
  Olympians 7, 212–13
  Olympic Games 120–24,
    313, 343
oracles
  Delphi 80, 99, 102, 105–7,
    313
  Dodona 106
  Egypt 179
Orestes 25–6
Ortygia 99, 102
ostrakismos 43–4
Ovid 255–6

paintings 22–3, 180, 251, 286
Palatine Hill 222, 223
Panacea 144
Pantheon 253
Paris 5–6
Parmenides 148–9
Parry, Milman 10
Parthenon 31–3, 66–8
Paul 294–5
Peleus 5, 7
Peloponnesian War 87–92, 106
Pergamon 187, 201–17
Perikles 62–4, 66, 89, 134
  image of 65
Persepolis 58
Persian empire 184–5
Persians 34, 55, 59–61, 67
Phalaris 117
Pheidias 65–6, 68, 121, 198,
    203, 308
Philetairos 208, 216
Philip II of Macedon 93,
    171–7, 332
Phocaea 115
Phoenicians 10, 111, 112,
    235–6
Phrygia 91

phylax panteles 154
Pindar 105, 128–9
Pisistratus 38–9
Plataea, battle of 86, 307
Plato 23, 80, 89, 95, 105, 117,
    134–5, 150, 153–6, 162
  and Aristotle 158
  Laws 134, 154
  Neoplatonism 314
  Platonic love 153
  Protagoras 149
  Republic 133, 135, 153–4
Pliny the Elder 262–3
Pliny the Younger 295–6, 301
Plotinus 314
Plutarch 62–3, 76, 79, 92, 102,
    175, 333
  Life of Alexander 181
  Life of Lycurgus 76
  Life of Nikias 90
  Perikles 62–3
polemarch 37, 43
Polybius 172, 225, 235, 275,
    333
Polyphemus 8–9, 105
Pompey 243–4
pontifex maximus 249, 312
Poseidon 66, 92
Praxithea 33
Presocratics 138–41, 145,
    148–9
Priam 5, 6, 7, 16, 217
Prometheus 50
Propylaia 65–6, 89
Protagoras 118, 134, 149, 150
prytaneis 42
Ptoelmy I 187, 191–2, 196–9
Ptolemy II 192, 196–9
Punic Wars 235, 236, 239
Pylos 17, 19, 35, 38
Pyrrha 23–4

Pyrrho 167
Pythagoras 117, 140, 142–3

Ramesses II 24
Rome 219–63, 292–3, 344–5
  agriculture 254
  art and literature 253–8
  'Augustan peace' 250–51
  early republic 227–30
  expansion 230–50
  origins and foundation 221–6
Romulus 223, 226

Santorini 23
Scepticism 167–8
Schliemann, Heinrich 15–18,
  31
scripts 18–22, 24
sculptures 66–8, 198, 277
Seleucus 206–7
Seneca the Younger 164
Septimius Severus 303, 307,
  315
Seven Wonders 198
Sikels 100, 116
Socrates 52, 135–8, 145, 148,
  150–52, 161
Solon 37–9, 124, 341
Sophists 150
Sophocles 48, 136
Sparta 25–6, 40, 73–95, 342
  athletes 123
  hoplite warfare 82–5
sports
  athletic contests 85
  Isthmian Games 119
  Nemean Games 119
  Olympic Games 119–24,
    313, 343
  Pythian Games 119, 127
  wrestling 123

Stamatakes, Panagiotes 17
statues 65, 68, 121, 127, 174,
  210, 214–15, 267, 270,
  272, 308
Stoics 162–5, 209
strategos 42, 89
Suetonius 259–60, 273, 333
  Twelve Caesars 259
Sulla 242
Sybaris 117, 123
Sybarites 117
Syracuse 89–90, 97–129, 240

Tacitus 273–4, 333
  Agricola 274
  Annals 273
  Germania 274
  Histories 273
Tarquins 226–7
Tegea 25
temenos 48
temples 69, 81, 104, 106, 113,
  121–2, 198, 206
Tertullian 321, 323
Thales 139–40
theatre 49–50, 146, 206
Thebes 11, 17, 18, 175
Theodosius 313, 320
Thermopylae, battle of 76,
  85–6
Theseus 33–5, 67
Thetis 5, 7
Thirty Tyrants 92, 95, 134
Thucydides 23, 81, 87, 89, 99,
  332
Thurii 118
Tiryns 17, 18
Tivoli 290–91
Trajan 271–2, 277–8, 285–8,
  295–7
Troad 187, 206, 214, 267

Trojan War 14, 214
Troy 3–27, 216, 217, 223
Tyrannicides 40–41, 54
Tyre 111, 116, 177–8

Utopia 131–68

vases 52–4, 113, 231, 240, 334
Ventris, Michael 19–20
Virgil 256–7
  Aeneid 256, 275
  Eclogues 256
  Georgics 256
Volscians 229–30

wall paintings 22–3
wanax 25
wars 91, 241–4
  Dacian 286
  Lelantine 110
  Peloponnesian 87–92, 106
  Punic 235, 236, 239
Weil, Simone 26–7
Winkelmann, J.J. 203–4, 206,
    211, 215–16
wrestling 123
Xenophanes 53–4, 125–6,
    142
Xerxes 58, 61

Yadin, Yigael 284–5

Zealots 282–3
Zeno (not the Stoic) 148–9,
    152
  'paradoxes' 148–9
Zeno (the Stoic) 162–3
Zeus 5, 11, 67, 106, 121–2,
    145, 198, 206, 212, 308